The Nature of Value

The Nature of Value

Axiological Investigations

Ramon M. Lemos

University Press of Florida

Gainesville/Tallahassee/Tampa/Boca Raton
Pensacola/Orlando/Miami/Jacksonville

00 99 98 97 96 95 6 5 4 3 2 1

Library of Congress Cataloging-in-Publication Data

Lemos, Ramon M., 1927–
    The nature of value: axiological investigations / Ramon M. Lemos.
        p.   cm.
    Includes bibliographical references and index.
    ISBN 0-8130-1366-6 (alk. paper)
        1. Values.   I. Title.
BD232.L398   1995   95-1079
121'.8—dc20   CIP

The University Press of Florida is the scholarly publishing agency for the State University
System of Florida, comprised of Florida A & M University, Florida Atlantic University,
Florida International University, Florida State University, University of Central Florida,
University of Florida, University of North Florida, University of South Florida, and University of West Florida

University Press of Florida
15 Northwest 15th Street
Gainesville, FL 32611

To the memory of
Mamie Lou

Contents

Preface   ix

1. Value and Psychological Phenomena   1
    1. Value, Valuing, and Evaluating   1
    2. Levels of Psychological Phenomena   6
    3. Terminological Remarks   12

2. Ontological Categories and Bearers of Value   15
    1. States of Affairs, Propositions, and Facts   15
    2. States of Affairs as Bearers of Value   19
    3. Propositions as Bearers of Value   24
    4. Abstracta and Concreta as Bearers of Value   29

3. Species of Value   34
    1. Intrinsic, Extrinsic, and Total Value   34
    2. Extrinsic Value and Utility   39
    3. Instrumental and Contributory Value   41
    4. Inherent Value   52

4. Definition, Proof, and Knowledge of Intrinsic Value   59
    1. The Definability of Intrinsic Value   59
    2. Proof and Knowledge of Intrinsic Value   67

5. Moral and Non-Moral Value   72
    1. Moral Concepts and Value Concepts   72
    2. The Value of Moral Objectives   81
    3. Theodicy   86

6. Persons, Things, and Value   91
    1. Universals, Kinds, and Value   91
    2. Normality and Value   94

3. Goodness and Excellence   97

4. Good-Making Properties and Virtues   100

5. Virtues and Vices   103

6. Loving and Hating   108

7. The Primacy of Practical Rationality   117

1. The Value of Religious Belief and Hope   117

2. Theoretical and Practical Rationality   122

3. Silence and Deception   126

4. Positive, Negative, and Conflicting Duties   130

5. Self-Deception   134

6. The Possibility of Self-Deception   137

7. The Value of Knowledge   142

8. Morality and Rationality   148

1. Acting Morally and Acting Rationally   148

2. Morality and Self-Interest   154

3. The Inadequacy of Egoism   162

4. Unmitigated Non-Egoism   168

9. Attitudes toward the Indifferent   172

1. Likings and Dislikings of Good and Bad Objects   172

2. Extreme Views of Attitudes toward the Indifferent   176

3. Moderate Views of Attitudes toward the Indifferent   181

4. Instances, Kinds, and Value   187

5. Egocentrism, Anthropocentrism, and Magnanimity   190

6. Disliking Indifferent Things   191

10. The Complete Human Good and Higher Education   196

1. Civilization and Morality   196

2. Being Good and Having Goods   200

3. Moral and Non-Moral Education   206

Notes   211

Works Cited   215

Index   217

Preface

During the past forty or fifty years a great deal has been published in moral and political philosophy. During most of this period, however, axiology or the general theory of value has been relatively neglected, and not as much work has been done in this area as was done during the last decades of the nineteenth and first decades of the twentieth century by philosophers such as Brentano, Moore, and Ross. In recent years there has been something of a renewed interest in value theory. Much, however, if not indeed most, of the recent work in this area has not been in the non-naturalist, rationalist, intuitionist, realist tradition of the three thinkers just mentioned. The present work is in that tradition. It seeks to develop and vindicate a view of the irreducibility, rationality, and objectivity of value as an alternative to reductionist, skeptical, relativist, and subjectivist treatments of value. This it does in what may be referred to as a "positive" as opposed to a "negative" way by concentrating mainly on the development of my own views rather than on presenting detailed criticisms of the views of others, and there are few explicit references to and discussions of recent work. It will be an easy matter for those familiar with the recent literature to discover from the exposition of my own views the respects in which I agree and those in which I disagree with the views of recent writers on the topics I treat. For recent incisive criticisms, with which in the main I agree and to which I have little to add, of recent reductionist, skeptical, relativist, and subjectivist approaches to value theory I refer the reader to the criticisms presented by Professor Panayot Butchvarov in his excellent book *Skepticism in Ethics*.

It might be helpful if I present here a brief account of the course of the book. One of the central theses of the book is that value is neither identical with nor reducible to psychological phenomena such as liking or disliking, preferring, evaluating, and valuing or disvaluing, whether taken singly or in various combinations. In the first chapter, which is mainly phenomenological in character, I consider some of the differences between value and various of these psychological phenomena, some of the differences between such phenomena and some of the relations in which they stand to one another, and different levels of such phenomena.

In chapter 2, which is mainly ontological in nature, I discuss the ontological categories to which the bearers of intrinsic value belong. To use the language of Meinong, such categories are species of either of two genera—objects and objectives. The categories of universals and particulars are species of objects. Objectives are sometimes, as by Ross, identified with facts. The term "fact," however, has different senses, to distinguish between which it is necessary to distinguish between states of affairs, the obtaining and the non-obtaining of states of affairs, and propositions, each of which I take to be species of objectives. Universals, taken completely in abstraction from their exemplification by particulars, and states of affairs, taken completely in abstraction from the question of whether they do or do not obtain, are abstracta. I argue that abstracta have no intrinsic value at all and that it is only concreta, such as existent particulars and the obtaining and non-obtaining of states of affairs, that have such value. Although, however, only concreta and never abstracta have such value, the intrinsic value of particulars depends upon the nature of the universals they exemplify and that of the obtaining and non-obtaining of states of affairs upon the nature of the states of affairs that do or do not obtain.

In chapter 3, I present a discussion of the species of value and their relationships to one another. There are two major species of value—intrinsic and extrinsic—and two major species of extrinsic value—instrumental and contributory. These species yield the concept of total value, which is the conjunction of the intrinsic, instrumental, and contributory value a bearer of value has. The treatment of these species of value includes a discussion of wholes and parts and of the world, taken as a whole than which no more inclusive whole can be conceived. The chapter concludes with a discussion of C.I. Lewis' concept of inherent value and a rejection of this concept as useless for value theory.

In the fourth chapter I argue that the concepts of value, of positive, negative, and neutral value, of intrinsic and extrinsic value, and of instrumental and contributory value cannot be understood unless the concepts of intrinsic goodness and badness are understood, so that the latter two concepts are the central concepts of value theory. Attempts to define these two concepts fall into either of two mutually exclusive and jointly exhaustive classes. One class consists of attempts to define them in terms of non-evaluative concepts, whether psychological or non-psychological, the other of attempts to define them in terms of evaluative concepts. I examine various attempts of both types, argue that they all fail, and conclude that the concepts in question are indefinable. I argue also that although the intrinsic goodness or badness of a given thing can sometimes be established by appealing to the intrinsic goodness or badness of something else, ultimately such proof rests on seeing without proof that something is intrinsically good or bad. All proof, however, whether in value theory or in any other area of inquiry, rests on seeing without proof that some given proposition is true and that certain propositions follow from certain others.

I argue in chapter 5 that although the concepts of intrinsic goodness and badness are the central concepts of value theory it does not follow that they are also the central concepts of moral philosophy. Instead, the central concepts of moral philosophy—such as the concepts of duty or obligation, ought, rightness and wrongness, supererogation, rights, moral goodness and badness, and moral virtues and vices—can be explicated without using the concepts of intrinsic goodness and badness, so that moral philosophy, rather than being simply a branch of value theory, is instead presupposed in certain respects by the latter. At the same time, however, what may be referred to as "moral objectives" are such that any moral objective has either intrinsic or extrinsic positive or negative value and therefore either positive or negative total value. The chapter ends with a brief treatment of theodicy.

In the sixth chapter an account is presented of the ground of the value of particulars, which are either persons or things that are not persons. The goodness or badness of particulars of both types is determined by the nature of the universals they exemplify, taken in conjunction with the nature of the kinds of which they are instances. The exemplification of a given universal by an instance of one kind might make it a good instance of its kind, whereas the exemplification of the same universal by an instance of another kind might make it a bad instance of that kind. It is argued that in at least some cases being a normal instance of a given kind is sufficient to make an instance of the kind a good instance and that an instance of a kind can be a good instance without being an excellent one. This is followed by a discussion of virtues and vices, which are treated as good-making and bad-making properties of persons, and of loving and hating, the first of which is treated as a central virtue of persons, the second a central vice. It is then argued that the complete good of a person consists of two components—one a non-moral component consisting of having non-moral goods of various sorts, the other a moral component consisting of being morally good, which consists of having various of the moral virtues in a degree sufficient to make one a good person.

The seventh and eighth chapters are devoted to a discussion of the nature and value of practical rationality. In chapter 7 it is argued that such rationality takes precedence over theoretical rationality, given that the object of theoretical rationality—the acquisition of theoretical knowledge or understanding—is only one value among others. The argument includes a discussion of the difference between silence and deception and of the possibility of self-deception and an assessment of the relative value of silence, deception, and knowledge. In the eighth chapter the relationship of practical rationality to morality is discussed. Two views of practical rationality and morality are discussed, one of which is egoistic, the other non-egoistic. It is argued that there is no antecedent impartial concept of practical rationality that is neither egoistic nor non-egoistic and that we can determine whether an egoistic or a non-egoistic view of practical rationality is preferable only by determining whether an egoistic or a non-egoistic view of morality is preferable. This means that, rather than tailoring our view of morality to fit some antecedent view of rationality, we ought instead to tailor our view of practical rationality to fit an acceptable view of morality. Since, I argue, a non-egoistic view of morality is preferable to an egoistic view, we ought to adopt a non-egoistic rather than an egoistic view of practical rationality.

In chapter 9 the value of different attitudes that can be taken toward intrinsically indifferent things is discussed. Different possible extreme views and different possible moderate views of the value of various attitudes toward the indifferent are distinguished, and I argue that it is good that people like various indifferent things of which they have experience or knowledge, if for no other reason than that such likings are manifestations of magnanimity, instances of which are intrinsically good, and that a pervasive dislike of indifferent things is intrinsically bad, given that such disliking is a manifestation of mean-spiritedness, instances of which are intrinsically bad.

In the tenth chapter, which perhaps could be regarded as an appendix rather than a concluding chapter, I discuss some of the implications for higher education of the view of the complete human good presented in chapter 6. By distinguishing between (1) civilization and morality, (2) having goods and being good, and (3) moral and non-moral education, I argue that a non-moral education that seeks only to assist students in acquiring only one aspect of their complete good, by endeavoring only to increase their understanding of the various arts and sciences and to prepare them for various careers, is one-sided and inadequate and that the task of higher education is also to assist students in acquiring their complete good by helping them to become good persons.

Chapter 2 is a slightly revised version of a paper, "Bearers of Value," that appeared in *Philosophy and Phenomenological Research* 51 (1991). I am grateful to the editor for permission to use that material here. I thank also Oya Kolatu and Lissette Castillo for the excellent work they did in typing the manuscript. Douglas Browning of the University of Texas read an earlier version of the manuscript with the exception of chapters 4, 5, and 10. I am deeply grateful to him for his many insightful and detailed comments and suggestions. I have followed some but not all of his suggestions. On certain philosophical issues we disagree. My respect for him as a philosopher, however, is so great that usually when we disagree I come away feeling that he sees things I fail to see. For the many flaws that doubtless remain I alone am responsible, especially in view of the fact that I have not unfailingly followed the suggestions he made. As always, my profoundest debt of gratitude is to my wife, to whose memory this book is dedicated, for her unfailing cheerfulness and encouragement over many years and for constantly providing throughout these years absolutely ideal conditions under which to work. One of my deepest regrets is that she did not live to see its completion.

Chapter 1

Value and Psychological Phenomena

One of the central theses of this work is that value is not identical with or reducible to psychological phenomena such as valuing, evaluating, preferring, liking or disliking, taken either singly or in various combinations. In this chapter we shall consider (1) some of the differences between value and certain of these phenomena, (2) some of the differences between such phenomena and some of the relations in which they stand to one another, and (3) different levels of such phenomena.

1. Value, Valuing, and Evaluating

The term "value" is used in different ways. Some of these uses will be of no interest to us here. We shall not, for example, be interested in its use to refer to the truth-value of propositions. Nor shall we be concerned with its use to refer to the value of a variable, as when it is said that the value of the variable "x" in "1 + x = 3" is 2. There are, however, at least three uses of the term and its cognates in which we shall be interested. In one of these uses it is used as a verb, as in "I value *a*," "you value *b*," and "he values *c*". In a second it is used as an adjective, as in "*x* is valuable". In a third it is used as a noun, as in "Some of John's values are *a*, *b*, and *c*," in which the values of the variables "*a*," "*b*," and "*c*" are some of the things John values. In this third sense of the term it is the things themselves valued by a person that constitute the values of that person. Such things are valuable or have value, at least for the person who values them, but they themselves, as values of the person, are distinct from the value they have for him. They are his values in the sense that he values them.

In addition to valuing various things, a person can also evaluate things. Evaluating a thing is different from valuing it. In evaluating something a person is not valuing it but instead is endeavoring to determine its value or at least to ascertain whether he, and perhaps also others, ought to value it and, if he concludes that he, and again perhaps also others, ought to value it, to determine the degree to which he, and perhaps also they, ought to do so. Evaluating some object of evaluation presupposes that the value, if any, it has and the degree of its value are independent of whether one already values it. Thus one can value an object without evaluating it, and one can evaluate an object without already valuing it. The evaluation of things by human beings has been a persistent and widespread practice throughout the course of human history, and unless things have value independently of their being evaluated this practice would rest on a persistent and widespread illusion and would have little or no point.

As used in any of the three ways indicated above, the term "value" usually, if not indeed always, connotes what is sometimes referred to as "positive" value, as opposed to "negative" or "neutral" value. In the broadest sense of the term, to say that someone values something, x, is to say either that he likes it or that he regards it as good, and to say that x has value or is valuable is to say that it is good. Similarly, to say that some of John's values are a, b, and c is to say that he likes them or that he regards them as good. In evaluating something, however, a person is endeavoring to determine whether it has value and, if it does, whether its value is positive or negative and perhaps also to determine the degree to which it has either positive or negative value. The term "value" thus has both a narrow and a broad use. In the narrow sense it connotes only positive value. In the broad sense it connotes not only positive but also negative and perhaps also neutral value.

To say that something has neutral value is to say that it has neither positive nor negative value. If the term "value" is used in the broadest possible sense, neutral value, like positive and negative value, will be a form of value, and everything will have value, since everything has either positive, negative, or neutral value. In a narrower sense of "value," however, to say of something that it has neutral value or that it is neutral in value is to say that it has no value at all. In this sense of "value," some things might have value and others not. Those things that have either positive or negative value have value, but those things, if any, that have neither positive nor negative value have no value at all. Since to say of something that it has neutral value is to say that it has neither positive nor negative value, it seems better to use the term "value" only in the narrower sense according to which the only forms of value are positive and negative value. Thus instead of saying that everything has value, since everything has either positive, negative, or neutral value, I shall say that those things, if any, that have neither positive nor negative value have no value at all or that they are indifferent in value.

If we restrict our use of "value" in the way suggested, we may say that "value" names a genus or determinable of which the most general species or determinations are positive and negative value. The terms "positive value" and "negative value" are technical or at least quasi-technical terms. The meaning of "positive value" is more or less the same as that of "good," in a wide sense of "good"; and the meaning of "negative value" is more or less the same as that of "bad," in a wide sense of "bad". We may therefore say that "value" names a genus or determinable of which the most general species or determinations are good and bad. This, indeed, might even serve as a definition of "value," taken as an adjective or a noun. It is unlikely in this context to be taken as a verb, since, as we have seen, to say that some person values something, *x,* is to say that he likes *x* or regards it as good. Taken as a verb, the genus named by "value" would be more appropriately named "valuing". If so, then it is valuing, not value, that is named by "valuing".

Valuings might themselves have value and be valued and evaluated by someone. Just as a person can like or regard as good certain things and dislike or regard as bad certain other things, so also one can like or regard as good some valuings and evaluations and dislike or regard as bad certain others. One might, for example, like or regard as good evaluations that are careful, conscientious, and judicious and dislike or regard as bad those that are careless, unconscientious, and injudicious. And one might like or regard as good and thus value valuings of others that agree with one's own and dislike or regard as bad valuings of others that disagree with one's own. Indeed, one might also evaluate one's own valuings and evaluations and come to value, i.e., to like or to regard as good, some of them and to dislike or regard as bad others. A person's initial valuings are likely to be strenghtened if, upon evaluating them, he comes to value them, i.e., to like them or to regard them as good. If, however, he comes to dislike them or to regard them as bad, he might modify or abandon them. This, however, does not always happen, since the strength of one's initial likings or valuings might be greater than that of one's subsequent dislike of them. In such a situation, I might initially value something, x, subsequently come to dislike or to regard as bad my valuing x, yet nonetheless continue to value x, perhaps because my initial liking of x is greater than my subsequent dislike of my liking of x. In such a situation I do not both like and dislike x; instead, I like x or regard it as good, yet also dislike or regard as bad my liking x. It is my liking x, not x itself, that I dislike or regard as bad. Yet despite my dislike of my liking x I nonetheless continue to like x.

Evaluations and valuings of evaluations and valuings are second-order phenomena that have as their intentional objects first-order phenomena consisting of evaluations and valuings of things that are not themselves evaluations and valuings. Such second-order phenomena therefore presuppose the corresponding first-order phenomena. The latter, however, are presupposed only as the intentional objects of the second-order phenomena and need not exist, occur, or have being independently of their being the objects of the second-order phenomena, just as the intentional objects of first-order valuings and evaluatings need not exist, occur, or have being independently or their being valued and evaluated. We frequently value and evaluate things that do not exist and that we know do not exist independently of our valuing and evaluating them.

This happens frequently in situations in which we are deliberating about which of two or more possible courses of action we ought to undertake. Usually such deliberation will include a consideration of what seem to us to be the probable consequences of choosing one possible course of action as opposed to others. Prior to our choice, each of the possible courses of action and its probable consequences have no being at all independently of our consideration of them. They are instead only intentional objects for us, and are such objects for us only if and only so long as we think of them. Yet it is precisely the value of such intentional objects that we in our deliberation are endeavoring to determine. Or, if one prefer, it is precisely what would be the value of each course of action and its probable consequences if it were undertaken and if its probable consequences did in fact ensue that we are attempting to ascertain. Yet even in this second way of describing the situation involved in deliberation, it is still the value of what are only intentional objects for us prior to our choosing and acting that we are endeavoring to determine. Even, that is, if it is not the value of each of the possible courses of action and its probable consequences as intentional objects for us that we are attempting to ascertain, but instead what *would* be the value of each possible course of action and its probable consequences *if* it were in fact chosen and *if* its probable consequences did in fact ensue, each possible course of action and its probable consequences are still during the process of deliberation only intentional objects for us. At least one of the purposes of deliberation is that it helps us to choose wisely between possible courses of action by attempting prior to choice and action to assess what would be the value of each of the courses of action open to us and of its probable consequences if it were chosen and if its probable consequences did in fact ensue. Believing that one of the courses of action, if chosen, would have greater value than any of the others, I choose it. Whether it does in fact have the value I believed prior to choice it would have might well be determinable only after the choice has been made and its consequences have unfolded. And whether it does in fact have greater value than some other possible course of action would have had had it been chosen might well be something we can never know.

We also value and evaluate states of affairs that never obtain but that could have obtained only in the past, i.e., only prior to our valuing and evaluating them. Thus we might believe that the state of affairs consisting of Germany's not invading Poland in 1939 would have had greater value had it obtained than did the opposite state of affairs. The state of affairs consisting of Germany's not invading Poland in 1939, since it did not and can never obtain, is only an intentional object, as is also its obtaining. Nonetheless, we might, while knowing that it did not obtain, still regard its obtaining as preferable to the obtaining of the opposite state of affairs that did in fact obtain. This clearly would seem to be a case in which we would be regarding an intentional object, i.e., a state of affairs that did not and never can obtain, as being preferable to a state of affairs that did in fact obtain and that therefore, although an intentional object, is not only an intentional object. We can also regard as good the obtaining of some state of affairs we believe has obtained or is obtaining but that in fact has not and is not obtaining. In such a case we regard as good something we believe not to be merely an intentional object but yet in fact is only such an object and nothing more. If so, then we can value and evaluate things that in fact are only intentional objects, regardless of whether we believe or know that they are only such objects.

2. Levels of Psychological Phenomena

In the previous section I used the term "valuing" to refer to likings and dislikings as well as to what may be referred to as "valuing proper" or as "valuing in the strict sense of the term". The difference between liking and disliking on the one hand and valuing proper on the other is something like the following. In liking and disliking the emphasis, as the language suggests, is on what one likes or dislikes without necessarily taking what one likes or dislikes as being good or bad. In valuing proper the emphasis, as again the language suggests, is on the goodness or badness of what one likes or dislikes, as contrasted with one's liking or disliking of it. Frequently, perhaps usually, but I think not always, what one likes or dislikes one also regards as good or bad. Yet, as I think the following example shows, one's first-order likings and dislikings can at the second-order level themselves be liked or disliked or regarded as good or bad.

Suppose that I come upon an automobile accident and like looking at the injured, bleeding, and perhaps also dead and dying victims as others render aid. I like looking at the injured victims regardless of whether I regard their plight as good or as bad or as neither. If I like looking at them without regarding their plight as good or as bad, a first-order instance of liking occurs unaccompanied by any first-order valuing proper. In such a case I like looking at them but am indifferent toward their plight. If, however, I make an evaluation of their plight, it is not necessary that I regard it as good if I am to like looking at them. Instead, I might like looking at them while at the same time regarding their plight as bad. I might even like looking at them while at the same time I do everything I can to render aid. This example suffices, I think, to show (1) that a first-order liking can occur regardless of whether a first-order valuing proper also occurs and (2) that a first-order liking can be accompanied by an evaluation regardless of whether the object of evaluation is regarded as good or as bad. Precisely similar considerations apply also to first-order dislikings. I can dislike something (1) without regarding it as good or bad, (2) while regarding it as bad, and also even (3) while regarding it as good. I can dislike a particular painting (1) without regarding it as good or as bad, (2) while regarding it as bad, and even (3) while regarding it as good, in the latter case perhaps because I defer to the judgment of those I believe to be more knowledgeable than I about painting. In such cases of deference I do not see that what I regard as good is good but instead defer to the judgment of those I take to be more knowledgeable than I whom I believe do see that what I regard as good even though I dislike it is in fact good.

The likings, dislikings, and valuings proper discussed in the preceding paragraph are all first-order phenomena. Second-order phenomena come on the scene only when first-order phenomena are themselves liked, disliked, evaluated, or regarded as good or as bad. The objects of first-order phenomena consist of anything, other than first-order phenomena themselves, that is liked, disliked, valued, or evaluated, whereas all objects of second-order phenomena are first-order likings, dislikings, valuings, or evaluations. Some creatures (perhaps all dumb animals) that have likes and dislikes are incapable of liking, disliking, valuing, or evaluating their likings and dislikings. To be capable of doing the latter one must be able to objectify one's likings and dislikings as objects of consciousness for oneself. This is something that normal adult human beings can do. Thus I, liking to look at the victims of an accident, might come to be ashamed of my liking to do this. In being ashamed of my first-order liking, I dislike the latter. My being ashamed is therefore a second-order phenomenon, since its object is the first-order phenomenon of my liking to look at the accident victims.

One might, if one prefer, say that I am ashamed of myself. Such a way of speaking is acceptable, provided that one realize that it is merely an elliptical way of saying that I am ashamed of myself because of my liking to look at the accident victims. I can be ashamed of myself only if there is something about me, such as my being or failing to be something, my doing or failing to do something, or my liking or disliking something, of which I am ashamed. It is my being or failing to be something, my doing or failing to do something, my liking or disliking something that I am ashamed of, not simply myself regardless of what I am or fail to be, do or fail to do, like or dislike. This, incidentally, does not mean that one can be ashamed only of one's own being or failing to be something, doing or failing to do something, liking or disliking something. Instead, one can also be ashamed of others, especially those to whom one stands in some special relationshp such as membership in the same family, because of what they are or fail to be, do or fail to do, like or dislike.

The phenomenon of shame, however, is not necessarily a second-order phenomenon, since I can be ashamed not only of my liking or disliking something but also of my being or failing to be something or of my doing or failing to do something. If I am ashamed of my being or failing to be something or of my doing or failing to do something, my being ashamed is a first-order rather than a second-order phenomenon. This is because my being or failing to be something, my doing or failing to do something, unlike my liking or disliking or my being ashamed of something, are not essentially intentional. They, like my liking or disliking something, can be liked or disliked and can be things of which I am ashamed. But unlike my liking or disliking or my being ashamed of something, they are not essentially intentional, and it is because of this that they are not first-order phenomena, all of which are essentially intentional.

The second-order phenomenon of my being ashamed of the first-order phenomenon of my liking to look at the accident victims can itself become the object of a third-order phenomenon. This would happen if I come to regard my being ashamed as being appropriate, fitting, right, or good. If I do so come to regard it, I might also come to like my being ashamed as something that is appropriate, fitting, right, or good. If so, then we have a series consisting of a liking, a disliking, and then a liking. First I like looking at the accident victims. This is followed by my being ashamed of this first liking. In being ashamed of the first liking I might come to dislike it. Being ashamed is an essentially painful phenomenon, and in being ashamed I might come to dislike something that initially I liked. So long, however, as my being ashamed does not itself become an object for me, it remains an essentially painful experience. I am pained that I liked doing something that now, because of my being ashamed, and perhaps also because of the pain essentially tied to my being ashamed, I dislike having done. Once, however, my being ashamed becomes an object for me, I might, but need not, come to regard it as appropriate, fitting, right, or good. If I do not come so to regard it, I might continue to be ashamed and to suffer the essentially accompanying pain. But if I do so come to regard it, the pain of my being ashamed might be lessened and might even disappear entirely as the satisfaction from so regarding it grows. In this way I might come finally to like my disliking of what initially I liked.

Higher-order phenomena presuppose those of lower-order, at least as intentional objects, whereas those of lower-order do not presuppose those of higher-order. This is to say that lower-order phenomena can exist or occur without being objects of those of higher-order, whereas those of higher-order cannot exist or occur without having those of lower-order as their objects. Thus I can like looking at the accident victims without being ashamed of doing so and can be ashamed of doing so without regarding my being ashamed as appropriate or inappropriate. But I cannot regard my being ashamed as appropriate or inappropriate if I am not or do not believe that I am ashamed, and I cannot be ashamed of liking to look at the victims if I do not or believe that I do not like looking at them.

This is connected with the fact that what may be referred to as "the immediate object" of a third-order phenomenon is some second-order phenomenon and that of a second-order phenomenon some first-order phenomenon. The object of a first-order phenomenon, although it is the immediate object of the first-order phenomenon alone, may perhaps be referred to as "the mediate object" or at least as part of the immediate object of the corresponding second-order and third-order phenomena. Thus a first-order phenomenon cannot be the object of a second-order phenomenon and a second-order phenomenon the object of a third-order phenomenon unless the object of the first-order phenomenon is at least indirectly intended in intending the first-order or the second-order phenomenon. If, that is, I am to like, dislike, evaluate, or value my liking to look at the accident victims, I must have as an intentional object not only my liking to look at the victims but also the victims themselves. Precisely similar considerations apply to third-order phenomena. I cannot think of my being ashamed of my liking to look at the victims without thereby also thinking (1) not only of my being ashamed of my liking to look at them and (2) of my liking to look at them but also (3) of the victims themselves. If so, then the immediate object of a first-order phenomenon carries over, so to speak, as part of the object of second-order and third-order phenomena. Because of this, second-order phenomena may be said to build on first-order phenomena and third-order phenomena on those of the second-order.

It is important that different levels of these phenomena be distinguished from different, sometimes conflicting, likings, dislikings, valuings, and evaluations at the same level of the same thing by the same or by different persons, whether from the same or from different points of view and whether in the same or in different respects. Such different likings, dislikings, valuings, and evaluations can occur at any of the three levels we have distinguished. Thus I might like, you might dislike, and he might neither like nor dislike looking at the accident victims of our example, and at different times I might like, dislike, and neither like nor dislike looking at accident victims. Such likings, dislikings, and neither-likings-nor-dislikings are all at the first-order level. Similarly, I might not be ashamed of my liking to look at accident victims whereas you, being my wife, might be ashamed of my liking to do so. And I at first might not be ashamed of my liking to look at such victims and later come to be ashamed of my liking to do so. My not being ashamed and your being ashamed of my liking to do so are both second-order phenomena. Again, I might not regard my not being ashamed as inappropriate whereas you do regard it as being such. And I for a time might not regard my not being ashamed as inappropriate and later come to regard it as being so. My not regarding my not being ashamed as inappropriate and your regarding it as such are both third-order phenomena. These examples, I think, suffice to show that different likings, dislikings, valuings, and evaluations on the part of the same or of different persons at the same or at different times can occur at the same level, whether it be at the first, the second, or the third level.

If the preceding is correct, we evaluate various likings, dislikings, valuings, and evaluations, both those of our own and also those of others, as being appropriate or inappropriate, fitting or unfitting, right or wrong, good or bad. That we like or dislike various likings, dislikings, valuings, and evaluations of others seems obvious enough. We tend to like those of others with which we agree and to dislike those with which we disagree. And that we like various of those of our own also seems obvious enough. It also seems obvious that we sometimes dislike various of those of our own in the past, especially when they conflict with our present likings, dislikings, and valuings. But that we can and sometimes do like those of others that disagree with our own and sometimes dislike our own present likings, dislikings, or valuings is not so obvious. Yet I believe that in fact we sometimes do. Thus I might like some valuing or evaluation of yours even though it disagrees with one of mine because I believe yours to be honest, conscientious, and judicious.

It might, however, be objected that if I like your evaluation on these grounds even though it disagress with mine, it is not your evaluation I like but rather its honesty, conscientiousness, and judiciousness. This, I think, would be a mistake. From the fact that we like something because it has certain characteristics it does not follow that we like only its characteristics and not the thing itself that has these characteristics. In general, we like the things we like and dislike the things we dislike because of the characteristics they have or that we believe they have.

Although we might also like or dislike various of their characteristics, we also like or dislike the things themselves. I cannot, however, like some evaluation of yours that disagrees with one of mine because I believe yours to be acceptable, correct, or true, since if it disagrees with one of my own evaluations, and I know or believe that it does, I cannot, believing that my own evaluation is acceptable, correct, or true, believe also that yours is too. I cannot, that is, believe that each of two con-flicting evaluations is acceptable, correct, or true if I know or believe that they conflict.

We can also dislike both some of our own present likings, dislikings, valuings, and evaluations and also various of those of others that agree with various of our own. Thus I might dislike both my own and also your evaluation that my liking to look at the accident victims is inap-propriate, unfitting, wrong, or bad. And even though I might dislike your and my evaluation and continue to like looking at accident victims despite my regarding it as inappropriate, I might nonetheless resolve to refrain from indulging this liking, endeavor earnestly to keep this reso-lution, and indeed also succeed fully in doing so. If so, then I refrain from doing something I like doing because I evaluate my doing the thing in question as inappropriate. W. D. Ross maintained that "there is no more mystery in the fact that the thought of an act as one's duty should arouse an impulse to do it, than in the fact that the thought of an act as pleasant, or as leading to pleasure, should arouse an impulse to do it."[1] Similarly, there is no more mystery in the fact that a person's evaluation of something he likes doing as inappropriate should lead him to refrain from doing it, even though he dislikes his evaluation, than in the fact that a person's liking to do something should lead him to do it. If so, then just as a person's liking to do something can lead him to do it, so also his evaluation of his doing the thing in question as inappropriate can lead him to refrain from doing it even though he dislikes his evalua-tion. In this way a person's valuings and evaluations can have as direct an effect on his conduct as his likings and dislikings and, because of this, can have as much importance for practice as his likings and dislikings.

But, as I shall argue more fully later on, just as the goodness or bad-ness of likings and dislikings depends on the goodness or badness of what is liked or disliked, so also the goodness or badness of one's valu-ings depends on that of whatever it is that one regards as good or bad. This applies to likings, dislikings, and valuings at each of the three levels distinguished above. Since, however, the goodness or badness of third-order phenomena depends on that of the second-order objects of such phenomena, that of second-order phenomena on that of the first-order objects of such phenomena, and that of first-order phenomena on that of the objects like, disliked, or valued at the first-order level, the goodness or badness of such objects is fundamental. Unless such objects are themselves good or bad, no likings, dislikings, or valuings, regardless of the level at which they occur, can be either good or bad. If, that is, no such objects were themselves good or bad, all likings, dislikings, and valuings would be indifferent in value, and the widespread and persistent practice of evaluating objects would lose much if not indeed all of its point.

3. Terminological Remarks

Liking something regardless of whether one regards the thing liked as good, valuing something in the broad sense of liking it without regarding it as good, and valuing something in the more restricted sense of regarding the thing valued as good regardless of whether one likes it, which I have called "valuing proper," are all species of what are sometimes termed "pro-attitudes". Similarly, disliking something regardless of whether one regards the thing disliked as bad, disvaluing something in the broad sense of disliking it without regarding it as bad, and disvaluing something in the more restricted sense of regarding it as bad regardless of whether one dislikes it, which may be called "disvaluing proper," are all species of what are sometimes termed "con-attitudes". One cannot take a pro- or a con-attitude toward a given thing without taking some specific pro- or con-attitude toward it, and to say of someone that he has a pro- or a con-attitude to a given thing, while informative, is not as informative as a specification of what species of pro- or con-attitude he has toward the thing in question. Since there is a difference of some importance between (1) liking a thing regardless of whether one also regards it as good and (2) regarding a thing as good regardless of whether one also likes it, to say only of someone that he has a pro-attitude toward a given thing might mean either of two things without specifying which of the two is meant. Since the terminology of "pro-attitude" and "con-attitude" is insufficiently specific in the respect indicated, in what follows I shall avoid such terminology and speak instead of liking and disliking things and of regarding things as being good or bad. The psychological phenomena of liking and disliking a given thing are specifically different from those of regarding a given thing as being good or bad, and phenomena of one of these species are not reducible to those of the other.[2]

Just as there are different species of pro- and con-attitudes, so also there are different species of liking and disliking—so many, in fact, that it would be a most formidable task to attempt to list them all. Being irritated, being terrified, and being disappointed, for example, differ specifically from one another, and to say that a person is irritated by something when in fact he is terrified by it would be to misdescribe his experience. Yet whatever it is that irritates, terrifies, or disappoints a person is something he dislikes, as is also his being irritated, terrified, or disappointed, at least during the period of time he suffers these experiences. Similarly, being amused, being ecstatic, and being relieved differ specifically from one another, and to say that a person is amused by something when in fact he is ecstatic about it would be to misdescribe his experience. Yet whatever it is that makes a person amused, ecstatic, or relieved is usually something he likes, as he usually also likes his being amused, ecstatic, or relieved, at least during the span of time he has such experiences. To say of someone simply that he dislikes something is not as informative as saying of him that he is irritated, terrified, or disappointed by it; and to say of someone that he is amused, ecstatic, or relieved by or over something is more informative than saying of him simply that he likes it. Yet although in what follows it will sometimes be important to distinguish between (1) liking or disliking a given thing regardless of whether one also regards it as being good or bad and (2) regarding a given thing as being good or bad regardless of whether one also likes or dislikes it, it will only rarely be important to distinguish between the different species of liking and disliking. For this reason I shall usually speak simply of someone's liking or disliking a given thing without specifying any of the many ways in which a person can like or dislike something.

I shall therefore use "liking" and "disliking" as generic terms intended to cover all the various species of liking and disliking. My use of these terms will thus be similar to, if not indeed identical with, Brentano's use of "loving" and "hating".[3] The terms "loving" and "hating," however, in ordinary English have a more specific use than "liking" and "disliking". It is possible that a person like something without loving it and dislike something without hating it, as "loving" and "hating" are frequently used in ordinary English. The terms "liking" and "disliking" therefore have a more generic use in ordinary English than "loving" and "hating" do, and because of this it seems better to use them rather than "loving" and "hating" to refer to the generic attitudes I shall be using them to indicate.

Chapter 2

Ontological Categories and Bearers of Value

This chapter is devoted to a treatment of a topic that has not received as much attention in recent years as it once did. This is the issue of the ontological categories of the bearers of intrinsic value. To use the language of Meinong, without necessarily attaching to it precisely the same meaning he did, such categories are species of either of two genera—objects and objectives. The categories of universals and particulars are species of objects. W. D. Ross identifies objectives with facts, and suggests that "the things that have ultimate value are facts."[1] But, as will appear, the term "fact" has different senses, to distinguish between which it is necessary to distinguish between states of affairs, the obtaining and the non-obtaining of states of affairs, and propositions, each of which I shall take to be species of objectives. The central question I shall address is that of which of these categories of objects and objectives are bearers of intrinsic value and which are not. I shall assume that for the purposes of this chapter the distinction I intend between the two species of objects—universals and particulars—will be sufficiently clear.[2] The argument, however, will require a short ontological excursion concerning the nature of the various species of objectives and their relationships to one another.

1. States of Affairs, Propositions, and Facts

A state of affairs is or consists of something's being, doing, or having something. States of affairs are neither true nor false. Instead, they either obtain or do not obtain. If one believes that a given state of affairs obtains when in fact it does or that it does not obtain when in fact it does not, then one's belief is true. But if one believes that a given state of affairs obtains when in fact it does not or that it does not obtain when in fact it does, then one's belief is false. States of affairs are therefore distinct from and not reducible to beliefs, although someone's believing that a given state of affairs obtains is a state of affairs that obtains at a given time. Although a person can believe that a given state of affairs obtains, the state of affairs itself is not a belief but instead is that which is believed to obtain. Rather than being reducible to the concept of belief, the concept of a state of affairs is the concept of something the obtaining or the non-obtaining of which can be the content of a belief. The content of a belief is also a proposition. From this, however, it does not follow that states of affairs and propositions are identical, since, as we shall see, a proposition is the content of a belief in a different sense from that in which the obtaining or the non-obtaining of a state of affairs is. *That* a given state of affairs obtains, however, is a proposition.

We must therefore distinguish between (1) states of affairs, (2) the obtaining and the non-obtaining of a state of affairs, and (3) that a given state of affairs obtains (or does not obtain), which is a propositon. States of affairs can be entertained as intended objects of thought but cannot be believed. They obtain or do not obtain, but are distinct from and are not reducible to their obtaining or their not obtaining. If this were not the case, one could not entertain as an object of thought some state of affairs, such as the Eiffel Tower's being in London, without considering also the question of whether it does or does not obtain. Moreover, in order to consider this latter questions it is necessary first to have as the intended object of one's thought the state of affairs the obtaining or the non-obtaining of which one is to consider. One must first think of a state of affairs before one can think of it as obtaining or as not obtaining. In addition, without states of affairs there would be nothing to obtain or not to obtain, and no proposition could be either true or false.

The obtaining of a given state of affairs, like the state of affairs that obtains, is neither true nor false, whereas the proposition that a given state of affairs obtains is true or false. But although the two are not identical, they are necessarily related. First, propositions presuppose the obtaining and the non-obtaining of states of affairs, in the sense that no proposition could be true or false in the absence of the obtaining and the non-obtaining of states of affairs. It is because various states of affairs do or do not obtain that various propositions are true or false.

Second, for any given state of affairs there is a pair of propositions, one to the effect that it obtains, the other to the effect that it does not obtain. Which of the two is true depends upon whether the state of affairs in question does or does not obtain.

We turn now to consider briefly some of the relations holding between (1) states of affairs, the obtaining and the non-obtaining of states of affairs, and propositions and (2) facts. The term "fact" is used in different senses. In one of its senses it is used to designate states of affairs that obtain. In this sense of the term those states of affairs that obtain are facts, whereas those that do not obtain are not facts. Thus the Eiffel Tower's being in Paris is a fact, since that state of affairs obtains, whereas the Eiffel Tower's being in London is not a fact, since that state of affairs does not obtain. To admit the category of facts in this sense, however, is not to introduce another category in addition to that of states of affairs that obtain, since the term "fact" in this sense is only another name for such states of affairs and designates nothing distinct from or in addition to them.

A second sense of the term "fact" is that in which it is used to designate the obtaining or the non-obtaining of a state of affairs, as distinct from the state of affairs that does or does not obtain. In this sense of the term, the obtaining of the state of affairs consisting of the Eiffel Tower's being in Paris is a fact distinct from the fact consisting of that state of affairs, which is a fact in the first sense of "fact". Similarly, in this second sense of the term the non-obtaining of the state of affairs consisting of the Eiffel Tower's being in London is also a fact, even though this state of affairs is not a fact in the first sense of "fact," since it does not obtain. In this second sense of the term, the obtaining of a state of affairs that obtains is a fact distinct from the state of affairs that obtains, which is a fact in the first sense of "fact"; and the non-obtaining of a state of affairs that does not obtain is also in this sense a fact even though the state of affairs that does not obtain is not a fact in the first sense.

To some it might seem that the term "fact" is never used in this second sense. If, however, we substitute for the pedantic "the obtaining (or the non-obtaining) of the state of affairs consisting of the Eiffel Tower's being in Paris" the ordinary expression "the existence (or the non-existence) of the Eiffel Tower in Paris," we can more easily see that "fact" is sometimes used in this second sense. People do, that is, sometimes say such things as "the existence of the Eiffel Tower in Paris is a fact" and "the non-existence of the Eiffel Tower in London is a fact". To admit, however, the category of facts in this second sense is not to introduce another category in addition to that of the obtaining or the non-obtaining of states of affairs, since facts in this sense are nothing other than the obtaining or the non-obtaining of states of affairs.

A third sense of the term "fact" is that in which it is used to designate true propositions. In this sense of the term, the following two sentences are equivalent in meaning: "That the Eiffel Tower is in Paris is a true proposition" and "That the Eiffel is in Paris is a fact". So also are these two sentences: "It is true that the Eiffel Tower is in Paris" and "It is a fact that the Eiffel Tower is in Paris". To generalize, any sentence used to state a true proposition also states a fact and vice versa. Thus "The Eiffel Tower is in Paris" states a true proposition if and only if it states a fact. This last, however, can be misleading in that it might suggest that the stated true proposition and the stated fact are distinct, when in point of fact they are identical. The true proposition stated by the true sentence "p," rather than being distinct from the fact stated by "p," is instead identical with this fact. Thus to admit the category of facts in this third sense is not to introduce a category distinct from and in addition to that of true propositions. Instead, the term "fact," used in this third sense, is only another name for what is designated by the expression "true proposition".

There is still another sense of "fact" that perhaps should be mentioned. This is the sense in which the term is used to designate anything that exists or has being independently of its being thought of by anyone. The term is used in this sense more widely in non-philosophical than in philosophical contexts and discourse. Facts in this sense of the term may be referred to as "existent entities" or "real entities". In this sense of "fact" the Eiffel Tower, since it exists independently of being thought of by anyone, is a fact, whereas mermaids and square-circles, since they do not, are not facts. Although acts of thinking of mermaids or square-circles, since they can occur without themselves being thought of, are facts, the intended objects of such acts are not, since they have no being independently of being for someone intentional objects. If anything does in fact exist independently of its being for anyone an intentional object, then there are facts in the sense in question. In this sense of the term, however, facts are objects rather than objectives.

The result of these considerations is that the category of facts is not an irreducible ontological category. Instead, the term "fact" has at least four distinct senses, according to which facts are either real entities, states of affairs that obtain, the obtaining or the non-obtaining of states of affairs, or true propositions. This, however, does not mean that there are no facts. If there are real entities, states of affairs that do or do not obtain, and true propositions, then there also are facts. Nor does the fact that facts do not constitute a distinct ontological category mean that the term ought no longer to be used. From the fact that neither of two alternative expressions indicates anything not indicated by the other it does not follow that either ought no longer to be used.[3]

2. States of Affairs as Bearers of Value

The preceding account of various species of objectives and of their relationship to one another will suffice for our purposes. Its main purpose has been to prepare the ground for a consideration of the question of which, if any, of these species of objectives are bearers of value and which, if any, are not. Let us begin our treatment of this question by considering first the obtaining and the non-obtaining of states of affairs.

The obtaining of any given state of affairs is either good, bad, or indifferent, and so also is the non-obtaining of any given state of affairs. That which determines the goodness, the badness, or the indifference of the obtaining or the non-obtaining of any given state of affairs would seem to be the nature of the state of affairs that does or does not obtain. Suppose that states of affairs a, b, and c obtain and that states of affairs x, y, and z do not. Suppose also that the obtaining of a and the non-obtaining of x are good, that the obtaining of b and the non-obtaining of y are bad, and that the obtaining of c and the non-obtaining of z are neither good nor bad. Since states of affairs a, b, c all obtain, and since the obtaining of a is good, that of b bad, and that of c indifferent, there must be some difference between a, b, and c by virtue of which the obtaining of a is good, that of b bad, and that of c indifferent. Similar considerations apply to the non-obtaining of x, y, and z. If so, then that which determines the goodness, badness, or indifference of the obtaining or the non-obtaining of any given state of affairs is the nature of the state of affairs that does or does not obtain.

From this, however, it does not follow that states of affairs themselves, taken completely in abstraction from any consideration of whether they do or do not obtain, are good or bad. This is the case because from the fact that the nature of something, such as the nature of a state of affairs, determines the goodness or badness of something else, such as the obtaining or the non-obtaining of the state of affairs in question, it does not follow that the former as well as the latter must itself be either good or bad. Moreover, if states of affairs, taken in abstraction from the question of whether they do or do not obtain, were themselves good or bad, that which determines their goodness or badness would be something other than their obtaining or their not obtaining. If so, then it is hard to see what could determine their goodness or badness other than their nature. But if this is so, then it would seem that it is their nature that would determine both their own goodness or badness and also that of their obtaining if they do obtain and of their not obtaining if they do not obtain.

It might be helpful if we illustrate these rather abstract considerations by means of examples. Let us suppose that the states of affairs consisting of John's being honest, John's being blind, and John's having brown eyes all obtain and that the states of affairs consisting of John's being dishonest, John's being sighted, and John's having blue eyes do not obtain. Let us suppose also that the obtaining of John's being honest and the non-obtaining of John's being dishonest are both good, that the obtaining of John's being blind and the non-obtaining of John's being sighted are both bad, and that the obtaining of John's having brown eyes and the non-obtaining of John's having blue eyes are both indifferent. Since the states of affairs consisting of John's being honest, John's being blind, and John's having brown eyes all obtain, and since the obtaining of the first state of affairs is good, that of the second bad, and that of the third indifferent, there must be some difference between them by virtue of which the obtaining of the first is good, that of the second bad, and that of the third neither good nor bad. Similar considerations apply to the non-obtaining of John's being dishonest, John's being sighted, and John's having blue eyes.

Since their obtaining is something the first three states of affairs have in common, and since the obtaining of the first is good, that of the second bad, and that of the third indifferent, their obtaining cannot be the ground of the goodness of the obtaining of the first, of the badness of the obtaining of the second, or of the indifference of the obtaining of the third. Similar considerations apply to the non-obtaining of the second three states of affairs. But if their obtaining cannot be the ground of the goodness, badness, or indifference of the obtaining of the first three states of affairs, and if their not obtaining cannot be the source of that of the non-obtaining of the second three states of affairs, then it would seem that the value of the obtaining or the non-obtaining of these states of affairs must be determined by their nature regardless of whether they do or do not obtain.

It was argued above (1) that states of affairs that obtain are facts and (2) that the obtaining of states of affairs that obtain and the non-obtaining of those that do not obtain are also facts. If this is correct, and if the considerations just presented are acceptable, then facts in these two senses of "fact" are either good, bad, or indifferent. John's being honest, John's being blind, and John's having brown eyes, since each is a state of affairs that obtains, is a fact. And if John's being honest is good, John's being blind bad, and John's having brown eyes neither good nor bad, the first is a good, the second a bad, and the third an indifferent fact. Moreover, since the obtaining of these three states of affairs are facts in the second sense of "fact" distinguished above, and since the obtaining of the first is good, that of the second bad, and that of the third neither good nor bad, the first is a good, the second a bad, and the third an indifferent fact. Similarly, since the non-obtaining of the states of affairs consisting of John's being dishonest, John's being sighted, and John's having blue eyes are also facts in the second sense of "fact," and since the non-obtaining of the first is good, of the second bad, and of the third neither good nor bad, the first is a good, the second a bad, and the third an indifferent fact.

To some it will doubtless seem strange to speak of facts in the above two senses of "fact" as being good, bad, or indifferent. Some who find it strange to speak of facts as being good or bad might not find it strange to speak of them as being indifferent since, in believing that facts are neither good nor bad, they might regard all facts as being indifferent in the sense of being neither good nor bad. But if states of affairs that obtain are facts in one sense of "fact," and if some states of affairs that obtain are good, some bad, and some indifferent, then so also are facts in this sense of "fact". Similarly, if the obtaining and the non-obtaining of states of affairs are facts in a second sense of "fact," and if the obtaining or the non-obtaining of some states of affairs is good, of some bad, and of some indifferent, then so also are facts in the second sense of "fact".

The strangeness of speaking of facts in either of the first two senses of "fact" as being good, bad, or indifferent might be diminished somewhat if we adopt a different way of speaking. Thus rather than speaking of facts in the first two senses of the term as being good, bad, or indifferent, let us speak instead of its being good, bad, or neither good nor bad that some given state of affairs obtains. Rather than saying that John's being honest is good, that John's being blind is bad, or that John's having brown eyes is neither good nor bad, let us say instead that it is good that John is honest, bad that John is blind, and neither good nor bad that John has brown eyes. If we do, then rather than saying of a given state of affairs that obtains that it is good, bad, or indifferent, we shall say instead that it is good, bad, or neither good nor bad that some given state of affairs that obtains does in fact obtain. In saying that it is good that John is honest, bad that he is blind, or neither good nor bad that he has brown eyes, we are supposing that he is honest, that he is blind, or that he does have brown eyes. We are supposing, that is, that some given state of affairs does in fact obtain and are saying that it is good, bad, or neither good nor bad that it obtains.

Still another alternative to saying that John's being honest is good, John's being blind is bad, and John's having brown eyes is neither good nor bad is to speak as follows: *that* John is honest is good, *that* John is blind is bad, and *that* John has brown eyes is neither good nor bad. To speak in these ways is to suppose that he is honest, that he is blind, or that he does have brown eyes. We are supposing that some given state of affairs does in fact obtain and are saying of it that its obtaining is good, bad, or indifferent. There appears, however, to be no difference in meaning between these two ways of speaking. "It is good that John is honest" and "That John is honest is good" seem to be identical in meaning. In either case, one is saying of a given state of affairs that obtains that it is good that it obtains. Since, however, a state of affairs that obtains is a fact in the first sense of the term, to say of a given state of affairs that obtains that it is good that it obtains is to say of a given fact that it is good that it is a fact.

Similar considerations apply to the obtaining and the non-obtaining of states of affairs. Rather than saying that the obtaining of the state of affairs consisting of John's being honest is good, we can say instead either (1) "It is good that John is honest" or (2) "That John is honest is good". These two ways of speaking, however, do not distinguish between (1) the state of affairs consisting of John's being honest and (2) the obtaining of this state of affairs. Because of this, neither way of speaking is an adequate substitute for either (1) "The state of affairs consisting of John's being honest, which obtains, is good" or (2) "The obtaining of the state of affairs consisting of John's being honest is good". Since there is in fact a difference between (1) a state of affairs that obtains, since it is possible that precisely the same state of affairs not obtain (unless, of course, it is a necessary state of affairs), and (2) its obtaining, the more pedantic locutions I have been using cannot be replaced adequately by the more familiar locutions in question. This, however, is not to suggest that in non-philosophical contexts we replace the familiar locutions with the pedantic ones, since in non-philosophical contexts we rarely, if ever, have any need to distinguish between (1) some state of affairs that obtains and (2) the obtaining of that state of affairs.

We do, however, in non-philosophical contexts sometimes have occasion for distinguishing between (1) some state of affairs that does not obtain and (2) the non-obtaining of that state of affairs. Thus of states of affairs that do not obtain we sometimes say that it would be good or that it would be bad if they obtained. We do not, of course, use precisely this at least slightly pedantic way of speaking but instead say something such as "It would be bad if John were dishonest" or "It would be good if John were sighted". In saying that it would be bad if John were dishonest we are saying either of two things, depending upon whether (1) we believe that it is not the case that he is dishonest or (2) we have no belief either that he is or that he is not dishonest. If we believe that it is not the case that John is dishonest, then in saying that it would be bad if he were dishonest we are saying that it would be bad if he were dishonest although in fact he is not. If, however, we have no belief either that John is or that he is not dishonest, then in saying that it would be bad if he were dishonest we are saying that it would be bad if he were dishonest although we do not know and have no belief either that he is or that he is not dishonest. Precisely similar considerations apply to our saying that it would be good if John were sighted. To generalize, to say of any given state of affairs, *x*, or of any state of affairs, *y*, that it would be good if *x* obtained, or bad if *y* obtained, is to say either (1) that it would be good if *x* obtained, or bad if *y* obtained, although in fact neither does or (2) that it would be good if *x* obtained, or bad if *y* obtained, although we do not know and have no belief either that they do or that they do not obtain.

As I believe the examples given show, we do sometimes distinguish between the obtaining and the non-obtaining of various states of affairs and say of those that do not obtain that it would be good (or bad) if they did obtain. We believe, that is, that the obtaining of certain states of affairs would be good if they were to obtain and that the obtaining of certain other states of affairs would be bad if they were to obtain. Whether, however, the obtaining of any given state of affairs would be good or bad depends upon the nature of the state of affairs in question. From this, however, it does not follow that the state of affairs itself, taken completely in abstraction from any consideration of whether it obtains, is either good or bad. This is indicated by the subjunctive mood of the locutions I have been discussing. To say that it *would* be bad *if* John were dishonest or that it *would* be good *if* he were sighted is not to say, at least not explicitly, of anything that it *is* good or that it *is* bad. It is not to say that the states of affairs in question are good or bad regardless of whether they obtain. At the same time, however, it is still the nature of these states of affairs, taken in abstraction from any consideration of whether they obtain, that makes (or would make) the obtaining of the first state of affairs bad and the obtaining of the second good.

It was maintained above that since states of affairs that obtain are facts in the first sense of "fact," and that since some such states of affairs are good and others bad, some facts, in the first sense of the term, are good and others bad. It was also contended that since the obtaining and the non-obtaining of states of affairs are also facts in the second sense of "fact," and that since the obtaining or the non-obtaining of some states of affairs is good and of others bad, some facts in the second sense of the term are good and others bad. It was noted that to some it will doubtless seem strange to speak of facts, in either of the first two senses of the term, as being good or bad. I am now about to discuss a view that to some will seem even stranger.

3. Propositions as Bearers of Value

This is the view that facts in the third sense of "fact" distinguished above are also such that some are good and some bad. But since facts in the third sense of the term are identical with true propositions, it would follow that true propositions are such that some are good and others bad. That facts in the third sense, and therefore true propositions, are such that some are good and others bad might seem to be indicated by the forms of certain locutions such as the following: (1) "It is good that John is honest." (2) "That John is honest is good." (3) "It is bad that John is blind." (4) "That John is blind is bad." The first two locutions are similar in form to the following locutions: (a) "It is a fact that John is honest." (b) "That John is honest is a fact." (c) "It is true that John is honest." (d) "That John is honest is true." If so, it will be obvious which locutions corresponding to (a)-(d) are similar in form to (3) and (4).

The form of (b) clearly seems to indicate that what is said to be a fact is that John is honest. This seems also to be indicated, although perhaps less clearly so, by the form of (a). It too seems to indicate that what is said to be a fact is that John is honest. Since propositions are the ultimate bearers of truth and falsity,[4] the forms of (c) and (d) seem to indicate that what is being said to be true is the proposition that John is honest. Whatever it is that is indicated by the locution "that John is honest" is said in (1) and (2) to be good, in (a) and (b) to be a fact, and in (c) and (d) to be a true proposition. The same thing, that is, that is said by (a) and (b) to be a fact and by (c) and (d) to be a true proposition is said by (1) and (2) to be good. If so, and if facts in the third sense of "fact" are identical with true propositions, then facts, again in the third sense of the term, and true propositions are such that some are good and others bad.

It might, however, be objected that if some true propositions are good and others bad, then some false propositions must also be good and others bad. It is not clear, however, what one would mean by saying that some false propositions are good and others bad. As indicated above, to say that the true proposition that John is honest is good is another way of saying that the fact that John is honest is good. The only reason advanced for saying that some true propositions are good and some bad is that true propositions are facts, in the third sense of "fact," and that some facts are good and others bad. Since, however, false propositions are not facts in any of the three senses of "fact" distinguished above, the reason given for saying that some true propositions are good and some bad cannot be given for saying that so also are some false propositions. Even if there were some reason for claiming that some false propositions are good and some bad, it still is not clear what could be meant by such a claim.

One thing that might be meant is the following. For any given proposition there is a contradictory proposition opposite in truth-value to the given proposition. Similarly, if a given true proposition is good its contradictory is bad, and if a given true proposition is bad its contradictory is good. On such a view, just as the contradictory of any given proposition is opposite in truth-value to the given proposition, so also the contradictory of any given proposition is bad if the given proposition is good and good if the latter is bad. In the way indicated, the view in question would assimilate the goodness or badness of propositions to their truth or falsity. This, however, would not mean that every true proposition is good and every false proposition bad. Instead, just as some true propositions are good and others bad, so also some false propositions are good and others bad. Let us examine this view.

As was indicated above, the only reason given for saying that some true propositions are good and others bad is that true propositions are identical with facts, some of which are good and some of which are bad. Such a reason cannot be given for saying that some false propositions are good and others bad. Nor does the fact that every true proposition has a contradictory opposite that is false mean that the latter must be bad if the former is good or good if the former is bad. From the fact that the true proposition that John is honest is good it does not follow that the false proposition that it is false that John is honest is bad. Instead, what follows is that it would be bad if it were false that John is honest. If so, then although some true propositions might be good and others bad, it does not follow that their contradictory opposites might also be either good or bad. Instead, if a given true proposition is good (or bad) its contradictory would be bad (or good) if it were true. This is another way of saying that it would be bad if a given good proposition were false rather than true and that it would be good if a given bad proposition were false rather than true.

It is not at all strange to say (1) that it would be bad if John, who is in fact honest, were instead dishonest or (2) that it would be good if John, who is in fact blind, were instead sighted. It is, that is, not in the least strange to say of propositions we believe to be false that it would be good (or bad) if they were true. It is, however, strange to say of any proposition we believe to be false either that it is good or that it is bad. What led us to the view that some false propositions are good and others bad was the view that some true propositions are good and others bad. The latter view, as was indicated earlier, is itself strange, although perhaps not as strange as the former view. What led us to the latter view was the view that true propositions are facts, in the third sense of "fact," coupled with the view that some facts are good and others bad. And what led us to this view is the fact that we sometimes say such things as "It is good that John is honest," "That John is honest is good," "It is bad that John is blind," "That John is blind is bad," coupled with the view that what is said by using such locutions is that some fact is good or bad. In addition, we sometimes use such locutions as "The fact that John is honest is good" and "The fact that John is blind is bad," which seem even more clearly to mean that what is said to be good or bad is some fact. Locutions such as these are frequently used, and what is said by using them is not at all strange if what we mean to say is that some fact is good or bad.

When, however, we replace "The fact that John is honest is good" and "The fact that John is blind is bad" with "The true proposition that John is honest is good" and "The true proposition that John is blind is bad," we seem to be saying that it is some true proposition that is good or bad, and to say that a true proposition is good or bad does seem strange. Such strangeness, however, disappears completely if we use instead such locutions as "That the proposition that John is honest is true is good" or "It is good that the proposition that John is honest is true". Just as "The fact that John is honest is good" seems to say that it is some fact that is good, so "It is good that the proposition that John is honest is true" seems to say that it is good that a given proposition is true. Although it does seem strange to say of a true proposition that it is good, it is not at all strange to say that it is good (or bad) that a given proposition is true (or false). To say the latter, however, is not to say that the proposition itself is good (or bad). Similarly, to say of some purported fact that it is good (or bad) that it is a fact is not to say that the fact itself is good (or bad). To say, that is, that it is good that it is a fact that John is honest is not to say that the fact that John is honest is good.

If the preceding is correct, there are two fundamentally different ways of interpreting sentences such as the following: (1) "It is good that John is honest." (2) "That John is honest is good." (3) "It is bad that John is blind." (4) "That John is blind is bad." The first is to interpret them as saying that it is a fact or a proposition that is good or bad. The second is to interpret them as saying that it is good (or bad) that a given purported fact is (or is not) in fact a fact or that it is good (or bad) that a given proposition is true (or false). If we opt for the first interpretation we commit ourselves to the view that some facts or propositions are good and others bad. But if we opt for the second interpretation we do not commit ourselves to such a view. It seems strange to say that a fact, in the third sense of "fact," is good (or bad) and even more strange to say that a proposition is good (or bad). But it is not in the least strange to say that it is good (or bad) that some purported fact is (or is not) a fact or that it is good (or bad) that a given proposition is true (or false).

The second interpretation therefore seems preferable to the first. But, it may well be asked, if neither facts nor propositions are either good or bad, in virtue of what is it good (or bad) (1) that some purported fact is (or is not) in fact a fact and (2) that a given proposition is true (or false)?

In answering this question it is important to remember that it is only facts in the third sense of "fact," according to which facts are true propositions, that are neither good nor bad. Facts in the first sense of the term, according to which facts are states of affairs that obtain, and facts in the second sense of the term, according to which facts are the obtaining or the non-obtaining of states of affairs, can be good or bad. It is the goodness or badness of the obtaining and the non-obtaining of various states of affairs that determines whether it is good or bad (1) that some purported fact, in the third sense of "fact," is in fact a fact and (2) that a given proposition is true (or false). This is to say that it is the goodness or badness of facts, in the second sense of "fact," that determines whether it is good or bad (1) that some purported fact, in the third sense of the term, is in fact a fact and (2) that a given proposition is true (or false). Thus the ground of its being good (1) that John is honest and (2) that the proposition that John is honest is true is the goodness of the obtaining of the state of affairs consisting of John's being honest.

The preceding is an account only of the ground of its being good (or bad) (1) that some purported fact, in the third sense of the term, is in fact a fact and (2) that some proposition is in fact true (or false). It is not an account of the ground of the goodness or badness of facts in the first and second senses of "fact". It is not, that is, an account of the ground of the goodness or badness of either (1) any state of affairs that obtains or (2) the obtaining or the non-obtaining of any state of affairs. As was indicated above, the ground of the goodness or badness of the obtaining or the non-obtaining of a state of affairs is the nature of the state of affairs that does or does not obtain. We have left unanswered the question of whether states of affairs themselves, taken completely in abstraction from any consideration of whether they do or do not obtain, can be either good or bad. If they can be, then it is their nature that determines not only the goodness or badness of their obtaining or their not obtaining but also their own goodness or badness, taken in abstraction from their obtaining or their not obtaining. If they cannot be, then the question of what the ground of their own goodness or badness is does not arise.

4. Abstracta and Concreta as Bearers of Value

The question of whether states of affairs themselves, taken in complete abstraction from any consideration of whether they do or do not obtain, can be good or bad is analogous to the question of whether universals themselves, taken completely in abstraction from any consideration of whether they are exemplified by particulars, can be either good or bad. Are honesty and blindness themselves, for example, either good or bad when considered completely in abstraction from the question of whether they are exemplified by particulars? Or is it only their exemplification by particulars that can be good or bad? Different philosophers have taken opposing positions on this issue. Everett Hall, for example, argues that it is only the exemplification of universals by particulars, not universals taken in abstraction from such exemplification, that can have value.[5] And recently Panayot Butchvarov has distinguished between abstract goods and concrete goods and argued that "goodness is, strictly speaking, a property of properties, and that good concrete entities, which we may call concrete goods, exemplify it only, so to speak, indirectly, by exemplifying some other properties that exemplify goodness directly, and which we may call abstract goods."[6] Thus for Butchvarov "a person's life can be said to be good on the grounds that it is happy only if happiness itself can be said to be good."[7] On this issue I side with Hall.

The states of affairs consisting of John's being honest and John's being blind, if the John who is honest is identical with the John who is blind, differ from one another only if his being honest differs from his being blind. Moreover, *his* being honest can differ from *his* being blind only if there is a difference between being honest and being blind and therefore only if there is a difference between honesty and blindness. Since the John who is a constituent of the first state of affairs is identical with the John who is a constituent of the second state of affairs, the obtaining of the first can be good and the obtaining of the second bad only because there is a difference between being honest and being blind and thus between honesty and blindness. This can be put by saying that the ground of the goodness of the obtaining of the first state of affairs is that one of its constituents exemplifies honesty, whereas the source of the badness of the obtaining of the second is that one of its constituents exemplifies blindness. The obtaining of the first state of affairs is good not because John is a constituent of it but because of his honesty, that of the second bad not because John is a constituent of it but because of his blindness. It is his being honest that makes the obtaining of the first state of affairs good, his being blind that makes the obtaining of the second bad.

From the preceding, however, it does not follow that universals can be either good or bad regardless of whether they are exemplified by particulars, just as from the fact that the nature of states of affairs determines whether their obtaining would be good or bad it does not follow that they can be either good or bad regardless of whether they obtain. What inclines some to suppose that unexemplified universals and states of affairs that do not obtain can be good or bad would seem to be considerations such as the following. If universals as such can be neither good nor bad, how can their exemplifications be good or bad? Similarly, if states of affairs as such can be neither good nor bad, how can their obtaining or their not obtaining be good or bad? How can the obtaining or the non-obtaining of something that itself can be neither good nor bad be good or bad? It would be as if by magic that goodness and badness appear suddenly on the scene out of elements that themselves can be neither good nor bad. But that this is what happens does seem in fact to be the case. If in fact it is the case, then perhaps goodness and badness, if they can correctly be said to be properties, may rightly be regarded as emergent properties. They emerge from conjunctions of elements that, taken in isolation from one another, are neither good nor bad. Such emergence would seem to occur in the following ways.

The exemplification of a universal, taken completely in abstraction from any consideration of the universal exemplified, can be neither good nor bad. No universal, taken completely in abstraction from any consideration of whether it is exemplified, can be either good or bad. And no particular, taken completely in abstraction from any consideration of any of the universals it exemplifies, can be either good or bad. Yet the exemplification, and also the non-exemplification, of a given universal by a given particular can be either good or bad. Similar considerations apply to states of affairs. No state of affairs, taken completely in abstraction from any consideration of whether it obtains, can be good or bad. And the obtaining or the non-obtaining of no state of affairs, taken completely in abstraction from any consideration of the nature of the state of affairs that does or does not obtain, can be good or bad. Yet the obtaining or the non-obtaining of a given state of affairs, taken in conjunction with the nature of the state of affairs in question, can be good or bad.

The preceding can also be put by saying that it is only the concrete, never the abstract, that can be good or bad. Abstracta, whether they be abstract universals, i.e., universals taken in abstraction from their exemplification by particulars, or abstract particulars, i.e., particulars taken in abstraction from the universals they exemplify, can be neither good nor bad. It is instead only the exemplification or the non-exemplification of a given universal by a given particular that can be good or bad. Similarly, abstracta, whether they be abstract states of affairs, i.e., states of affairs taken in abstraction from any consideration of whether they obtain, or abstract obtainings or non-obtainings, i.e., obtainings and non-obtainings taken in abstraction from any consideration of which states of affairs do or do not obtain, can be neither good nor bad. It is instead only (1) the obtaining or the non-obtaining of a given state of affairs and (2) a state of affairs that does in fact obtain that can be good or bad. The emergence of something that can be good or bad out of what may be referred to as its ontological elements or constituents, none of which, taken singly or abstractly, can be good or bad, is only one of a variety of forms of emergence. Provided that certain assumptions be made, it is perhaps also an example of Moore's principle of organic wholes, according to which "the value of a whole must not be assumed to be the same as the sum of the values of its parts."[8]

The assumptions in question are these. In the case of universals, the exemplification by a given particular of a given universal may be considered to be what may be referred to as an ontological whole consisting of ontological constituents, elements, or parts, one of which is the universal in question, taken completely in abstraction from the question of whether it is exemplified by anything at all, and another of which is the particular in question, taken completely in abstraction from the question of which universals it exemplifies. So considered, neither of these abstract parts can be good or bad, whereas the whole consisting of the exemplification of the universal in question by the particular in question can be good or bad. In the case of states of affairs, the obtaining of a given state of affairs is an ontological whole consisting of ontological parts, one of which is the state of affairs in question, taken completely in abstraction from the question of whether it obtains, and another of which is the obtaining or the non-obtaining of a state of affairs, taken completely in abstraction from the nature of the state of affairs in question. So considered, neither of these abstract parts can be good or bad, whereas the whole consisting of the obtaining of the state of affairs in question can be good or bad.

Since Moore does not make clear precisely what is to count as a whole and what is to count as a part, I am not sure that the preceding would be examples covered by his principle of organic wholes. Whether, however, they would so count, it still seems to be the case (1) that the exemplification of a given universal by a given particular can be good or bad, whereas the universal and the particular, taken singly in abstraction from the question of whether the former is exemplified and of which universals the latter exemplifies, cannot be and (2) that the obtaining of a given state of affairs can be good or bad, whereas the state of affairs itself and its obtaining, taking each singly in abstraction from the other, cannot be.

If the preceding is correct, a world consisting only of universals and relationships between them and containing no particulars whatever would be a world devoid of value. This would be the case even if goodness and various of its specific forms, such as moral goodness, beauty, and rationality, and badness and various of its specific forms, such as moral badness, ugliness, and irrationality, were themselves universals. This is to say that goodness and badness and their various specific forms, taken as universals, are not self-predicable—that, taken as universals, goodness is not itself good, beauty is not itself beautiful, and rationality is not itself rational and that, again taken as universals, badness is not itself bad, ugliness is not itself ugly, and irrationality is not itself irrational. It is only particulars, not universals, that can be good or bad in various ways even though their goodness or badness be determined, at least in part, by the nature of the universals they exemplify.

From the fact, however, that neither universals, taken in abstraction from their exemplification by particulars, nor states of affairs, taken in abstraction from any consideration of whether they obtain, can be good or bad, it does not follow that it is always inappropriate to speak of them as being good or bad. We sometimes do say that honesty, beauty, and rationality are good and dishonesty, ugliness, and irrationality bad and that a person's being honest, beautiful, or rational is good and that a person's being dishonest, ugly, or irrational is bad. There is nothing wrong with such ways of speaking, as long as they do not mislead us into supposing that such abstract universals and states of affairs are themselves good or bad. Certainly such ways of speaking, provided that they do not thus mislead us, are preferable to the rather tortuous circumlocutions with which this chapter is replete. If, however, my argument is sound, such ways of speaking are elliptical. To say that a given universal, such as happiness, is good is an elliptical way of saying either that exemplifications of it are or would be good or that it is or would be good that it is or that it be exemplified. And to say that a given state of affairs, such as John's being happy, is good is an elliptical way of saying either that its obtaining is or would be good or that it is good that it obtains or that it would be good that it do so. Understood in this way, abstract universals and states of affairs can with truth be said to be good or bad.

But although abstract universals and states of affairs do not, except in an elliptical sense, have intrinsic value, they do have contributory value in a straightforward non-elliptical sense. The parts of a whole have contributory value if they contribute to the value of the whole, and the degree of their contributory value is determined by, or consists of, the degree to which they determine the value of the whole. It is possible that certain parts of a given whole have no intrinsic value at all, yet have contributory value because they contribute to the value of the whole. Moore goes as far as to say that "it seems as if indifferent things may . . . be the sole constituents of a whole which has great value, either positive or negative."[9] I have suggested that abstract universals and states of affairs may be regarded as ontological constituents, elements, or parts of wholes and have argued that the value of a whole is determined, at least in part, by the nature of its abstract parts. If so, then even though abstract universals and states of affairs have no intrinsic value at all they do nonetheless have contributory value.

Chapter 3

Species of Value

We turn now to discuss the species of value and their relationships to one another. There are two major species of value—intrinsic and extrinsic—and two major species of extrinsic value—instrumental and contributory. These species yield the concept of total value, which is the conjunction of the intrinsic, instrumental, and contributory value of a thing, event, or state of affairs. Our treatment of these species of value will require a discussion of wholes and parts and of the world, which is that whole than which no more inclusive whole can be conceived.

1. Intrinsic, Extrinsic, and Total Value

Things and events and their existence and occurrence and their non-existence and non-occurrence, as well as the obtaining and the non-obtaining of states of affairs, can have intrinsic value. For the sake of expository simplicity, however, in this section I shall speak mainly of the value of the obtaining and the non-obtaining of states of affairs, with the understanding that what is said about them applies, with the necessary changes, to things and events and their existence and occurrence and their non-existence and non-occurrence. Strictly speaking, as I argued in chapter 2, it is only the obtaining and the non-obtaining of states of affairs, not states of affairs themselves taken completely in abstraction from any consideration of whether they do or do not obtain, that can have intrinsic value. To avoid tedious repetition, however, I shall frequently speak of states of affairs themselves as having such value even though in fact it is only their obtaining or their non-obtaining that can have it.

The intrinsic value of a state of affairs is absolute, in the sense that it is determined completely by the nature of the state of affairs in question taken completely in abstraction from any consideration of the value of other states of affairs that are not constituents, elements, or parts of it. Although the intrinsic value of a compound state of affairs, x, containing two or more states of affairs as its parts, is determined, at least in part, by the intrinsic value of its parts, a consideration of the relation of x to other states of affairs that are not parts of x can be relevant only to determining the extrinsic value of x. Thus if the obtaining of some state of affairs, x, the obtaining of which is intrinsically good, prevents the obtaining of another state of affairs, y, the obtaining of which would be intrinsically better than that of x, the obtaining of x, although still intrinsically good, is also extrinsically bad relative to y. The extrinsic, unlike the intrinsic, value of a state of affairs therefore can be determined only by considering various of the relations in which its obtaining stands to the obtaining of other states of affairs. The concepts of extrinsic goodness and badness may therefore be said to be relative concepts. So also are the concepts of intrinsically better and intrinsically worse, since to be better or worse is to be better or worse than something else.

At times it will prove helpful to use the concepts of positive and negative value rather than the equivalent concepts of good and bad. The obtaining of a given state of affairs has positive intrinsic value if its obtaining is intrinsically better than its not obtaining and negative intrinsic value if its not obtaining is intrinsically better than its obtaining. For the obtaining of any state of affairs, x, to have extrinsic value there must be some other state of affairs, y, the obtaining of which has or would have intrinsic value. In order that the obtaining of any state of affairs, x, (1) have positive extrinsic value, there must be some other state of affairs, y, the obtaining of which has or would have positive intrinsic value, and (2) have negative extrinsic value, there must be some other state of affairs, y, the obtaining of which has or would have negative intrinsic value. The phrase "or would have" is used in the preceding two sentences because, as was suggested above, it is possible that the obtaining of a given state of affairs, x, have positive intrinsic value but negative extrinsic value because its obtaining prevents the obtaining of some other state of affairs, y, the obtaining of which would have greater positive intrinsic value than the obtaining of x has.

Given the preceding terminology, we can now introduce the concept of the total value of the obtaining of a state of affairs. The total value of any state of affairs is determined by taking into account both its intrinsic and its extrinsic value. If the positive intrinsic value of one state of affairs, x, is the same as that of another, y, and if x has greater positive extrinsic value than y has, then the total positive value of x is greater than that of y. Similarly, if the positive extrinsic value of x is the same as that of y, and if the positive intrinsic value of x is greater than that of y, then the total positive value of x is greater than that of y. It is therefore relatively easy to determine which of two states of affairs has greater total value if either the intrinsic or the extrinsic value of each is the same as that of the other. If each has the same intrinsic and extrinsic value as the other, then the total value of each is the same as that of the other. If each has the same intrinsic value as the other but one has greater extrinsic value than the other, then it also has greater total value than the other. And if each has the same extrinsic value as the other but one has greater intrinsic value than the other, then it also has greater total value than the other.

It is, however, by no means as easy to determine which of two states of affairs, x and y, has greater total value when the intrinsic value of x is greater than that of y and the extrinsic value of y is greater than that of x. In attempting to make such a determination it is important to remember, as was suggested above, that the extrinsic value of a state of affairs, x, can be determined only by determining the intrinsic value of some other state of affairs, by virtue of the obtaining of which x has extrinsic value. It is from the intrinsic value of this other state of affairs that x derives its extrinsic value. If so, then the total value of any state of affairs, x, can be determined only by taking into account both (1) the intrinsic value of x and (2) the intrinsic value of some other state of affairs, a, the intrinsic value of which determines the extrinsic value of x. Thus given that the intrinsic positive value of x is greater than that of y and that the extrinsic positive value of y is greater than that of x, which of the two has greater total positive value can be determined in the following way: (1) subtract the intrinsic positive value of y from that of x, (2) subtract the intrinsic positive value of a, the state of affairs from the intrinsic positive value of which x derives its extrinsic value, from the intrinsic positive value of b, the state of affairs from which y derives its extrinsic value, and (3) determine whether the degree of positive intrinsic value that remains upon the completion of step (1) is greater or less than that which remains upon the completion of step (2). If that which remains upon the completion of step (1) is greater than that which remains upon the completion of step (2), then x has greater total value than y; if it is less than that which remains upon the completion of step (2), then y has greater total value than x; if it is the same as that which remains upon the completion of step (2), then the total value of x is the same as that of y.

It might happen that although the difference between the intrinsic positive value of x and y is greater than that between the intrinsic positive value of a and b, the proportion of the value of b to a is greater than that of the value of x to y. For the sake of convenience, let us make the admittedly unrealistic assumptions (1) that the degree of the positive intrinsic value of a state of affairs can be measured in terms of positive units of value and (2) that the degree of the negative intrinsic value of a state of affairs can be measured in terms of negative units of value. Let us suppose also that the degree of positive value of x is 100 units, of y 50 units, of a 10 units, and of b 40 units. If so, then x is twice as valuable as y, b four times as valuable as a. This, however, does not mean that the conjunction of y and b is intrinsically better than that of x and a. Instead, since the positive intrinsic value of the conjunction of x and a is 110 units, whereas that of the conjunction of y and b is only 90 units, the conjunction of x and a is intrinsically better than that of y and b. If so, the total value of x is greater than that of y.

It might be helpful to consider another example. Suppose (1) that x has positive intrinsic value but negative extrinsic value, (2) that y has negative intrinsic value but positive extrinsic value, (3) that a, the state of affairs from the obtaining of which x derives its extrinsic value, has negative intrinsic value, and (4) that b, the state of affairs from the obtaining of which y derives its extrinsic value, has positive intrinsic value. Suppose also (1) that the value of x is 100 positive units, (2) that the value of y is 50 negative units, (3) that the value of a is 10 negative units, and (4) that the value of b is 40 positive units. If so, then the value of the conjunction of x and a is 90 positive units (100 positive and 10 negative units), that of the conjunction of y and b 10 negative units (50 negative and 40 positive units). The conjunction of x and a therefore has greater positive value than that of y and b, and the total value of x is greater than that of y.

The assignment of positive and negative units of value to states of affairs has been done only for the sake of convenience in illustrating the suggested method of determining which of two states of affairs, x and y, would have greater total value when x has greater intrinsic value than *y* and *y* greater extrinsic value than *x*. From the fact that the assignment of units of value to states of affairs has the convenience indicated it does not follow that their value can in fact be measured in terms of such units. Such value, whether it be intrinsic or extrinsic, positive or negative, cannot in fact be measured in terms of such units. There is not, nor can there be, a calculus of value, if by this be meant a process that measures in numerical terms the value of various states of affairs. It is true that people sometimes say that one thing, *x*, is twice or three times as valuable as another thing, *y*. Such language is appropriate if what its use is intended to indicate is the economic or monetary value of the things in question. The economic or monetary value of one thing, *x*, is twice or three times that of another thing, *y*, if people are willing to pay twice or three times as much money to obtain *x* as they are willing to pay to obtain *y*. But economic or monetary value is one thing, intrinsic value another, and from the fact that people are willing to pay twice or three times as much money to obtain *x* as they are willing to pay to obtain *y* it does not follow that the intrinsic value of *x* is twice or three times as great as that of *y*.

Sometimes, however, when people say that one thing, *x*, is twice or three times as valuable as another, *y*, they do not intend to say anything at all about the economic or monetary value of *x* and *y* but instead seem to be saying, although they would not or might not use such language, that the intrinsic value of *x* is twice or three times as great as that of *y*. This is especially true when a person says, as people sometimes do, that one of his experiences, *x*, is twice or three times as good as another of his experiences, *y*. Such language is not misleading if the speaker intends only to say, and is understood by those he addresses as intending only to say, that *x* is much better than *y*. It is, however, misleading if the speaker means to say, and is understood as meaning to say, that *x* literally is twice or three times as intrinsically valuable as *y*. The statement that *x* is twice or three times as valuable as *y* cannot be true if it is intended to be taken literally. Although one thing or state of affairs can be much more valuable than another, it cannot be twice or three times as valuable. The fundamental reason this is so is that there are no numerical units in terms of which intrinsic value can be measured. This, however, does not mean that there cannot be quantitative differences between the intrinsic value of one thing or state of affairs, *x*, and that of another, *y*. One thing or state of affairs, *x*, can be slightly more valuable or much more valuable than another, *y*, and the difference between being slightly more valuable and much more valuable is a quantitative difference. It is not, however, a quantitative difference that can be measured numerically by using or counting units of intrinsic value, since there are no such units. Thus from the fact that there is a quantitative difference between the degree to which one thing, x, has some property, f, and the degree to which another thing, y, has that property, it does not follow that the difference can be measured numerically. Whether it can be or not depends upon the nature or kind of the property in question.

2. Extrinsic Value and Utility

It was maintained above that if the obtaining of a given state of affairs, x, has positive or negative extrinsic value, then there must be some other state of affairs, a, the obtaining of which has or would have positive or negative intrinsic value, and that it is from its relation to a that x acquires whatever extrinsic value it has. This means that I am using the expression "extrinsic value" in a narrower sense than that in which it is sometimes used. This is so because it is sometimes used in such a way that anything that can be used to attain some end has extrinsic value as a means of attaining the end in question regardless of whether the latter has any intrinsic value at all. In this sense of the expression, the use of poison might be extrinsically good as a means of killing someone regardless of whether killing that person has any intrinsic value at all, and also even if the killing of him were intrinsically bad. C. I. Lewis, who uses the expression "extrinsic value" in essentially the same way in which I have been using it, has suggested that we speak of a thing's utility rather than of its extrinsic value when we wish to speak of its usefulness as a means of attaining some end, regardless of whether the end we seek has any intrinsic value at all, whether positive or negative, and regardless also of whether the end we seek has any extrinsic value as a means to attaining some further end that has intrinsic value.[1] I suggest that we follow his suggestion, since there is a difference between (1) something's standing in a certain relation, R, to something else that is intrinsically good or bad and (2) something's standing in that relation, R, to something else regardless of whether the latter has any intrinsic value at all. Following Lewis' suggestion, I shall say that poisoning a person has utility or is useful as a means of killing him, regardless of whether killing him has any intrinsic value at all, whether positive or negative. It can have extrinsic value only if killing him or, more properly, his death at the time in question either (1) has intrinsic value, whether positive or negative, or (2) has extrinsic value as a means to some further end that has intrinsic value.

As the preceding suggests, in order that something, x, have extrinsic value it is not necessary that it stand in an immediate relation to something else that has intrinsic value. Thus x has extrinsic value if it is a means of producing y, which itself has no intrinsic value but has extrinsic value as a means of producing something else, z, which does have intrinsic value. In such a situation x stands in an immediate relation to y, which in turn stands in an immediate relation to z. The relation of x to z is mediate rather than immediate because it is mediated by the immediate relations of x to y and of y to z. In the case in question, x and y are both instrumental in the production of z, which has intrinsic value, and because of this x and y have extrinsic value regardless of whether they also have intrinsic value. If, however, z itself has no intrinsic value, x and y would still have utility or be useful as means of producing z even though they would then have no extrinsic value by virtue of their relation to z. They might, however, have such value by virtue of their relation to something other than z that does have intrinsic value. As was indicated above, extrinsic value, unlike intrinsic value, is relative, not absolute. Thus one and the same thing, a, can have extrinsic value by virtue of its relation to a second thing, b, but not by virtue of its relation to a third thing, c. It has extrinsic value in relation to b but not in relation to c. Similar considerations apply to utility. It too is relational, not absolute. Thus a can have utility or be useful as a means of producing b but not as a means of producing c.

It might be thought that if something, x, has utility or is useful as a means of producing something else, y, regardless of whether y has any intrinsic value, then y must be something desired or liked by someone, or at least have utility as a means of producing something else, z, which is desired or liked by someone. This, however, would be a mistake. Whether one thing, x, has utility as a means of producing another thing, y, depends entirely upon the relation in which x and y stand to one another, regardless of whether anyone desires or likes y. It is true that I might not regard x as being useful for the production of y if I neither desire nor like y nor regard y as having intrinsic value. From this, however, it does not follow that in fact x is not useful as a means of producing y. Some indication that this is in fact the case is provided by the fact that it sometimes happens that we desire or like something or regard it as having intrinsic value, yet do not know what we must do to acquire or produce it and therefore, because of this, endeavor to discover what we must do. Such a search would seem to rest on the assumption that there are, or at least might be, means or ways of acquiring or producing the thing in question, if only we knew what they are. Another indication that the preceding is in fact the case is provided by the fact that we can be mistaken concerning what is and what is not a means to the acquisition or production of something we desire or like or value. I can believe that x is useful as a means of acquiring or producing y when in fact it is not. Whether it is such a means is completely independent both of any beliefs I might have and of my desiring, liking, or valuing y.

3. Instrumental and Contributory Value

The species of extrinsic value we have been discussing is instrumental value. Neither that which has instrumental value nor that in relation to which it has such value is such that either is part of the other. A second form of extrinsic value is contributory value. To have contributory value is to contribute in some way to the value of some whole of which that which has contributory value is a part. To say that some part of a given whole contributes to the value of the whole is to say that the value of the whole is determined, at least in part, by the nature of the part in question, taken in conjunction with the nature of the whole of which it is a part. Thus what essentially distinguishes contributory value from instrumental value is that anything that has contributory value has such value by virtue of its contributing to the value of some whole of which it is a part, whereas anything that has instrumental value has such value by virtue of its being a means to the existence or occurrence of something that has intrinsic value but of which it is not a part. Some attention must therefore be given to the concept of wholes and parts if the concept of contributory value is to be understood adequately.

Perhaps the most obvious type of a whole that has parts is a material thing. Husserl distinguishes between two types of parts of material things—independent parts and dependent parts. Independent parts are pieces of the whole of which they are parts; dependent parts are moments, aspects, or qualities of the whole of which they are parts. Independent parts or pieces are themselves particulars and would still exist as particulars if they were separated from the wholes of which they are parts. Dependent parts or moments are not particulars but instead are either universals or singular cases of universals. Whether they are universals or singular cases of universals depends upon whether the qualities ingredient in particulars are themselves universals or singular cases of universals. Husserl regards them, as do I, as being singular cases of universals. So regarded, a moment of one particular, such as its brownness, is unique to it and cannot be a moment of another particular. It is because pieces are themselves particulars and therefore would still exist as particulars if they were separated from the wholes of which they are pieces that Husserl regards them as independent parts of the wholes of which they are parts. And it is because moments can exist only as aspects or qualities of particulars that Husserl regards them as being dependent parts of the particulars of which they are parts.[2]

The preceding distinctions can be illustrated by means of a simple example. Suppose that a certain table exists and that it has a top and four legs. Suppose also that the color of the exterior surface of the top and of each of the four legs is a uniform shade of brown. The top and each of the four legs are independent parts or pieces of the table, since each would still exist as a particular, although no longer as a part of the table, if it were separated from the other pieces of the table. The brown color of the table and of each of its pieces, however, is a dependent part of the table and of each of its pieces. It is a moment, aspect, or quality of the table and of each of its pieces, and as such it is not a piece of the table or of any of its pieces. It can exist only as a moment, aspect, or quality of the table and of each of its pieces and therefore is not itself a particular.

The parts of a whole, whether they be pieces or moments of the whole, can contribute to the value of the whole. Both the top and each of the legs of the table of our example, let us suppose, contributes to the value of the table, and as doing so each has contributory value. The color of the table might also contribute to the value of the table, and if it does it too has contributory value. The degree to which each of its pieces and its color contributes to the value of the table is the degree to which each has contributory value relative to the table. The contributory value of each of its parts is positive if each contributes to making the table a good table, and the degree to which each has positive contributory value is the degree to which each contributes to making the table a good table. If any of the parts of a whole, whether it be a piece or a moment, contributes nothing at all to the value of the whole, then it has no contributory value at all.

In order that a part of a whole have contributory value it is sufficient that it contribute to the positive value of the whole if its contributory value is positive, to the negative value of the whole if its contributory value is negative. Thus for a part to have positive contributory value it is not necessary that it be such that no other possible part put in its place would contribute to making the whole even better. Just as a given whole of a given kind can be a good whole of that kind without being such that no whole of that kind could be even better, so also a given part of a given whole has positive contributory value if it contributes to making the whole a good whole even though it does not contribute to making the whole as good as it would be if the part in question were replaced by some other possible part. Precisely similar considerations, with of course the obvious necessary changes, apply to negative contributory value. Thus the specific shade of brown covering the surface of our table has positive contributory value if it contributes to making the table beautiful even though there be some other shade of brown that would make the table even more beautiful.

Similar considerations apply to instrumental value. In order that something have positive instrumental value it is sufficient that it be a means to the existence or occurrence of something good. Thus something, a, has positive instrumental value if it is a means to the existence of something, x, that is intrinsically good even though a be such that its replacement by something else, b, would result in the existence of something, y, that would have greater positive intrinsic value than the existence of x has. In the situation envisaged, b would have greater positive instrumental value than a has because b is a means to the existence of something, y, that has greater positive intrinsic value than x has. From this, however, it does not follow either (1) that a has no instrumental value at all or (2) that any instrumental value it has must be negative if the instrumental value of b is positive or positive if the instrumental value of b is negative. Although the existence of y would have greater positive intrinsic value than the existence of x has, the existence of a would still have positive instrumental value as a means to the existence of x, provided that x has positive intrinsic value. The intrinsic goodness of x suffices to make a instrumentally good if a is a means to x. Anything that has value, whether the value be intrinsic, instrumental, or contributory, has the value it has regardless of whether it can be replaced by something else that has greater intrinsic, instrumental, or contributory value.

It was maintained above that perhaps the most obvious kind of whole that has parts consists of material things. Such things, however, are not the only wholes that have parts. There are many kinds of things, events, acts, and states of affairs that are such that two or more of them constitute a whole of which each is a part. Thus suppose that three men, Abraham, Isaac, and Jacob exist. Suppose also that in some way each has unjustifiably caused his parents to suffer; each, that is, in some way has inflicted unmerited suffering on his parents. Suppose further that each later thinks of the suffering he has caused his parents. Suppose, finally, that Abraham is pleased that he caused his parents to suffer, that Isaac is sorry that he has done so, and that Jacob is indifferent about his having done so, being neither pleased nor sorry. Given the preceding, we can distinguish between three wholes, each with two parts. The first consists (1) of Abraham's causing his parents to suffer and (2) of his being pleased that he has done so; the second consists (1) of Isaac's causing his parents to suffer and (2) of his being sorry that he has done so; the third consists (1) of Jacob's causing his parents to suffer and (2) of his being neither pleased nor sorry that he has done so.

These three wholes differ in value. Since, however, let us suppose, the value of the first part of each of these wholes is the same as that of the first part of either of the others, the difference in value between the wholes issues from a difference in value between the second part of each whole. The first part of each whole is bad, since each is an instance of a son's unjustifiably causing his parents to suffer, and any such instance is bad. The second part of each whole, however, differs in value from the second part of either of the other wholes. The second part of the first whole is bad, since a son's being pleased that he has unjustifiably caused his parents to suffer is bad. The second part of the second whole is good, since a son's being sorry that he has unjustifiably caused his parents to suffer is good. The second part of the third whole, like the second part of the first whole, is bad, since a son's being neither pleased nor sorry that he has unjustifiably caused his parents to suffer is also bad. It is not, however, as bad as the second part of the first whole, since it is worse to be pleased that one has unjustifiably caused one's parents to suffer than to be neither pleased nor sorry that one has done so.

If the preceding is correct, the first part of each of the three wholes is bad, since any instance of unjustifiably causing one's parents to suffer is bad. The second part of the first and third wholes are also bad, with the second part of the first whole being worse than the second part of the third whole. The second part of the second whole, however, is good. The kind of goodness and badness in question is intrinsic goodness and badness. In addition to the intrinsic goodness or badness of each part of the three wholes, each has contributory value, since each contributes to the goodness or badness of the whole of which it is a part. Given the nature of each of the parts of the three wholes, the intrinsic badness of the first part is sufficient to make each of the three wholes intrinsically bad. Since, however, the second part of the second whole is good, whereas the second part of each of the other wholes is bad, the second whole, though bad, is not as bad as either of the other two wholes. The second part of the second whole, since it is intrinsically good, contributes to making the second whole not as bad as either of the other two wholes. Since, however, the negative intrinsic value of the first part of the second whole is greater than the positive intrinsic value of the second part of that whole, the intrinsic goodness of the second part, although it makes the whole intrinsically better than it would be if the second part were either bad or neither good nor bad, does not suffice to make the whole intrinsically good.

It might be pointed out in passing that these considerations concerning the second whole apply also to retributive punishment. Suppose that someone, John, has done something bad, the doing of which makes him deserve to suffer punishment because he has done it. This gives rise to two possible wholes, each containing the same first part, which is John's doing the thing in question. In one of these possible wholes the second part is his suffering the punishment he deserves, whereas in the other the second part is his not suffering the punishment he deserves. Suppose that the second part of the first possible whole would be good, the second part of the second bad. Each of these possible wholes is such that it would be bad if it existed. The first would be bad because the negative value of the first part would be greater than the positive value of the second part, and the second would be bad because each of its parts would be bad. Since, however, each possible whole has the same first part, and since the second part of the first whole would be good whereas the second part of the second would be bad, the first whole, although it would be bad, would not be as bad as the second whole. Thus given that John has done something the doing of which makes him deserve to suffer punishment, it is better that he suffer the punishment he deserves than that he not suffer it even though the whole consisting of his doing the thing in question and his suffering the punishment he deserves is itself bad.[3]

In situations of the sort we have been considering, if two parts of a given whole are such that one is intrinsically good and the other is intrinsically bad, the intrinsic value of the whole is positive if the positive intrinsic value of its good part is greater than the negative intrinsic value of its bad part, negative if the negative intrinsic value of its bad part is greater than the positive intrinsic value of its good part. This, however, does not mean that the intrinsic value of a whole is positive if it has more intrinsically good than intrinsically bad parts, negative if it has more intrinsically bad than intrinsically good parts. Instead, the intrinsic value of a whole consisting of three or more parts is determined by considering what may be referred to as the combined positive intrinsic value of its good parts and the combined negative intrinsic value of its bad parts. Even though a whole has a greater number of intrinsically good than intrinsically bad parts, the combined negative intrinsic value of its bad parts might be greater than the combined positive intrinsic value of its good parts. If it is, then the whole itself is intrinsically bad. If, however, the combined positive intrinsic value of the good parts is neither greater nor less than the combined negative intrinsic value of the bad parts, the intrinsic value of the whole is neither positive nor negative, which is to say that it is neither intrinsically good nor intrinsically bad.

There are cases of other types, however, to which the preceding does not apply. In these cases a given whole can be intrinsically bad even though the combined positive intrinsic value of its good parts is greater than the combined negative intrinsic value of its bad parts and, indeed, even though each of its parts, taken in isolation from the other parts and from the whole of which they are parts, is intrinsically good. This would happen if the parts do not stand in an appropriate relationship to one another and to the whole, so that they do not fit together properly. This sometimes happens in the case of bad works of art. Even though each of the parts of a work of art, when taken in isolation from one another and from the whole of which they are parts, be good, the work of art itself, which is the whole of which they are parts, might nonetheless be bad because the parts do not fit together. Indeed, it is even possible that a work of art be good even though each of its parts, taken in isolation from one another and from the whole of which they are parts, have little or no intrinsic value, provided that they fit together properly.

The first part of each of the three wholes we considered above can also be a part of other wholes. Thus a fourth whole might consist (1) of Abraham's unjustifiably causing his parents to suffer and (2) of Isaac's being pleased that Abraham has done so; a fifth whole might consist (1) of Isaac's unjustifiably causing his parents to suffer and (2) of Jacob's being sorry that Isaac has done so; a sixth might consist (1) of Jacob's unjustifiably causing his parents to suffer and (2) of Abraham's being neither pleased nor sorry that Jacob has done so even though he knows that Jacob has done so. As before, the first part of each of these wholes is intrinsically bad, the second part of the fourth intrinsically bad, the second part of the fifth intrinsically good, and the second part of the sixth intrinsically bad, although not as bad as the second part of the fourth. Although the second part of the fifth whole is intrinsically good, the whole itself is intrinsically bad, since the negative value of the first part is greater than the positive value of the second part.

The second part, like the first, of each of our first three wholes can also be a part of other wholes. Thus a seventh whole might consist (1) of Abraham's being pleased that he has unjustifiably caused his parents to suffer and (2) of Isaac's being pleased that Abraham is pleased; an eighth whole might consist (1) of Isaac's being sorry that he has unjustifiably caused his parents to suffer and (2) of Jacob's being sorry that Isaac is sorry; a ninth might consist (1) of Jacob's being neither pleased nor sorry that he has caused his parents to suffer, even though he has done so, and (2) of Abraham's being neither pleased nor sorry that Jacob is neither pleased nor sorry, even though Abraham knows that Jacob is neither pleased nor sorry. The seventh whole, and each of its parts, is intrinsically bad. The first part of the eighth whole is intrinsically good, the second part intrinsically bad. Since, however, the positive value of the first part is greater than the negative value of the second part, the eighth whole is intrinsically good. It is not, however, as good as a whole would be that consisted of the same first part and a second part consisting of Jacob's being pleased that Isaac is sorry. The ninth whole, and each of its parts, is intrinsically bad. Neither it, however, nor either of its parts, is as bad as the seventh whole and each of its parts.

Each of the parts of each of the nine wholes we have considered, like the wholes of which they are parts, is either intrinsically good or intrinsically bad. Each of the parts of these wholes also has positive or negative contributory value, since each contributes to the goodness or the badness of the wholes of which they are parts. None of them, however, is a means to the production or the existence of the wholes of which they are parts. Each stands to the whole of which it is a part in the relation of part to whole, not in the relation of means to end. This, however, does not mean that something, *a,* that has instrumental value as a means to something else, *b,* cannot be considered as a part of a whole consisting of it and *b,* the end from the intrinsic value of which it derives its instrumental value. Thus *a* and *b* can be considered as constituting a whole of which each is a part. If they are so considered, then each, so considered, has positive, negative, or neutral contributory value, depending upon whether and how they contribute to the value of the whole. Each has positive contributory value if it contributes to the goodness of the whole, negative contributory value if it contributes to the badness of the whole, neutral contributory value if it contributes neither to the goodness nor to the badness of the whole. From the fact, however, that a means and the end to which it is a means can be considered as constituting a whole of which they are parts, it does not follow that instrumental value is a species of contributory value. Neither of these two forms of value is reducible to the other. If *a* has instrumental value as a means to something else, *b,* that has intrinsic value, *a* has instrumental value relative only to *b,* of which it is not a part, and not relative to some whole containing *a* and *b* as parts. And if *a* and *b* have contributory value relative to some whole of which they are parts, they have such value relative only to the whole containing them, and not relative to one another.

In each of the nine wholes we have considered, each of the parts has either positive or negative intrinsic value. This, however, does not mean that each part of any given whole must have such value if it is to have either positive or negative contributory value. The top and each of the legs of our table has contributory value, since each contributes to the value of the table, which is the whole of which they are parts. From this, however, it does not follow that any of these parts has any intrinsic value whatever, whether taken as parts of the table or taken singly in abstraction from any consideration of their status as parts of the table. If so, then various parts of a given whole can have contributory value regardless of whether any of them have any intrinsic value at all. Moreover, even when each part of a whole does have some intrinsic value, whether positive or negative, the intrinsic value of the whole, whether positive or negative, can be greater than the combined intrinsic value of the collection of its parts when the latter are considered in abstraction from one another and the whole of which they are the parts. This is in accordance with Moore's principle of organic wholes. This principle applies to instrumental value as well as to intrinsic value. The instrumental value of a whole can be greater than the combined instrumental value of the collection of its parts when the latter are considered in abstraction from one another and the whole of which they are parts. Thus our table can have greater instrumental value than its top and legs would have collectively if they were separated from one another and thereby from the table.

Any part of any given whole can also be regarded as a part of some other whole. This has already been illustrated in the examples given above. Thus Abraham's causing his parents to suffer is a part not only of the whole consisting of itself and of Abraham's being pleased that he has caused his parents to suffer but also of the whole consisting of itself and of Isaac's being pleased that Abraham has caused his parents to suffer. Indeed, any state of affairs, regardless of whether it obtains, can be regarded as a part of some whole consisting of itself and of some other state of affairs, regardless of what the latter state of affairs might be and of whether it obtains. Thus the state of affairs consisting of my now being sorry that it is raining in Miami, which is a state of affairs that does not obtain, may be regarded as a part of a whole consisting of itself and of the state of affairs consisting of some Mongolian's now being pleased that the sun is shining in Ulan Bator, which might or might not obtain.

Although the state of affairs consisting of my now being sorry that it is raining in Miami does not in fact obtain, it still has being as an intentional object for me. Similarly, the state of affairs consisting of some Mongolian's now being pleased that the sun is shining in Ulan Bator, regardless of whether it obtains, still has being as an intentional object for me.[4] Anything that is an intentional object for someone, whether it be a thing, an event, or a state of affairs, and regardless of whether it exists, occurs, or obtains, can be considered by the person for whom it is such an object as a part of some whole, the other part of which might also be, but need not be, only an intentional object for that person.

Whether, however, the existence, occurrence, or obtaining of something that is an intentional object for someone would be good, bad or neither good nor bad depends upon the nature of the object, regardless of whether the latter be merely an intentional object or instead also have being independently of its being such an object for anyone. The number of objects and the number of different combinations of such objects of which a person can think is limited only by the extent of his imagination. Whether one would be pleased, sorry, or neither pleased nor sorry if such objects were to exist, occur, or obtain would depend, at least in part, upon one's likes and dislikes. Whether, however, the existence, occurrence, or obtaining of such objects would be good, bad, or neither would depend upon the nature of the objects themselves.

Just as anything that is an intentional object for some person can be considered by him to be a part of some whole that is also an intentional object for him, so also anything that does in fact exist, occur, or obtain can be considered to be a part of some whole, the other parts of which are other things, events, or states of affairs that also in fact exist, occur, or obtain.[5] The number of combinations of such things is so large that none of us can ever know them all. And of the tiny fraction of such combinations that anyone can ever know, only a fraction of that fraction are such that they are regarded by the person who knows them as being good or bad, the remainder being regarded as being neither good nor bad. The totality of such parts and wholes—known and unknown, liked or disliked, good, bad, or neither good nor bad—is the actual world, which is the whole that has as parts every part and every whole that exists, occurs, or obtains except itself and which is not itself a part of any whole. As in the case of any other whole, the goodness, badness, or indifference of this whole that is not itself a part of any other whole is determined by the goodness, badness, or indifference of its parts. The same laws of value, if "laws" they may be called, that apply to its various parts and wholes apply also to the whole that contains all these parts and wholes but is not itself a part of any whole. Each of its parts has positive contributory value to the degree to which they contribute to the intrinsic goodness of the whole that contains them all, negative contributory value to the degree to which they diminish its intrinsic goodness. The all-inclusive whole is itself intrinsically good if the positive value of its good parts is greater than the negative value of its bad parts, intrinsically bad if the negative value of its bad parts is greater than the positive value of its good parts.

Although the various parts of the world have positive or negative contributory value relative to the world, depending upon whether they increase or diminish its intrinsic goodness, they have no instrumental value relative to the world. This is because they are not means to its existence as something of which they are not parts, since they all are part of it. Moreover, the world itself, since it is not a part of some larger whole and is not a means to the existence of anything outside itself, can have no contributory value and no instrumental value. Instead, the only kind of value it can have is intrinsic value. It might, however, be thought that since we cannot know all its parts, nor even always know the value, positive or negative, of various of its parts of which we do have knowledge, we cannot know whether it itself on the whole is intrinsically good, intrinsically bad, or neither good nor bad.

If, however, the whole that contains as parts everything that exists, occurs, or obtains but yet is not itself a part of any other whole contains God, conceived in the Anselmian way as that than which no greater can be conceived, then necessarily it is intrinsically good. Lest heresy be suspected here, let it be noted that to say that the whole than which no more inclusive can be conceived contains God as one of its parts is compatible with the view that every other part of this whole is created by God and depends completely upon the continuing conserving action of God for its continuing existence from moment to moment. Although God, conceived in this way, would not be a part of the whole He creates and sustains in being, this whole being the created world, He would be a part of the whole containing as parts both Himself and the world He creates, and this whole, given that God is that than which no greater can be conceived, necessarily would be intrinsically good. The reason this is the case is that the positive value of the existence of God, again conceived as that than which no greater can be conceived, would be so unsurpassably great that necessarily it would be unsurpassably greater than any negative value the existence of the created world might have, regardless of the degree to which the existence of the created world might be intrinsically bad. Indeed, one might well argue, in Leibnizian fashion, that if that than which no greater can be conceived does in fact exist, then the created world, regardless of the degree to which it might be intrinsically bad, is still the least bad, and therefore the best, of all possible worlds, since, if it were not, God, being that than which no greater can be conceived, would not create and conserve it. Given, that is, that God creates and conserves the world, and given also that God is that than which no greater can be conceived, the world He creates and conserves must be the least bad, and therefore the best, of all possible worlds, regardless of the degree to which it is intrinsically bad. Even if it were as bad as Schopenhauer in certain of his philosophical moments seems to have thought, it would still be the least bad, and thus the best, of all possible created worlds, regardless of the degree to which it is intrinsically bad. It might also be mentioned in passing that Schopenhaur did not seem to be in any particular hurry to separate himself from the world, regardless of how bad in certain of his philosophical moments he believed, or pretended to believe, it to be. Nor do most of the rest of us seem to be in any particular hurry to separate ourselves from it.

It was maintained above that the world, considered as an all-inclusive whole, can have only intrinsic value and thus neither instrumental nor contributory value. Since it is not a part of some larger whole, it cannot contribute to the value of such a larger whole. And since it is all-inclusive, there is nothing outside it in relation to which it can have instrumental value. The created world, on the other hand, can have not only intrinsic value but also contributory value, since it can contribute to the value of the all-inclusive whole containing as parts itself and God if God exists. It cannot, however, have instrumental value, since it cannot be a means to the existence of anything of which it is not a part. The existence of God, however, would have both contributory and instrumental as well as intrinsic value, since His existence would contribute to the value of the all-inclusive whole of which He would be a part and also be a means to the existence of the created world, of which He is not a part.

4. Inherent Value

Before concluding this chapter I should like to discuss briefly the concept of a species of value not heretofore mentioned. This is the concept of inherent value employed by C. I. Lewis.[6] For Lewis inherent value is a species of extrinsic value essentially distinct not only from intrinsic value but also from the two species of extrinsic value distinguished above—those of instrumental value and contributory value. For Lewis it is only experiences that can have intrinsic value. Those experiences, and only those, that are liked, pleasant, satisfying, or wanted are intrinsically good; and those, and only those, that are disliked, unpleasant, unsatisfying, or unwanted are intrinsically bad. For the sake of simplicity, I shall express this by saying that it is those and only those experiences that are liked that are intrinsically good and that it is those and only those that are disliked that are intrinsically bad. If experiences alone can have intrinsic value, the value of anything other than experiences can be only extrinsic. It does not, however, follow that their value must be either instrumental or contributory. Instead, something, x, can have instrumental or contributory value without having inherent value, and something else, y, can have inherent value without having instrumental or contributory value. The difference between inherent value and these other two species of extrinsic value can be explained as follows.

Suppose that a is a means to something else, b, of which a is not a part, and that a and b are not themselves experiences. If so, then neither a nor b can have intrinsic value. A has instrumental value as a means to b, and b might also have such value as a means to something else, c. In order, however, that a have instrumental value as a means to b and b as a means to c, as opposed to having only utility, then c, or something else, d, to which c is a means, must have inherent value as something that is directly or immediately liked or disliked. (To avoid redundancy, I shall refer to immediately or directly liking or disliking something simply as liking or disliking it.) If neither a nor b are liked or disliked they have no inherent value but instead have only instrumental value as a means to something else, c or d, that has inherent value. If, however, a or b themselves are liked or disliked they have inherent as well as instrumental value. But although a, b, and c, and also d if it is a means to something else, e, can each have both instrumental and inherent value, none can have intrinsic value if none is itself an experience. It is only the experience of any of them that can have such value. Such experiences are intrinsically good if they are liked, intrinsically bad if they are disliked, intrinsically indifferent if they are neither liked nor disliked. Similar considerations apply to contributory value. If x is a part of y, and if x contributes to the value of y, then x has contributory value relative to y. The part, x, and the whole, y, might also have inherent value. Each has such value if each is liked or disliked. Neither, however, can have intrinsic value if neither is an experience. Instead, it is only the experience of either that can have such value. The experience of either is intrinsically good if it is liked, intrinsically bad if it is disliked, intrinsically indifferent if it is neither liked nor disliked.

In order, however, that something have inherent value it is not necessary that it actually be liked or disliked by anyone. Instead, it suffices that it be such that it would be liked or disliked by someone if he were to have experience of it. Thus something can have inherent value without ever being liked or disliked by anyone because no one ever in fact has experience of it, provided that it would be liked or disliked by someone were he to have experience of it. The inherent value of such things is therefore dispositional. Intrinsic value, however, is not. It is only actual experiences that can be intrinsically good or bad. Just as the nature of certain possible states of affairs that do not in fact obtain might be such that it would be good were they to obtain, and just as the nature of certain universals that are not in fact exemplified is such that it would be good were they exemplified, so also certain possible experiences that are not in fact actual might be such that they would be liked or disliked by someone were he to have them. But just as states of affairs that do not in fact obtain and universals that are not in fact exemplified are neither good nor bad, so also possible experiences that are not in fact actual are neither good nor bad.

The preceding, I hope, will suffice, at least for our purposes here, as an explication of Lewis' concept of inherent value and how it differs from the concepts of instrumental, contributory, and intrinsic value. It will be evident that such value, like instrumental and contributory value, would be relative. Just as a can have instrumental value only relative to something else, b, to which it is a means, and just as x can have contributory value only relative to some whole, y, of which it is a part, so also something can have inherent value only relative to the liking or disliking of it by someone. Lewis' concept of intrinsic value is also such that such value turns out to be relative, since whether a given experience is intrinsically good or bad is determined by whether it is liked or disliked. Thus if an instance of a given type of experience is liked by one person, and if another instance of that type of experience is disliked by a second person, the first instance is intrinsically good relative to or for the first person and the second intrinsically bad relative to or for the second person even though the two instances are instances of the same type of experience.

But although instrumental and contributory value, like inherent value, are relative in the senses indicated, they are nonetheless objective in a sense in which inherent value would not be. Whether a has instrumental value as a means to b, and whether x has contributory value as contributing to the value of some whole, y, are independent of anyone's experiences and beliefs. Either *a* does or it does not have instrumental value as a means to *b*, and either *x* does or it does not have contributory value as contributing to the value of some whole, *y*, regardless (1) of whether anyone believes that they do and of whether anyone has any experience of *a*, *b*, *x*, or *y* and (2) of whether anyone would believe that they do were he to have experience of them. Something, *a*, cannot both have and also not have instrumental value as a means to *b*, and something, *x*, cannot both have and also not have contributory value as contributing to the value of some whole, *y*. Should someone believe that *a* is a means to *b* when in fact it is not his belief would be false, and should someone believe that *x* contributes to the value of *y* when in fact it does not he too would be mistaken. Similarly, whether *a* is a means to *b* and whether *x* contributes to the value of *y* is independent of whether anyone who has experience of *a*, *b*, *x*, or *y* likes or dislikes them and of whether anyone would do so were he to have experience of them.

The situation is radically different in the case of inherent value. Such value would be subjective in a sense in which instrumental and contributory value are not. Whether something, *o*, has such value is determined entirely by whether those who have experience of it like or dislike it and by whether anyone would do so were he to have experience of it. It would be inherently good if those who have experience of it like it or if anyone would like it were he to have experience of it, inherently bad if those who have experience of it dislike it or if anyone would dislike it were he to have experience of it. Should those who have experience of it neither like nor dislike it and if no one would like or dislike it were he to have experience of it, then it would have no inherent value at all. The subjectivity of inherent value is even more evident in those cases in which one person likes a given object, *o*, a second dislikes it, and a third neither likes nor dislikes it. Thus if Abraham, Isaac, and Jacob all have experience of *o*, and if Abraham likes it, Isaac dislikes it, and Jacob neither likes nor dislikes it, *o* is inherently good relative to or for Abraham, inherently bad relative to Isaac, and neither inherently good nor inherently bad for Jacob. One and the same thing would be at once inherently good, inherently bad, and inherently indifferent if some who have experience of it like it, some dislike it, and some neither like nor dislike it. Even in the case of those things, if there are any, that are such that each person who has experience of them likes them or that are such that any person would like them were he to have experience of them, their inherent goodness would depend completely upon their being liked by those who have experience of them or upon their being such that they would be liked by anyone were he to have experience of them. The universal inherent goodness of such things, if it may be called such, would depend completely upon the subjective factor of whether they are universally liked by those who have experience of them or would be liked by all who have experience of them were they to have such experience, not upon the objective nature of such things. Similar considerations, with of course the obvious necessary changes, would apply to those things, if there are any, that universally are inherently bad and to those, if again there are any, that universally are inherently indifferent.

Similar considerations, with the necessary changes, apply to Lewis' account of the intrinsic value of experiences. Their value too would be completely subjective even though there might be experiences of certain kinds that are such that anyone who has such experiences likes them or that are such that anyone would like them were they to have them. Indeed, Lewis' account of inherent and intrinsic value is such that intrinsic value turns out to be even more subjective than inherent value. On his view, various objects can have positive or negative inherent value independently of whether anyone does in fact have experience of them, provided that they be such that someone would like or dislike them were he to have experience of them. It is therefore at least abstractly possible that there be a world completely devoid of subjects of experience that nonetheless contains inherently valuable objects, provided that it contain objects that would be liked or disliked by some subjects of experience were such subjects ever to exist and to have experience of such objects. The inherently valuable objects of such a world would still exist even if there were in fact to be no subjects of experience to have experience of them. In such a world, however, nothing would have intrinsic value and everything would be intrinsically indifferent, given that experiences alone can be intrinsically good or bad. Although such a world could contain inherently good or bad objects, it could contain nothing intrinsically good or bad. For this reason intrinsic value, on Lewis' view, turns out to be even more subjective than inherent value.

Given the complete subjectivity of intrinsic value on Lewis' view, his distinction, discussed earlier, between instrumental value and utility would not have as wide an application as it would have were intrinsic value objective. This does not mean that it would have no application at all. *A* could still have utility as a means to *b* without being instrumentally good because neither it nor *b* (1) is a means to the existence or occurrence of something inherently good or (2) leads to anyone's having an intrinsically good experience. If, however, *a* or *b* is a means to the existence or occurrence of something, *c,* liked by someone, then *c* is inherently good, regardless of what *c* might be; and if *a* or *b* is a means to someone's having an experience he likes, regardless of what the experience might be, then *a* and *b* each have instrumental value and not merely utility as a means to the occurrence of that experience. Thus a son's undetected, unpunished, and never regretted killing of his father would have not only utility but also instrumental value as a means to his having his father's wealth, which for him is inherently good because he likes having it, and also instrumentally good because his father's wealth enables him to have certain experiences that for him are intrinsically good because he likes having them. In cases such as this the distinction between instrumental value and utility would have no application.

Lewis is correct in pointing out that there is a difference between (1) *a*'s being a means to *b,* when neither *a* nor *b* is an experience, (2) someone's liking or disliking *a* or *b,* and (3) someone's liking or disliking his experience of *a* or *b.* The son's killing of his father is a means to his having his father's wealth, neither of which is an experience; the son likes having his father's wealth and might also like killing him; and the son likes having certain experiences his having his father's wealth enables him to have. All this, however, can be acknowledged without also admitting that therefore the son's killing his father is instrumentally good, his having his father's wealth inherently good, and his having the experiences in question intrinsically good. If in these circumstances the son's having his father's wealth and his having the experiences in question are both intrinsically bad regardless of whether the son likes them, as I believe they would be, then his killing his father, although it would have utility as a means of having them both, would have no positive instrumental value at all as such a means but instead would be instrumentally bad.

If the considerations presented above are acceptable, Lewis' concept of inherent value is useless for value theory. The only species of value we need acknowledge are intrinsic value and the two species of extrinsic value—instrumental value and contributory value. If something, whether it be an experience or something other than an experience, is intrinsically bad, then liking it is also intrinsically bad and disliking it intrinsically good; and if something, whether an experience or something else, is intrinsically good, then liking it is also intrinsically good and disliking it intrinsically bad. If this is so, then Lewis has things backwards. Rather than the liking or disliking of objects and experiences making the latter inherently or intrinsically good or bad, it is instead their intrinsic goodness or badness that makes liking or disliking them intrinsically good or bad.

Chapter 4

Definition, Proof, and Knowledge of Intrinsic Value

In chapter 3 intrinsic value was distinguished from extrinsic value and from total value, which is the combined intrinsic and extrinsic value a thing might have, using "thing" in the broadest possible sense. Explications of the two species of extrinsic value—instrumental and contributory value—and of how they differ from intrinsic value were presented, and the concept of inherent value employed by C.I. Lewis was rejected as useless for value theory. Examples of phenomena of certain sorts that seem to be intrinsically good and of phenomena of certain other sorts that seem to be intrinsically bad have also been given. Part of the purpose of doing the latter prior to attempting an explication of the concept of intrinsic value has been to cite instances of phenomena of certain types that many people would agree have intrinsic value, whether positive or negative, and that some would claim to know have such value. In agreeing or in claiming to know that such instances have such value they are agreeing or claiming to know that the concept of intrinsic value does in fact have an application—that it does in fact apply to phenomena of various kinds—regardless of whether the concept itself can be adequately defined and of whether claims to the effect that a given thing is intrinsically good or bad can be proved. It is time now to address ourselves to these questions.

1. The Definability of Intrinsic Value

One might attempt to define the concept of intrinsic value by distinguishing such value from extrinsic value. This might be done by saying that the intrinsic value of a given thing, again taking "thing" in the broadest possible sense, is the value it has in itself, taken in abstraction from its relationship to anything else and thus in abstraction from any instrumental or contributory value it might have. Such a definition, while doubtless acceptable as far as it goes, does not go far enough. As was suggested in chapter 1, value may be regarded as a genus or determinable of which the most general species or determinations are positive, negative, and neutral value. To say that a thing has positive value is to say that it is good, in a wide sense of "good"; to say that it has negative value is to say that it is bad, in a wide sense of "bad"; and to say that it is neutral in value is to say that it is neither good nor bad. This means that the concept of value is definable or explicable only in terms of the concepts of good, bad, and indifferent, so that to understand the concept of value it is necessary to understand the latter concepts in terms of which it is defined or explicated. There is no difficulty in understanding the concept of neutral value, given that to say of a given thing that it is neutral in value is to say that it is neither good nor bad. The problem lies in understanding the latter two concepts. Unless they are understood the concept of value cannot be understood. Moreover, as the considerations presented in chapter 3 indicate, the concept of extrinsic value cannot be understood unless the concept of intrinsic value is understood.

If the preceding is correct, the concepts of value, of positive, negative, and neutral value, of intrinsic and extrinsic value, and of instrumental and contributory goodness and badness cannot be understood unless the concepts of intrinsic goodness and badness are understood. The latter two concepts are therefore the central concepts of value theory. Attempts to define these two concepts fall into two mutually exclusive and jointly exhaustive classes. One class consists of attempts to define them in terms of non-evaluative concepts, the other of attempts to define them in terms of evaluative concepts other than the concepts of intrinsic goodness and badness.

Definitions of the first type were termed by Moore naturalistic definitions, and many value theorists and moral philosophers have followed Moore in using this terminology. Such language, however, is unfortunate. Moore distinguishes between naturalistic and metaphysical ethics and claims that both commit what he calls the naturalistic fallacy, which, according to one of the several accounts of the fallacy he presents, consists in defining the concept of good in terms of what he calls natural properties. Yet despite the fact that he regards metaphysical ethics as committing the naturalistic fallacy, he distinguishes this type of ethics from naturalistic ethics by saying that it defines the concept of good in terms of non-natural supersensible properties.[1] To avoid such inconsistency in terminology, it seems better to refer to attempts to define evaluative concepts in terms of non-evaluative concepts as non-evaluative definitions. Such terminology expresses more clearly what those who define evaluative concepts in terms of non-evaluative ones are attempting to do, which is to reduce evaluative concepts to concepts that are not evaluative, regardless of whether the latter be concepts of sensible "natural" properties or of supersensible "non-natural" properties.

It might also be mentioned in this connection that in at least certain contexts two other forms of frequently used terminology can be misleading. One is the terminology of "fact/value," the other that of "is/ought". The first is misleading if it suggests or is meant to suggest that value judgments do not or cannot state facts and therefore are not or cannot be true or false. If any judgment is true and states a fact, the judgment that instances of unmerited suffering are intrinsically bad would certainly seem to be true and to state a fact. Such a fact is a value fact. Such facts differ from those facts that are not value facts, such as the fact that John is suffering. If so, then the class of facts is divisible into those facts that are value facts and those that are not, just as the class of judgments is divisible into value judgments and those that are not value judgments. Similarly, the terminology of "is/ought" is unfortunate if it suggests or is intended to suggest that all value judgments are "ought" rather than "is" judgments. In judging that undeserved suffering is intrinsically bad I am making an "is" judgment, not an "ought" judgment. I am judging that such suffering *is* bad, not that it *ought* to be bad. The truth of the value judgment that unmerited suffering is intrinsically bad might entail that we ought to endeavor not to inflict such suffering on anyone. This, however, does not mean that the value judgment is itself an "ought" judgment. Instead, what it means is that the value fact, which in one sense of the term "fact" is a true value proposition,[2] entails that we ought to refrain from doing a certain thing. Although it is not possible to derive "ought" judgments from "is" judgments when the latter state only facts that are not value facts, it is sometimes possible to derive "ought" from "is" judgments when the latter state value facts. Thus given the truth of the "is" value judgment that undeserved suffering *is* intrinsically bad, it follows that we have a *prima facie* duty not to inflict such suffering on any creature, whether man or beast, and thus that we ought not to do so unless our doing so is necessary if we are to fulfill some weightier duty.

Non-evaluative definitions of the concepts of intrinsic goodness and badness are divisible into those that define these concepts in terms of various psychological phenomena and those that define them in terms of various non-evaluative phenomena that are not psychological in character. It was at least implied in chapter 1 that non-evaluative definitions of the first type are unacceptable. The psychological phenomena in terms of which the concepts of intrinsic goodness and badness are most likely to be defined are divisible into the two major classes distinguished in chapter 1. These are likings and dislikings on the one hand and valuings proper on the other. Although people do sometimes seem to mean nothing more by saying that a given thing, such as a movie, is good or bad than that they like or dislike it, there is still nonetheless a difference between likings and dislikings on the one hand and valuings proper on the other. As was pointed out in chapter 1, it is possible that a person like or dislike a given thing without regarding it as being good or bad, regard a given thing as being good or bad without liking or disliking it, and even like a given thing while regarding it as bad or dislike it while regarding it as good. Given all this, the concepts of intrinsic goodness and badness cannot be defined adequately in terms of the concepts of liking and disliking.

Nor can the first pair of concepts be defined adequately in terms of the concept of valuing proper. In such valuings something other than the valuings themselves is regarded as being good or bad. In valuing a thing, it is the thing itself, not our valuing it, that we regard as being good or bad. Although we can evaluate and value various valuings of things by ourselves and others and regard them as being good or bad, such evaluations and valuings of valuings are second-order phenomena that have as their intentional objects the corresponding first-order valuings. Such second-order phenomena thus presuppose and are parasitic upon the corresponding first-order phenomena, in the sense that if the latter did not occur the former could not occur. Unless things other than evaluations and valuings were regarded as good or bad there could be no evaluating and valuings at all and thus no first-order evaluating and valuings to be evaluated and regarded as good or bad in second-order acts of evaluating and valuing. Moreover, as was also indicated in chapter 1, to evaluate a thing is to attempt to determine whether the thing itself is good, bad, or indifferent independently of the evaluating and valuing of it, so that the evaluation of a thing presupposes that the thing evaluated is itself independently good, bad, or indifferent and could not be undertaken in the absence of such a presupposition. Given this, the concepts of intrinsic goodness and badness cannot be defined adequately in terms of the concepts of evaluation and valuing. If so, then the first pair of concepts cannot be defined adequately in terms of either of the two major types of psychological phenomena in question—they cannot be defined either in terms of liking or disliking or in terms of valuing proper. Instead, such psychological phenomena are themselves correct or incorrect, fitting or unfitting, right or wrong, good or bad. Although such properties are predicable of them, they are not themselves identical with any such properties. Just as they cannot be defined in terms of such properties, so also the latter cannot be defined in terms of them.

This brings us to non-evaluative definitions of the concepts of intrinsic goodness and badness in terms of various non-evaluative concepts of phenomena that are not psychological in character. There is no need to attempt here the tedious task of running through the long list of such non-evaluative concepts suggested by various philosophers both before and after Moore down to the present. The central defect of all attempts to define the concepts of intrinsic goodness and badness in terms of such non-evaluative concepts is that the concepts of intrinsic goodness and badness are evaluative concepts, and such concepts are essentially different from and therefore cannot adequately be defined in terms of, identified with, or reduced to non-evaluative concepts. Again using "thing" in a broad sense, things of various kinds are intrinsically good because they have certain non-evaluative properties or exemplify certain non-evaluative universals and thus because certain non-evaluative concepts apply to them. To say, however, that they are intrinsically good because they have such properties or because they exemplify such universals and thus because such concepts apply to them is not to say that their having such properties or exemplifying such universals or satisfying such concepts is identical with their being intrinsically good. If it were, then to say that they are intrinsically good because they have such properties, exemplify such universals, or satisfy such concepts would be to say that they are intrinsically good because they are intrinsically good. Surely, however, to say that a given thing is intrinsically good because it has a given property, exemplifies a given universal, or satisfies a given concept is not to say that it is intrinsically good because it is intrinsically good. To say that a given thing is good because it has a certain property, exemplifies a certain universal, or satisfies a certain concept is to explain why it is good, but to say it is good because it is good not only explains nothing but does not even attempt to explain anything. Although the goodness of a given thing supervenes upon its having certain properties, exemplifying certain universals, or satisfying certain concepts, its goodness is not identical with, reducible to, or definable in terms of any of the latter.

From the fact, however, that evaluative concepts cannot be defined adequately in terms of non-evaluative concepts, regardless of whether the latter be concepts of psychological phenomena or of phenomena that are not psychological in character, it does not follow that they cannot be defined in terms of other evaluative concepts. We have already seen that certain evaluative concepts—such as those of extrinsic value (whether instrumental or contributory), total value, and positive, negative, and neutral value—are definable in terms of other evaluative concepts. The question before us is that of whether the concepts of intrinsic goodness and badness can be so defined. Such a definition of these concepts would be better in at least one respect than definitions of them in terms of non-evaluative concepts, since all definitions of the latter type commit what may be labeled "the non-evaluative fallacy," whereas definitions in terms of evaluative concepts do not. A number of such definitions can be and have been offered—so many, in fact, that it would be tedious to attempt to list them all. Fortunately, however, there is no need to attempt to compile such a list, since they all suffer from a certain fatal defect I shall endeavor presently to indicate. Since all possible evaluative definitions suffer from this defect, it will suffice for our purposes here if I indicate a few that have at least some initial plausibility. It will also suffice, and be helpful for purposes of expository simplicity, if I list only definitions of the concept of intrinsic goodness. It should be an easy matter for the reader to frame corresponding definitions of the concept of intrinsic badness.

The concept of intrinsic goodness has been or could be defined in any of the following at least initially plausible ways. To say that x is intrinsically good is to say that (1) the existence or occurrence of x is in itself preferable to its non-existence or non-occurrence; (2) the existence or occurrence of x is or would be better in itself that its non-existence or non-occurrence; (3) x, taken in abstraction from its relations to everything else, ought to exist or occur; (4) x is worth having in itself; or (5) it is correct, fitting, or right to like or value in itself *x* and/or its existence or occurrence. The reader will doubtless be able to think of still other at least initially plausible definitions. The list given, however, will suffice for our purposes. Each definition on the list is compatible with each of the others, so that one could consistently accept them all as alternative definitions or perhaps as together constituting a conjunctive definition.

Most of these definitions suffer from flaws unique to themselves. A defect from which (2) suffers is that it seems to be circular, since to say that the existence or occurrence of *x* is or would be better in itself than its non-existence or non-occurrence seems to be to say only that its existence or occurrence is or would be more good in itself than its non-existence or non-occurrence. If so, then the concept of good is more primitive or fundamental than the concept of better than and therefore cannot be defined adequately in terms of the latter. In addition, the concept of better than is wider than the concept of good since, as was pointed out earlier, one thing, *a,* can be better than another thing, *b,* even though neither *a* nor *b* is good. For this reason too the concept of good cannot properly be defined in terms of the concept of better than.

Two flaws afflict (3). It too seems to suffer from circularity, since in this context to say that *x* ought to exist or occur seems to be to say only that it is good that *x* exists or occurs or that it would be good were it to exist or occur. It also suffers from the fact that it employs "ought" in a loose and perhaps improper way since, as Prichard and Ross have pointed out,[3] in the strict sense of the term the value of "x" in locutions such as "x ought to . . ." is always some moral agent. This certainly is the case when "x ought to . . ." is short for "x morally ought to. . . ".

A defect from which (4) suffers is that it is too narrow. The existence or occurrence of various things can be intrinsically good, yet the existence or occurrence of a thing cannot be had by anyone, at least not in the sense of being possessed. Moreover, something such as a sunset might be intrinsically good because of its beauty, yet it is only the experience of a sunset and its beauty that can be had by anyone, not the sunset itself or its beauty. Even if experiences alone and nothing else were intrinsically good, (4) would still be unacceptable as a definition of the concept of intrinsic goodness, since it begs the question of whether anything other than experiences, the nature of which is such that it cannot be had, can be intrinsically good.

The fatal flaw of (5) is that it is too broad. This is the case because, as I shall argue in a later chapter, it is sometimes correct, fitting, or right to like or value in itself a given thing, *x*, and/or its existence or occurrence even though *x* be indifferent rather than intrinsically good. If the argument of that chapter does in fact establish this, then the concept of intrinsic goodness cannot be defined adequately in the way in which it is defined in definition (5).

Even if, however, the preceding objections to definitions (2) through (5) could successfully be met, they, along with (1), would still suffer from a certain fatal flaw. This is that even if, in each of the five definitions, the sentences that result when some value is substituted for the variable "*x*" were such that the truth of the sentence expressing the *definiendum* both entails and is entailed by the sentence expressing the *definiens,* the sentence expressing the *definiens* would be true because the one expressing the *definiendum* is true, whereas the sentence expressing the *definiendum* would not be true because the one expressing the *definiens* is true. Although this applies to all five definitions, it will suffice if we consider only (1), given that the others are all unacceptable for the reasons given. Thus if the existence or occurrence of *x* is in itself preferable to its non-existence or non-occurrence, the reason is that *x* is intrinsically good; *x*, however, is not intrinsically good because its existence or occurrence is preferable in itself to its non-existence or non-occurrence. This can be put by saying that although *x*'s being intrinsically good makes its existence or occurrence preferable in itself to its non-existence or non-occurrence, the preferability of its existence or occurrence in itself to its non-existence or non-occurrence does not make it intrinsically good. Similar considerations, I believe, would apply to any otherwise acceptable definition of the concept of intrinsic goodness.

What the preceding argument, if sound, establishes is that definitions of the concept of intrinsic goodness, whether they be in terms of non-evaluative or in terms of evaluative concepts, fail to capture or express the essence of such goodness. Although the truth of sentences used to assert that a given thing is intrinsically good might entail and be entailed by the truth of certain other sentences used to assert something else about the thing in question, no sentences of the latter type capture or express the essence of intrinsic goodness. For this reason the concept of intrinsic goodness is indefinable in the strictest sense of the term "definition," according to which a definition states the essence of the object being defined. From this, however, it does not follow that we do not know the meaning of a given indefinable term, that we do not have the concept it expresses, or that we do not know the essence of the object of the concept.

To some this might seem to be an untenable position and an undesirable outcome. Just a little reflection, however, should show that it is not. If in order to know the meaning of any term it were necessary that we be able to define both it and also every other term in terms of which it is defined, then we could not know the meaning of any term. I might define "a" in terms of "b," "b" in terms of "c," "c" in terms of "d," and so on. It is evident, however, that this process cannot go on forever. There are only two ways of stopping it. One is to present a circular definition and define, say, "d" in terms of "a". For obvious reasons, however, such definitions are unacceptable. The only other alternative is to accept some term as primitive or undefined, say "d". From the fact, however, that "d" is primitive or undefined it does not follow that we do not know its meaning. Unless we knew its meaning we could not know adequately the meaning of "a," "b," "c," which are defined ultimately in terms of it. If then, we are to know the meaning of any term, there must be some term the meaning of which we know even though we cannot define it. This applies not only to value theory but also to any other area of inquiry. It is sometimes hard to know which terms require definition and which do not and which are definable and which are not. If the argument of this section is sound, in value theory a term that neither needs to be nor can be defined is "intrinsic goodness". From this, however, it does not follow that we do not know what it means.

2. Proof and Knowledge of Intrinsic Value

In the previous section it was argued that the concept of intrinsic goodness is indefinable. A similar argument, with of course the necessary changes, could also be presented to establish that the concept of intrinsic badness is also indefinable. From the fact, however, that these concepts are indefinable it does not follow that we cannot prove or know that things of various kinds, again using "thing" in a wide sense, are intrinsically good or bad. We turn now to discuss briefly the question of whether such proof and knowledge are possible.

As is well known, Moore maintained that there can be no proof of any claim to the effect that a given thing is or is not intrinsically good (or bad or indifferent). Since the classes of the intrinsically good, the intrinsically bad, and the intrinsically indifferent are conjointly exhaustive and mutually exclusive, anything conceivable is a member of one and only one of these classes. If however, Moore's claim is correct, the question of which things are members of which classes is not a question that can be answered by presenting proof. This is the case, according to Moore, because there are no propositions more evident than any true proposition to the effect that a given thing is intrinsically good (or bad or indifferent) that could be used as premises in an argument that would establish the truth of such a proposition. There might be other propositions, each of which is as evident as, but no more evident than, a given proposition p to the effect that a given thing is intrinsically good which are such that if they are true p also is true. If, however, none of them is more evident than p, the fact that if they are true p also is true does not mean that the truth of p can be proved by appealing to their truth, since if their truth is no more evident than that of p the truth of p is not rendered more evident by appealing to them even though its truth be entailed by their truth. This seems to be the sense of "proof" Moore had in mind when he denied that any proposition to the effect that a given thing is intrinsically good can be proved.[4]

Despite Moore, however, there do seem to be certain ways in which the intrinsic goodness (or badness or indifference) of certain things can be proved. One way consists of arguing that a given instance of a given species is intrinsically bad because (1) the species in question is comprehended by some genus, all the instances of which are intrinsically bad, and (2) it is more evident that all instances of the genus are intrinsically bad than it is that all instances of the species are bad. Thus, as will be argued in a later chapter, a given instances of pervasive dislike of indifferent things is intrinsically bad because (1) such pervasive dislike is comprehended by a genus labeled "mean-spiritedness," all the instances of which are intrinsically bad, and (2) it is more evident that all instances of mean-spiritedness are intrinsically bad than it is that all instances of such pervasive dislike are bad. A second way of proving that a given thing, a, is intrinsically bad consists in arguing that it is the opposite of something else, b, that is intrinsically good. Thus in the chapter in question it will be argued that mean-spiritedness is intrinsically bad because it is the opposite of magnanimity, which is intrinsically good. A third way of proving that a given thing, a, is intrinsically good consists of arguing (1) that it is an instance of the kind, k, and has properties f, g, and h and (2) that any instance of the kind, k, that has the properties f, g, and h is intriniscally good because the possession of these properties by any instance of that kind suffices to make it intrinsically good.

It is evident, however, that each of these ways of proving that a given thing is intrinsically good or bad rests ultimately on the claim that something else is intrinsically good or bad. In the first way the argument rests on the claim that all instances of a given genus, such as mean-spiritedness, are intrinsically bad; in the second on the claim that the opposite, such as magnanimity, of something held to be intrinsically bad, such as mean-spiritedness, is intrinsically good; and in the third on the claim that any instance of the kind, k, that has the properties f, g, h is intrinsically good. Sometimes the claims on which such arguments rest can themselves be proved by appealing to still other claims the truth of which is more evident. Thus one might attempt to prove the truth of the claim that mean-spiritedness is intrinsically bad by arguing that it is the opposite of magnanimity, the intrinsic goodness of which is seen or at least assumed to be more evident than is the intrinsic badness of mean-spiritedness. Is there, however, a claim the truth of which is more evident than the truth of the claim that magnanimity is intrinsically good to which an appeal can be made to prove the truth of the latter claim? If there is, is there still some other claim the truth of which is more evident than that of the claim in terms of which the intrinsic goodness of magnanimity is proved? It is evident that this process cannot go forever. Finally we must accept without proof some claim to the effect that a given thing is intrinsically good or bad if we are to prove that anything at all is so.[5]

To some this might seem an unsatisfactory state of affairs. If, however, nothing can be known without proof, then nothing can be known. If, that is, we can know that p is true only if we know that q is true and that q entails p, and if we can know that q is true only if we know that r is true and that r entails q, and so on without end, then we can know nothing other than perhaps that q entails p and that r entails q, etc. Even our knowledge of such entailments, however, rests on our knowing something without proof, since the proposition that q entails p either is sufficiently evident in itself to justify our accepting it without proof or it is not. If it is not, then we can know that it is true only if we know that some other proposition, s, is true and that s entails that q entails p. The same considerations, however, would apply to s and to the proposition that s entails that q entails p. If, then, anything at all is evident, it is evident both that proof cannot go on forever and that if anything at all is to be known then something must be known without proof. Although it is sometimes, but fortunately not always, difficult in the extreme to know with certainty that one has reached a point at which no further proof is possible, one finally does reach a point at which one accepts a given proposition without proof simply because it is seen to be true or because, after the most careful reflection of which one is capable, it seems to be true.

Proof of the truth of a given proposition is necessary if we are to know it to be true only if we do not already know it to be true without proof through seeing it to be true. Moreover, ultimately we can know that a given proof establishes the truth of a given proposition only if we see without proof that each step in the proof follows from the preceding step. This means that ultimately the process of proving the truth of a given proposition consists in or depends upon a series of insights or seeings. This holds regardless of whether the proof is designed to establish that the proposition to be proved is true necessarily or true only with some degree of probability. To know that the premises of a given argument establish that the conclusion is true necessarily we must see that their truth entails its truth, and to know that they establish that the conclusion is true with a certain degree of probability we must see that their truth establishes that the conclusion is true with that degree of probability. It is also necessary that ultimately we see that the premises are true if we are to know that the conclusion is true. Unless the premises are seen to be true the most the proof can establish is that *if* they are true the conclusion is too, either necessarily or with some degree of probability. If the premises are only assumed and not seen to be true, the proof establishes only that *if* they are true the conclusion is too, not that it *is* true. Moreover, even in those proofs in which the premises are only assumed and not seen to be true, it is only the premises that can be assumed to be true and not the fact that the conclusion follows from them. Unless the conclusion is seen to follow from the premises we have only a series of assumptions, and such a series does not constitute a proof.

The preceding considerations apply not only to value theory but also to any area of inquiry, regardless of whatever the area might happen to be. In value theory these considerations mean that if anything is to be proved to be either intrinsically or extrinsically good or bad, then certain things must be known without proof to be intrinsically good or intrinsically bad through seeing that they are one or the other. In previous chapters various examples have been given of things that are intrinsically good and of other things that are intrinsically bad, and in succeeding chapters other examples will be given. I trust that the reader will see that at least some of these things are indeed intrinsically good and that at least some are intrinsically bad.

Chapter 5

Moral and Non-Moral Value

In chapter 5 it was argued that the concepts of intrinsic goodness and badness are the central concepts of value theory and that the concepts of extrinsic value (including both instrumental and contributory value), total value, and positive, negative, and neutral value are explicable only in terms of the concepts of intrinsic goodness and badness. From this, however, it does not follow that these two concepts are the central concepts of moral philosophy, as distinguished from value theory, which is to say that it does not follow that the central concepts of moral philosophy—such as the concepts of duty or obligation, ought, rightness and wrongness, supererogation, rights, moral goodness and badness, and moral virtues and vices—are all explicable in terms of the concepts of intrinsic goodness and badness. In this chapter we turn to treat briefly the relationship of such goodness and badness to such specifically moral concepts. If such moral concepts are explicable in terms of such goodness and badness, then moral philosophy is simply a branch of value theory; if they are not, then the former is not simply a branch of the latter.

1. Moral Concepts and Value Concepts

In treating the relationship of the concepts of intrinsic goodness and badness to specifically moral concepts it is important at the outset not to present definitions of concepts of the latter type that beg the question of whether they are explicable in terms of the former pair of concepts. It is therefore important that concepts such as those of duty and rightness not be defined in the way in which Moore defines them. According to him, "Our 'duty'. . . . can only be defined as that action, which will cause more good to exist in the Universe than any possible alternative. And what is 'right' or 'morally permissible' only differs from this, as what will *not* cause *less* good than any possible alternative."[1] It might be the case that in any given concrete existential situation a person's duty is to perform the act that will lead to more good than would any other act open to him in his situation. It might also be the case that in a given concrete situation a person acts rightly only if his act leads to as much good as would any other act open to him in the situation. It is also conceivable, however, that in certain situations a person's duty might be to perform some act that leads to less good than would some other act open to him and thus that he acts rightly in such situations even though his act leads to less good than would some other act open to him. If so, then Moore's definitions beg the question against opposing positions. Although his position concerning how a person must act in concrete situations if he is to do his duty and act rightly might be correct, those who take an opposing position do not thereby necessarily misuse the terms "duty" and "acting rightly" or contradict themselves. This means that the terms in question cannot be defined adequately in the way Moore suggests. Instead, they can be defined adequately only if the definition presented is what may be referred to as a purely "formal" definition that does not beg any substantive moral questions to which opposing answers have been or could be given.

One way of attempting a purely formal definition of such concepts goes as follows. It relies on Ross's distinction between *prima facie* and absolute duties.[2] In any given concrete situation a person's absolute duty is to fulfill, or to do his best to fulfill, his weightiest *prima facie* duty in that situation. A given *prima facie* duty, *a,* might override another, *b,* in a situation of type *x,* yet be overridden by *b* in a situation of type *y.* If a situation is such that a person in that situation has two *prima facie* duties, *a* and *b,* if both *a* and *b* override any other *prima facie* duties he has in the situation, if neither *a* nor *b* overrides the other, and if *a* and *b* conflict so that they cannot both be fulfilled, the person's absolute duty in that situation is to do either *a* or *b,* and he acts rightly in doing, or in doing his best to do, either *a* or *b.*

It might seem at first that in the preceding account the concept of *prima facie* duty is more fundamental than that of absolute duty, since the latter concept is explicated in terms of the former. In point of fact, however, the two concepts are correlative, since the concept of *prima facie* duty can itself be explicated only by using the concept of absolute duty. Thus to say of a given duty that it is *prima facie* is to say that in any given situation in which it is such a duty it would be an absolute duty if it were not overridden by some other conflicting *prima facie* duty or countered by some other conflicting *prima facie* duty of equal weight. Thus just as the concept of absolute duty was explicated by using the concept of *prima facie* duty, so also the latter concept can be explicated only by using the former. The two concepts are therefore correlative, and neither is more fundamental than the other. This, however, is not to deny that there might be some duties, such as respect for persons, that are unconditionally absolute, in the sense that they cannot be overridden in any situation in which we might find ourselves.

The account of the concept of duty presented above is such that it is more fundamental than the concepts of rightness and wrongness, which are definable in terms of the concept of duty. Thus in a given situation a person acts wrongly if and only if he fails to fulfill his weightiest *prima facie* duty, and thus his absolute duty, in that situation, rightly if and only if he does not fail to do so. It is conceivable, however, that a person might find himself in a situation to which none of his *prima facie* duties apply, so that in that situation he has no *prima facie* duty to do anything at all. In such a situation he cannot act wrongly, so that anything he does he does rightly, in the sense that he does not act wrongly. The concept of acting rightly is therefore broader than that of acting wrongly, and more occasions, happily, are presented in which we can act rightly than in which we can act wrongly. On such occasions we can relax and not worry about acting wrongly. If this is correct, then although in any situation in which we can act wrongly we can also act rightly, there are also situations in which we can act rightly, in the sense of not acting wrongly, even though in such situations we cannot act wrongly. If we had no duties we could not act wrongly and could act rightly only in the sense that, given that we have no duties, we could not fail to fulfill them. Since the concepts of rightness and wrongness are definable in terms of the concept of duty, the latter concept is more fundamental.

The concept of supererogation is also definable in terms of the concept of duty, and indeed is usually so defined, as when it is said that supererogatory acts are those acts that are above and beyond the call of duty. Although all such acts are right, in the sense that their performance does not violate duties, none are duties. From this, however, it does not follow, as it seems sometimes to be thought, that supererogatory acts have greater moral value and are harder to perform than acts that are simply duties but not supererogatory. Thus suppose that as I walk along a certain street I see a beggar and that I give him a dollar even though I have no duty to give him any money at all. Suppose also that this act requires no sacrifice of any significance on my part, that I find the performance of it easy, and that it has some moral value. There is no difficulty, however, in conceiving of many duties the performance of which would require some sacrifice on my part, that I might find it hard to fulfill, and the fulfillment of which would have considerably greater moral value than the performance of the simple supererogatory act of giving a dollar to a beggar. To say, then, that an act is supererogatory is to say only that, although it is right, it is above and beyond the call of duty but not necessarily that its performance is harder than, requires greater sacrifice than, and has greater moral value than the fulfillment of certain duties.

Given the preceding, the concept of ought, in the strict moral sense of the term, can be explicated in terms of the concepts of duty and of rightness and wrongness. The claim that in a given situation a person has a given *prima facie* duty entails the claim that he ought to fulfill it unless it is overridden by some weightier conflicting *prima facie* duty or countered by some conflicting *prima facie* duty of equal weight. Similarly, the claim that in a given situation a person has a given absolute duty entails the claim that he ought to fulfill it. From this it follows that the claim that in a given situation a person can act rightly only by performing a given act, or any one of two or more acts, entails the claim that he ought to do so. And the claim that in a given situation a person would act wrongly were he to act in a certain way entails the claim that he ought not to act in that way. The concepts of duty and of rightness and wrongness are therefore more fundamental than the concept of ought even though the claim that in a given situation a person ought to perform a given act also entails the claim that it is his duty to perform it and that he must do so if he is to act rightly. This is the case because he ought to perform such acts because it is his duty to do so and he must do so if he is to act rightly, but such acts are not his duty and it is not necessary that he perform them if he is to act rightly because he ought so to do. The situation here is analogous to that discussed in the first section of the previous chapter concerning the mutual entailment of a proposition p to the effect that a given thing, x, is intrinsically good and a proposition q to the effect that its existence or occurrence is preferable in itself to its non-existence or non-occurrence. Although p and q mutually entail each other, q is true because p is true but not vice versa. Similarly, although a proposition p to the effect that in a given situation a person's duty is to perform a given act and acts rightly only if he does so entails and is entailed by a proposition q to the effect that he ought to perform the act in question, q is true because p is true but not vice versa. If so, then the concepts of duty and of acting rightly are more fundamental than the concept of ought.

In addition to the strict sense of "ought" just discussed, there is also a looser sense of the term. In this looser sense, we sometimes say that a person ought to do a certain thing without intending thereby to say that he has a duty to do it or that he would act wrongly were he not to do it. Instead, what is meant is that it would be good were he to do the thing in question even though he has no duty to do it and would not act wrongly should he not do it. This sense of "ought" is connected with the concept of supererogation. Even though I might have no duty to give any money at all to a beggar I meet on the street and thus would not act wrongly in not giving him any, it might still be the case that I ought to give him some, in the sense that it would be a good thing to do. In this sense of "ought," we ought to perform various supererogatory acts in the sense that it would be good were we to do so even though we have no duty to perform any given supererogatory act in particular as opposed to others and would not act wrongly were we not to do so. Indeed, a plausible case could be made for the view that we ought from time to time to perform at least some supererogatory acts, not simply in the sense that doing so would be good, but also in the strict sense of "ought" discussed above, according to which we have a duty to perform some such acts and would act wrongly were we never to do so. On such a view, although I do not have a duty to perform any given supererogatory act and would not act wrongly in not doing so, I do however have a duty to perform some such acts from time to time and would act wrongly were I never to do so. Given, however, that I have no duty to perform any particular supererogatory act as opposed to others, the choice of which such acts to perform is mine to make. Particular supererogatory acts would therefore on the view in question still differ from particular acts it is my duty to perform. In the case of acts of the latter type the choice of whether to perform them is not mine to make, since were I to choose not to perform them I would fail to fulfill my duty and thus would act wrongly.

Since I have no duty to perform any particular supererogatory act as opposed to others, the possible beneficiaries of such acts have no claim or right against me that I perform them, and I do not wrong them in not doing so. This brings us to the concept of moral rights. I have argued elsewhere[3] in some detail for the view that to say that some moral agent, a, has a moral right to something, *x,* is to say (1) that *a* acts at least *prima facie* rightly in attempting to acquire or retain *x* and (2) that if any other moral agent, *b,* is in a position to affect *a*'s acquisition or retention of *x,* then *b* has at least a *prima facie* duty to act compatibly with *a*'s acquiring or retaining *x.* Since beings that are not moral agents—such as dumb animals, fetuses, infants, small children, and severely retarded people—are incapable of acting rightly or wrongly in a moral sense, to say that such a being, *a,* has a moral right to something, *x,* is to say only (2) above.[4] If in a given situation *b*'s *prima facie* duty to act compatibly with *a*'s acquiring or retaining something, *x,* to which *a* has a moral right, is not overridden by some conflicting weightier *prima facie* duty or countered by some conflicting *prima facie* duty of equal weight, then *b* has an absolute duty to act compatibly with *a*'s acquiring or retaining *x.* In failing to fulfill this duty *b* not only acts wrongly but also wrongs *a,* especially if *b* attempts to prevent *a* from acquiring or retaining *x,* as distinguished from simply doing nothing to assist *a* in acquiring or retaining *x.*

There is, or at least seems to be, a mutual entailment (a) between the proposition that a given moral agent, *a,* has a moral right to something, *x,* and propositions (1) and (2) above and (b) between the proposition that a being, *a,* who is not a moral agent has a moral right to something, *x,* and proposition (2) above. Propositions (1) and (2), however, are true in the case of any given moral agent, *a,* and proposition (2) in the case of any being, *a,* who is not a moral agent, only because *a* has a moral right to *x;* whereas *a* does not have a moral right to *x* because, given that *a* is a moral agent, propositions (1) and (2) are true or because, given that *a* is not a moral agent, proposition (2) is true. This can perhaps be seen more clearly in cases in which the *prima facie* duty of a moral agent, *b,* to act compatibly with *a*'s acquiring or retaining *x* is not overridden by some conflicting weightier *prima facie* duty or countered by some conflicting *prima facie* duty of equal weight, so that *b* has an absolute duty to act compatibly with *a*'s acquiring or retaining *x* and thus acts wrongly in not doing so and perhaps also wrongs *a*. If *b* wrongs *a* it is because *a* has some right that *b* violates; *a*, however, does not have the right in question because *b* violates it and thereby wrongs *a*. The violation of a right presupposes the existence of the right violated, but a right can exist without being violated. Thus although the concept of a moral right can, I think, be explicated in the ways indicated, it cannot be dispensed with by substituting for it the concepts in terms of which it is explicated, as I earlier thought.[5]

An attempt has been made to explicate the moral concepts discussed above, which are among the central concepts of moral philosophy, without doing so in terms of the concepts of intrinsic goodness and badness. Indeed, with the possible exception of the concept of supererogation, each of these concepts has been explicated without the introduction of any concept of goodness or badness at all, whether intrinsic or extrinsic. In treating the concepts of moral goodness and badness, however, we are dealing with specific forms of goodness and badness. These forms of goodness and badness can themselves, however, be explicated, at least in part, in terms of the specifically moral concepts already discussed. Such goodness and badness are predicable of three distinct types of entity—persons, overt acts (including omissions), and psychological phenomena of various sorts such as likings and dislikings, valuings, motives, feelings and emotions, and desires, hopes, and wishes. The moral goodness and badness of persons is determined by that of their overt acts and that of the psychological phenomena predicable of them, since a person is morally good or bad in the respects in which and in the degree to which his acts and the psychological phenomena predicable of him are morally good or bad.

The psychological phenomena predicable of a person are morally good, at least in part, in the respects in which and the degree to which they dispose him to fulfill his duties and thus to act rightly and as he ought, to respect moral rights, and from time to time to perform supererogatory acts, morally bad in the respects in which and in the degree to which they dispose him to act in contrary ways. In order, however, that psychological phenomena be morally good or bad it is not necessary that they actually issue in overt acts. Thus, for example, particular instances of envy or hatred, even though they never issue in overt acts, are still morally bad in themselves, especially if they take the form of desiring, hoping, or wishing that some evil befall the person envied or hated even though they never issue in an attempt to bring about such evil. Even if, in a world far different from ours, psychological phenomena never issued in overt acts they would still be morally good or bad in themselves, depending upon their intrinsic character.

One of the important ways in which psychological phenomena differ from acts is that rightness and wrongness as well as moral goodness and badness are predicable of acts, whereas usually only moral goodness and badness, not rightness and wrongness, except in a loose and perhaps metaphorical sense, are predicated of psychological phenomena. When, however, moral goodness and badness are predicated of acts, the predication is usually made of the motive animating the act, as distinct from the act itself, which is said to be simply right or wrong. In this connection, Ross makes a distinction between acts and actions, according to which acts are simply what I have been referring to as overt acts, taken in abstraction from the motives animating them, whereas actions are acts taken in conjunction with the motives animating them.[6] Thus on Ross's terminology acts are simply right or wrong, not morally good or bad, whereas actions are morally good or bad. Since, however, acts taken in abstraction from their motives are not morally good or bad, it is the moral goodness or badness of the motive that determines that of the action.

A question therefore arises as to what determines the moral goodness or badness of motives. It will not do to say that a given motive is morally good if it moves the agent to act rightly, morally bad if it moves him to act wrongly. A morally bad motive might move a person to act rightly, a morally good motive to act wrongly. A given person, John, for example, might rightly appoint Peter rather than Paul to a certain position that Peter rather than Paul because of his qualifications deserves to have, yet not because Peter deserves the appointment but instead solely because John is envious of Paul and because of his envy does not want Paul to have the position. If so, then although his act is right the motive animating it is morally bad. Or a person might perform a given act because he believes it to be right when in fact it is wrong. Thus if John appoints Paul rather than Peter to the position because he believes that Paul deserves it and Peter does not when in fact it is Peter rather than

Paul who deserves it, he acts wrongly even though the motive moving him to act is morally good. If, that is, the motive moving a person to act as he does is that he believes the act to be right, then his motive is morally good regardless of whether his act is right or wrong.[7] In such situations, however, the concepts of moral goodness and badness presuppose the concepts of acting rightly or wrongly, since to be moved to perform a given act by a belief that the act is right presupposes the belief in question and thus the concepts of rightness and wrongness. Since, however, these two concepts do not presuppose those of moral goodness and badness, the first pair of concepts is more fundamental than the second. This, however, for the reasons given, does not mean that the second pair of concepts is reducible to the first.

We turn now to the last of the concepts central to moral philosophy mentioned at the beginning of this chapter. These are the concepts of moral virtues and vices. These concepts presuppose in various ways the other concepts discussed above. To have various moral virtues is to be disposed to fulfill various duties, including the duty to respect rights and from time to time to perform supererogatory acts, and thus to act rightly and as one ought to act. A person is morally virtuous in the respects in which and in the degree to which he is so disposed and can have certain virtues without having others. He can be kind, for example, without being courageous and can be courageous without being kind. To have various vices, on the other hand, is to be disposed not to act in the ways in which one must act if one is to have the opposed virtues, and a person is morally vicious in the respects in which and in the degree to which he is so disposed. A person who has certain virtues is even more virtuous than he would otherwise be if he not only exercises these virtues in situations in which it is appropriate to do so but in addition does so at least in part because he believes that he has a duty to do so and thus that he acts rightly and as he ought to act in doing so and, moreover, when it is possible, also enjoys doing so. In certain situations, however, it is hard if not impossible to like exercising certain virtues. It is doubtful, for example, that Jesus enjoyed being crucified. Even, however, when it is hard or impossible to like exercising a given virtue, it might still be possible to take satisfaction in knowing that one is doing so. A person who is in the habit of exercising various of the virtues at least in part because he believes it to be his duty so to do and, when possible, also likes doing so is not only a virtuous person but also a morally good person. Such a person not only exercises various of the virtues in situations in which it is appropriate to do so but does so at least in part because he believes it to be his duty so to do and, in addition, when possible likes doing so.

If the preceding is correct, then moral philosophy, rather than being simply a branch of value theory, is instead presupposed in certain respects by the latter. This is illustrated by the concept of a good person, which is one of the concepts it is the task of value theory to explicate. Yet if the preceding argument is sound this concept can be explicated only by using certain moral concepts. This, however, does not mean that value theory is simply a branch of moral philosophy, since part of its task is to examine non-moral as well as moral goodness and badness.

2. The Value of Moral Objectives

If the argument of the preceding section is sound, various of the concepts central to moral philosophy can be explicated without using the concepts of goodness and badness and thus without using the concepts of intrinsic goodness and badness, which are the central concepts of value theory. At the same time, however, what may be referred to as "moral objectives" are such that any moral objective has either intrinsic or extrinsic positive or negative value and therefore either positive or negative total value. As was pointed out in chapter 2, objectives are facts, which, in various senses of "fact," are either states of affairs that obtain, the obtaining or the non-obtaining of states of affairs, or true propositions. Accordingly, moral objectives are moral facts, which are either moral states of affairs that obtain, the obtaining or the non-obtaining of moral states of affairs, or true propositions to the effect that some moral state of affairs obtains or about the obtaining or the non-obtaining of some moral state of affairs. A moral objective or fact, in any of these senses of "objective" and "fact," is an objective or fact that can be stated or described only by using some moral concept. Every moral fact, in each of these senses of "fact," is such that intrinsic or extrinsic goodness or badness and thus some total value is predicable of it. This can be seen by taking in turn each of the moral concepts discussed in the previous section.

Given any person, x, it is intrinsically good that x fulfills some absolute duty he has in a given situation and thus acts rightly and as he ought, that x performs a given supererogatory act, that x respects a given moral right, that x is morally good or performs some morally good act (or action) or that some morally good psychological phenomenon is predicable of x, or that x has a given moral virtue or that x is morally virtuous and thus is a morally good person. It is intrinsically good that any of these states of affairs obtains, that propositions to the effect that they obtain are true, and the obtaining of each is also intrinsically good. On the other hand, it is intrinsically bad that x fails to fulfill some absolute duty he has in a given situation and thus acts wrongly and fails to act as he ought, that x never performs any supererogatory acts, that x violates some right, that x is morally bad or performs some morally bad act (or action) or that some morally bad psychological phenomenon is predicable of x, or that x has a given moral vice or that x is morally vicious and thus is a morally bad person. It is intrinsically bad that any of these states of affairs obtains, that propositions to the effect that they obtain are true, and the obtaining of each is also intrinsically bad. The intrinsic goodness or badness of these and other moral objectives supervenes upon the nature of the objective, taken completely in abstraction from other objectives.

Each of the objectives indicated above is either intrinsically good or intrinsically bad regardless of whether it has any extrinsic value. Most if not indeed all objectives, however, have extrinsic as well as intrinsic value. Such extrinsic value is either instrumental, contributory, or both. Indeed, it seems that any intrinsically good objective, taken completely in abstraction from any instrumental value it might have, contributes to making the world, which is the most comprehensive whole of which it is a part, intrinsically better than it would be were the objective replaced by some intrinsically bad objective or by some intrinsically good objective having less positive value. Thus, taking the fulfillment or the non-fulfillment of a given person's absolute duty in a given situation completely in abstraction from the obtaining of all other possible states of affairs, the world is intrinsically better if he fulfills his duty than it would be were he not to do so. The preceding applies, with the necessary changes, to any intrinsically bad objective. The contributory value of an objective, however, can be outweighed by its instrumental value. This would happen if its negative instrumental value were greater than its positive contributory value or if its positive instrumental value were greater than its negative contributory value. It is also possible that the contributory value of an objective outweigh its instrumental value. This would occur if it had no instrumental value at all, as sometimes happens. Thus a person's wishing that some undeserved evil befall another person contributes to making the world at least slightly worse than it would otherwise be even though his having that wish has no effect on anything at all and thus no instrumental value at all. Even, however, when the obtaining of some state of affairs does have some instrumental value, the contributory value of its obtaining might be greater than its instrumental value. Thus the performance from compassion of some simple supererogatory act of giving a dollar to a beggar might have greater positive contributory than instrumental value were the beggar alcoholic and uses it to buy another bottle of cheap wine.

It is only, however, when taken simply in relation to the world, the most comprehensive whole of which it is a part, that the contributory value of an objective is determined completely by its intrinsic value. In relation to less comprehensive wholes its contributory value can be determined only by considering also the other parts of the whole and the whole of which they are parts. Thus the contributory value of an act of keeping a promise can be determined only by considering its relation to the act of making the promise and to the whole consisting of both acts. Other things equal, a whole consisting of an act of making a promise and an act of breaking it is intrinsically worse than one consisting of the same first part and an act of keeping it. Since the two wholes have the same first part, the second whole can be better than the first only because of a difference between the second parts, so that the second part of the second whole has some positive contributory value regardless of whether it also has any intrinsic value. It also has positive contributory value relative to the whole in question even though it has negative instrumental value, as it would have were its consequences worse than those of breaking the promise would be.

To determine the total value of an objective it is necessary that one consider not only its intrinsic value and any contributory value it might have but also any instrumental value it might have. Leaving aside for the sake of simplicity any contributory value a given objective might have, its total value is (1) positive if its positive intrinsic value is greater than its negative instrumental value or if its positive instrumental value is greater than its negative intrinsic value, (2) negative if its negative intrinsic value is greater than its positive instrumental value or if its negative instrumental value is greater than its positive intrinsic value.

Thus in a given situation the positive intrinsic value of acting compatibly with some person's acquiring or retaining something, *x,* to which he has a right, might be greater than the negative instrumental value of doing so. If so, then in that situation his right to *x* is not overridden by the negative instrumental value of our acting compatibly with his acquiring or retaining *x,* and we have an absolute duty to do so and can act rightly and as we ought only by doing so. If, however, a situation is such that the negative instrumental value of our acting compatibly with his acquiring of retaining *x,* which might be due to the fact that our doing so would violate some weightier right of some other person or the same right of two or more others, is greater than the positive intrinsic value of our doing so, then his right to *x* is overridden, so that in that situation we have an absolute duty and thus act rightly and as we ought only if we act incompatibly with his acquiring or retaining *x.* From this it is evident that the right in question is only *prima facia.* From the fact, however, that most rights are only *prima facia* it does not follow that there are no absolutely unconditional rights, such as the right to equality of consideration or the right to do one's duty, that cannot under any conditions be overridden.

The view advanced here is compatible with the view that we have an absolute duty to do what we can to bring about the obtaining of those states of affairs the obtaining of which would have greater positive total value than would the obtaining of other incompatible states of affairs that we can also bring about. Such a view, however, is not identical with what is usually regarded as consequentialism or utilitarianism. The primary reason it is not is that included among the states of affairs the obtaining of which would be intrinsically good are not only non-moral states of affairs, such as someone's liking something such as a pleasing aesthetic object or engaging in some activity such as swimming or having some pleasant experience such as tasting good food when hungry, but also moral states of affairs, such as our keeping promises or someone's having something he has a right to have. Although the obtaining of various non-moral states of affairs is intrinsically good, so also is the obtaining of various moral states of affairs. Just as it can be intrinsically good that a person engage in some activity he likes such as swimming, so also it is intrinsically good that a person have something he has a right to have or that he keep a promise. Although the intrinsic value of moral objectives might presuppose that of various non-moral objectives, in the sense that if nothing whatever had intrinsic value in a non-moral sense nothing could have such value in a moral sense, the intrinsic value of moral objectives is not reducible to that of those that are non-moral. For this reason the view advanced here is deontological rather than consequentialist or utilitarian.

The duty to do what one can to bring about the obtaining of both moral and non-moral states of affairs the obtaining of which would be intrinsically good is what is sometimes referred to as an objective duty. When it was said above that a person acts rightly in a given situation only if he fulfills or at least does not violate his absolute duty in that situation, the sense of "duty" and "rightness" used was that of objective duty and rightness. The terms "duty" and "rightness" are also, however, sometimes used in a different sense. This is the sense in which a person's duty is to do what he believes to be his duty. In this sense of the term a person acts rightly only if he does what he believes to be right. This sense of "duty" and "rightness" may be referred to as subjective duty and rightness. Such duty and rightness presuppose belief about objective duty and rightness, since a person, in doing what he believes to be his duty and to be right, is doing what he believes to be his objective duty and to be objectively right. Unless he believes that he has certain duties and that certain acts are right regardless of whether he believes them to be, he could not believe that it is his duty that he act in certain ways rather than others and that he acts rightly and as he ought only if he does so. But although subjective duty and rightness presuppose beliefs about objective duty and rightness, the former are not reducible to the latter, and a person, in doing what he believes to be his duty and to be right, might well be mistaken in his beliefs, and in acting on them might well fail to do what is in fact his objective duty and what is in fact objectively right.[8]

Subjective duty and rightness are related to morally good acts (or actions), since a person's act is morally good if he does what he believes to be his duty or believes to be right. Since, however, what he believes might be mistaken, his act, though morally good, might be wrong. If he is in fact mistaken, his act is morally good but objectively wrong. It is intrinsically good that his act is morally good but intrinsically bad that it is objectively wrong. If, however, he does what is in fact objectively right even though he believes that the act he performs is wrong, his act is objectively right but morally bad. It is intrinsically good that his act is objectively right but intrinsically bad that it is morally bad. In such situations the obtaining of one state of affairs, the obtaining of which is intrinsically good, is possible only at the cost of the obtaining of another, the obtaining of which is intrinsically bad. So long as he continues to hold his mistaken beliefs and acts on them, certain of his acts will be morally good but objectively wrong; if, however, he fails to act on them certain of his acts will be objectively right but morally bad. In either case he will bring about something intrinsically good but also something intrinsically bad.

Given the possibility of such conflicts, it is our absolute duty to reflect as carefully and conscientiously as we can about what our objective duties in fact are and to seek advice from the wisest people to whom we have access, given the amount of time we have for such reflection and for seeking such advice before choice and action are inescapable, and, having done so, to act accordingly. Doing so gives us the best chance we have of avoiding such conflicts at least to some extent, given that it is unlikely that we can unfailingly avoid them in all the complex situations in which from time to time we might find ourselves. We have also a duty to give others, when requested, the advice we have a duty to seek. Should our advice be rejected or should it not be sought, it might become our duty to do what we can to dissuade and even by force to prevent others from acting in ways we believe to be objectively wrong even though in doing so we might be compelled to require of them that they act in ways they believe to be wrong. Whether in particular cases we act rightly in an objective sense in doing so depends upon whether the total positive value of their acting rightly but in ways they believe to be wrong is greater than that of their acting wrongly but in ways they believe to be right. If, however, we have a duty and thus a right in particular cases so to act concerning others, they too have a duty and thus a right so to act concerning us.

3. Theodicy

Conflicts (1) between its being intrinsically good that certain acts are morally good and its being intrinsically bad that they are objectively wrong and (2) between its being intrinsically good that certain acts are objectively right and its being intrinsically bad that they are morally bad are similar to conflicts of another type. These are conflicts between

(1) its being intrinsically bad that certain states of affairs obtain and (2) its being intrinsically good that certain other states of affairs obtain which, however, can obtain only if states of affairs of the first type obtain or at least are believed to obtain. States of affairs of the first type include the existence of what are sometimes termed natural or non-moral evils and the occurrence of moral wrongs of various sorts. States of affairs of the second type include the occurrence of acts intended to eliminate, lessen, or prevent the existence of natural evils or to right or prevent the occurrence of moral wrongs. Unless either (1) natural evils exist or at least could exist and moral wrongs occur or at least could occur or (2) it is believed that they do or could exist or occur, acts of the sort in question could not occur or at least would be pointless if they did occur.

If natural evils could never exist and if moral wrongs could never occur and if no one ever believed that they could exist or occur, acts intended to prevent their existence or occurrence could not occur or would be pointless if they did occur. It would be intrinsically good that natural evils never exist and that moral wrongs never occur. The obtaining, however, of such a state of affairs would be extrinsically bad in at least one respect, since it would be incompatible with the obtaining of another state of affairs, the obtaining of which would be intrinsically good. This state of affairs would consist of the occurrence of acts intended to prevent the existence of natural evils that in fact can exist and the occurrence of moral wrongs that in fact can occur. Whether the total value of the first state of affairs would be positive or negative would be determined by whether its positive intrinsic value would be greater than that of the second state of affairs. If it were greater its total value would be positive; if it were lesser its total value would be nega-tive. In the first case it would be intrinsically good that such a world exist; in the second it would be intrinsically bad that it exist. Since, however, natural evils do exist and moral wrongs do occur, such a world does not in fact exist and, indeed, is far removed from the actual world in which we live and move and have our being.

If natural evils could exist but never in fact do and if moral wrongs could occur but never in fact do, acts intended to prevent their existence or occurrence could still occur. In such a world it might still be intrinsi-cally bad that natural evils could exist and that moral wrongs could occur, and it would be intrinsically good that acts intended to prevent their occurrence or existence occur. It would, however, be intrinsically good that in fact natural evils never exist and moral wrongs never occur. The obtaining of such a state of affairs would, however, be extrinsically bad in at least one respect, since it would be incompatible with the obtaining of another state of affairs, the obtaining of which would be intrinsically good. This state of affairs would consist of the occurrence of acts intended to eliminate or lessen evils that do in fact exist and to right wrongs that have in fact occurred. Whether the total value of the first state of affairs would be positive or negative would be determined, as before, by whether its positive intrinsic value would be greater than that of the second state of affairs. If it were greater its total value would be positive; if it were lesser its total value would be negative. In the first case it would be intrinsically good that such a world exist; in the second it would be intrinsically bad that it exist. Since, however, natural evils not only can but do exist and moral wrongs not only can but do occur, such a world is far removed from our actual world, although not as far removed as the first world.

In our actual world natural evils do exist and moral wrongs do occur. In this respect it is intrinsically worse than either of the other two worlds. In another respect, however, it is intrinsically better, since in it acts intended to eliminate or lessen natural evils that do in fact exist and to right moral wrongs that have in fact occurred do occur, whereas in the other two worlds they cannot, and the occurrence of such acts is intrinsically good. The existence of such natural evils and the occurrence of such moral wrongs is thus extrinsically good in at least one respect, since their existence and occurrence is necessary if acts intended to eliminate or lessen the former and to right the latter are to occur. Whether the total value of the first state of affairs is positive or negative is determined by whether its negative intrinsic value is greater or less than the positive intrinsic value of the second state of affairs. If it is greater its total value is negative; if it is less its total value is positive. In the first case, however, it does not follow that the intrinsic value of the actual world, taken as a whole, is negative, and in the second it does not follow that its intrinsic value is positive. Whether it is positive or negative is determined by whether the negative intrinsic value of the total amount of natural and moral evil is greater or less than the positive intrinsic value of the total amount of natural and moral goodness. Given what we know about the actual world, limited as our knowledge of it admittedly is, the positive intrinsic value of the latter seems to be greater than the negative intrinsic value of the former. This is doubtless one reason most of us like the actual world, taken as a whole, and are in no hurry to leave it.

If the preceding is correct, the existence of the actual world, taken as a whole, seems to be intrinsically good, even when the existence of natural and moral evils is taken into account. From this, however, it does not follow that it is as good as it would be were it to contain less natural and moral evil. It therefore does not follow that it is the best of all possible worlds. Even though no human being, nor all human beings taken together, has the knowledge, power, or goodness necessary to transform it into the best of all possible worlds, each of us does have the power to make it somewhat better than it is by acting to eliminate, lessen, and prevent various natural evils and to right various moral wrongs. As long as human beings continue to exist, it seems unlikely, given the past history and the present state of the world, that a time will ever come when such action is no longer necessary. As was argued above, such action is itself intrinsically good even though at times, because of the limitations of our knowledge, it be extrinsically bad. Indeed, it might well with some plausibility be argued that at least part of the purpose or meaning of human life is that our being human enables us to increase at least to some extent the amount of positive intrinsic value in the world. Unless we ourselves endeavor so to do, our complaints that God has not created the best of all possible worlds, or even a world somewhat better than the actual world, seem hypocritical, since we ourselves would then fail to act as He would act were he incarnate in human form and thus subject to various of the limitations of knowledge and power, although not of moral goodness, to which we are heir.

We also contribute something, slight though it be, to the intrinsic goodness of the world by hoping that God, conceived in the Anselmian way as a being than which no greater can be conceived, does in fact exist. Not only would the existence of such a being have greater positive intrinsic value than the existence of anything else could conceivably have, it would also have greater positive extrinsic and thus total value than anything else could possibly have, since it is only such a being, in whom infinite power and goodness would be united, that would have the power and the goodness required to create the best of all possible worlds. Despite the many appearances to the contrary, this He might already have done or be in the process of doing. Even though, however, the positive extrinsic value of natural evils be unfailingly greater than their negative intrinsic value, so that their total value is positive, in particular cases we by no means always see that this is so. In such cases, if asked what in particular justifies the occurrence of various such evils, "the wise theodicist," to use language used by Roderick Chisholm in a slightly different context, "would say that he doesn't know."[9]

Chapter 6

Persons, Things, and Value

In this chapter we begin a treatment of the nature and the ground of the value of objects, as contrasted with objectives. Objects are either universals or particulars. If, however, the argument of chapter 2 is acceptable, universals taken completely in abstraction from their exemplification by particulars have no intrinsic value. The objects with which we shall be concerned in this chapter are therefore particulars. The genus particular is divisible into two major species. One consists of persons, the other of things that are not persons. The terms "person" and "thing" will be construed broadly—"person" to refer to any human being and "thing" to any particular that is not a human being.

1. Universals, Kinds, and Value

In chapter 2 it was argued that none of the following abstract ontological constituents, elements, or parts of wholes can be either good or bad: (1) universals taken in abstraction from the question of whether they are exemplified, (2) particulars taken in abstraction from any consideration of which universals they exemplify, (3) states of affairs taken in abstraction from the question of whether they obtain, and (4) the obtaining or the non-obtaining of a state of affairs taken in abstraction from the nature of the state of affairs that does or does not obtain. None of these abstract parts of a whole can be either intrinsically good or intrinsically bad. Each of them can, however, have contributory value, since each can contribute to the goodness or badness of some whole of which it is a part. We can go even further and say that the positive, negative, or neutral value of any whole is determined, at least in part, by the nature of its abstract parts. Thus whether the exemplification of a given universal by a given particular is good, bad, or indifferent is determined by the nature of the universal exemplified and the kind of the particular exemplifying it.[1] Similarly, whether the obtaining or the non-obtaining of a given state of affairs is good, bad, or indifferent is determined by the nature of the state of affairs in question.

That both the nature of the universal exemplified and the kind of the particular exemplifying it contribute to the goodness, badness, or indifference of the exemplification of that universal by that particular can be shown by means of an example or two. The exemplification of sweetness by a dish of ice cream (treating a dish of ice cream as a particular) is good, whereas the exemplification of sweetness by a glass of beer (treating a glass of beer as a particular) would be bad. If so, then two distinct exemplifications of the same universal are such that one is good and the other bad, depending upon the nature or the kind of the particular exemplifying it. Sweet ice cream is good, sweet beer bad. Suppose now that there are two dishes of ice cream, one of which is sweet, the other bitter. Because of this, the first is good, the second bad. If so, then the exemplification of different universals by two distinct particulars of the same kind is such that the exemplification of one is good, of the other bad, depending upon the nature of the universals exemplified. One is such that its exemplification by ice cream is good, the other such that its exemplification by ice cream is bad. Sweet ice cream is good, bitter ice cream bad. Suppose next that we are told that two particulars are such that one is sweet, the other bitter, and that we know nothing else about them. If so, we do not have sufficient information to determine whether either particular is good, bad, or indifferent. Suppose, finally, that we are told either (1) that two particulars of a given kind are such that one exemplifies some universal the other does not or (2) that two particulars of different kinds exemplify the same universal, and that in each case we have no knowledge of which universals are exemplified. If so, then we do not have sufficient information to enable us to determine whether the particulars in question are good, bad, or indifferent. To know whether the exemplification of any given universal by any given particular is good, bad, or indifferent we need to know both which universal is exemplified and the nature or the kind of the particular exemplifying it.

The fact that the exemplification of the same universal by two particulars that differ in kind is such that its exemplification by a particular of one kind can be good and its exemplification by a particular of the other

kind can be bad supports the view that universals themselves can be neither good nor bad when taken in abstraction from any consideration
either of whether they are exemplified or, if they are exemplified, of
what kinds of particulars exemplify them. If, that is, sweetness as exemplified by ice cream is good but as exemplified by beer is bad, then it
would seem that sweetness itself, taken in abstraction from any consideration of what does or does not exemplify it, can be neither good nor
bad. From this, however, it does not follow that there are no universals
at all the nature of which is such that any exemplification of them by
any particular of any kind capable of exemplifying them would be good
(or bad). If, however, there are such universals, it does not follow that
they are themselves good (or bad) regardless of whether they are ever by
anything exemplified. Even though any exemplification of them by any
particular, regardless of its kind, would be good, it is still only their
exemplification that would be good, not the universals themselves
regardless of whether they are ever exemplified.

With the exception of very abstract universals such as being self-
identical, any given universal is such that it can be exemplified only by
particulars of certain kinds. Few universals are such that they can be
exemplified by anything and everything, regardless of its nature or kind.
The nature of particulars of a given kind, regardless of the kind in question, is such that they cannot exemplify certain universals that can be
exemplified by particulars of some other kind. The nature of ice cream
cones and of human beings is such that ice cream cones cannot and
human beings can exemplify kindness. It is good that human beings can
exemplify kindness and also good that they do. And if they do they are
in at least that respect good. From this, however, it does not follow that
it is bad that ice cream cones cannot exemplify kindness and that none
ever do. Nor does it follow that they are bad because they do not exemplify kindness. They can and do exemplify sweetness, whereas human
beings cannot. It is good that they can and that they do, and if they do
they in at least that respect are good. From this, however, it does not
follow that it is bad that human beings cannot be sweet and that none
ever are. Nor does it follow that human beings are bad because they are
not sweet.

If the preceding is correct, then the fact that particulars of one kind
can exemplify certain universals that particulars of another kind cannot
exemplify does not entail either (1) that it is bad that the latter cannot
and do not exemplify these universals or (2) that they are bad because

they cannot and do not do so. If this were entailed, then it would be bad that ice cream cones cannot be kind and bad that human beings cannot be sweet. Gargoyles but not human beings can be made of stone, but only someone as despondent as Quasimodo was over the fact that the lovely Esmeralda could not love someone as ugly as he in the way he loved her could lament the fact that he, unlike a gargoyle, was not made of stone. In order, then, that a particular be a good instance of its kind it is necessary only that it exemplify certain universals that instances of its kind are capable of exemplifying. It is not necessary that it be capable of exemplifying each universal that instances of every other kind are capable of exemplifying. If it were, then no particular of any kind could be a good instance of its kind. From this it follows that the good-making properties of a kind vary from kind to kind, depending upon the nature of the kind, and that a given property can be a good-making property of a given kind only if instances of the kind in question can have the property in question.

2. Normality and Value

In many cases, the properties we regard as good-making properties of a given kind are properties that instances of the kind usually or normally have. Thus sweetness is regarded as a good-making property of ice cream but not of beer at least in part because ice cream is normally sweet and beer is not. If it were beer and not ice cream that normally is sweet, we should probably regard sweetness as a good-making property of beer but not of ice cream. This suggests that more is involved than is sometimes recognized in the etymological connection between "normal" on the one hand and "norm" or "normative" on the other. This is not to suggest that everything good is so because it is normal or that everything normal is good. As Moore points out, the excellence of Shakespeare was extraordinary, not normal. Moore refers to this excellence as "abnormal".[2] This way of referring to it is acceptable, provided that by "abnormal" one means only "not normal" in the non-pejorative sense of the term and not, as "abnormal" is frequently today taken as connoting, "not normal" in some pejorative sense that implies that what is said to be abnormal is not simply not normal but also in some way bad because it is not normal. That it is good that certain instances of certain kinds are normal can be shown by means of a few simple examples. The first example concerns bodily deformities, the second mental or linguistic incapacitites, the third length of life.

One of the first things that parents of a newly born baby do upon seeing their child for the first time is to count its fingers and toes. They want it to have five fingers on each hand and five toes on each foot. Why? The answer, I think, is that it is normal for human beings to have five fingers on each hand and five toes on each foot. If it were normal to have six fingers on the right hand and seven on the left and eight toes on the right foot and nine on the left, the parents of the newly born baby would very probably be greatly disappointed to learn that it has only five fingers on each hand and five toes on each foot. They would regard it as being *de*formed or *mal*formed. We regard it as good that a baby have five fingers on each hand and five toes on each foot because it is normal to have five fingers on each hand and five toes on each foot. We should still regard a person with eight fingers on each hand as deformed or malformed even though his having that number of fingers would enable him to be a much better pianist than he would otherwise be. This indicates that we do not regard such a deformity as bad because in some way it incapacitates the person so afflicted. Even though it might enable him to achieve certain excellences he would otherwise be incapable of attaining, we would still regard it as bad. The reason we would do so, I suggest, is that such a deformity would be an abnormality. Such a person's hands would be badly formed, and they would be so because it is not normal to have eight fingers on each hand. Similar considerations apply to the number of arms, legs, eyes, and other bodily parts of a person.

Suppose that the parents of a newly born baby acquire as pets a dog and a cat, each born at about the same time as the baby. Six years pass. Neither the dog nor the cat, despite their living within the family, and perhaps even being considered members of it, has learned to speak. This is not a source of sadness for the parents. Suppose also, however, that neither has their child learned to speak. This is a source of sadness for them. They regard it as bad that their child has not learned to speak, but do not regard it as bad that neither the dog nor the cat has learned to do so. They regard the first but not the second state of affairs as bad because it is normal for six-year-old children to be able to speak but not for six-year-old dogs and cats to be able to do so.

We grieve when our close friends and relatives die. We also usually regard it as bad that they die. We do not, however, think it is as bad that an eighty-year-old person has died as we do that a child or a young or even middle-aged adult has died. At least part of the reason is that it is normal for a healthy person, barring accidents, to live to be seventy-five or eighty. We need not multiply examples further. The reader will be able to supply in abundance other examples, each illustrating the fact that we regard it as good that certain states of affairs obtain because it is normal for them to obtain and as bad that certain others obtain because it is not normal for them to do so.

The examples given, as well as many others that could be adduced, are sufficient, I believe, to show that we frequently regard being normal as good. We frequently regard it as good that instances of certain kinds are normal instances of their kind, and we also sometimes regard a normal or typical instance of a given kind as being a good instance of its kind. As was suggested above, this is indicated in the case of bodily normalities and abnormalities by our speaking of typical instances of a species as being well-formed and of abnormal instances as being badly formed, *de*formed, or *mal*formed. The goodness of the normal has frequently been neglected by value theorists, who sometimes write as though they believe that an instance of a kind can be a good instance of its kind only if it is a better instance than most instances. To be a better instance of a kind than most instances of that kind is, of course, to be a good instance of that kind. This, however, does not mean that typical or normal instances of that kind are not also good instances. To be a good instance of certain kinds it suffices to be a typical or normal instance. Although to be better than most instances of a kind is to be better than most good instances of the kind, it is not always necessary that an instance be better than most good instances if it is to be a good instance.

To recognize and appreciate the goodness of the normal is to recognize and appreciate the way the world and the things in it, especially the living things, normally are. A normal accompaniment of such recognition and appreciation is a certain satisfaction and contentment with the way the world and the things in it, again especially the living things, normally are. Such satisfaction and contentment in turn normally develops, at least in the case of the reflective person, and perhaps also in the case of the unreflective, into gratitude for the way the world and the things in it normally are and into feeling at home in the world and among the things in it. A failure to recognize and appreciate the goodness of the normal, and to believe instead that only the better than the normal is and can be good, also has its attendant phenomena. To believe that only those instances of a given kind can be good that are better than most instances of the kind leads, if one recognizes the implications of such belief, to a perpetual dissatisfaction with the way the world and the things in it normally are. It is hard to be and to feel at home in a world one believes to be populated with things most of which necessarily cannot be good instances of their kinds if it is in fact true that only those things that are better than most instances of their kind can be good instances of their kind. It is hard, that is, to be satisfied or content in a world one believes to be populated mainly by things that are not and cannot be good instances of their kind. But that the world would be so populated would be the case necessarily if to be a good instance of a kind is to be better than most instances of the kind, since then it would be impossible that most instances of any kind be good. The believer in such a world would thereby be provided with a far longer list of items for a litany of lamentations, to use a phrase of Hegel's, than that provided those who recognize the goodness of the normal.

I have been emphasizing the goodness of the normal partly because value theorists frequently neglect such goodness. The emphasis I have placed on it is in no way intended to deny the goodness of those instances of a kind that are better than most instances of the kind. Indeed, if anything at all is evident it ought to be evident that if most instances of a given kind are good, then those instances of the kind that are better than most instances of the kind must also be good. Such instances may be referred to as the better or the best instances of their kind. They are the better or the best instances of their kind because they have certain excellences that most instances of the kind do not have. They exhibit not only the good-making properties that most instances of their kind manifest but also have what may be referred to as certain excellent-making properties that most good instances of their kind do not have.

3. Goodness and Excellence

Such excellent-making properties are divisible into two types. The first type consists simply of the good-making properties possessed by most of the good instances of a given kind, possessed to a greater or higher degree by the excellent instances of the kind. An excellent instance of a kind, to be such an instance, need not have any good-making properties that most instances of the kind do not have, but instead might only have the good-making properties of its kind to a higher degree than do most of the good instances of the kind. The second type of excellent-making property consists of properties distinct from any of the good-making properties of good instances of a kind, by virtue of the possession of which the excellent instances of a kind are excellent and not merely good instances. An excellent-making property of the first type is simply a good-making property, possessed in a higher degree by excellent instances of the kind than by those instances that are merely good instances. An excellent-making property of the second type is a property possessed only by excellent instances of a kind, not by instances that are merely good instances, by virtue of the possession of which an excellent instance of a kind is such an instance and not merely a good instance.

To be a good instance of a kind a thing or a person need only possess good-making properties sufficient to make it a good instance of its kind. To be an excellent instance of its kind a thing or a person must either (1) possess certain good-making properties to a higher degree than do most good instances of that kind or (2) possess some excellent-making property that merely good instances of its kind do not possess. If to be an excellent instance of its kind a thing or a person must first be a good instance, then it must possess some good-making properties the possession of which is sufficient to make it a good instance of its kind. If it does not, then the possession of some excellent-making property that no merely good instance of its kind possesses would not suffice to make it an excellent instance of its kind. It would have an excellent-making property of its kind that no merely good instance of its kind has, but it still would not be a good instance because it would not possess enough of the good-making properties, the possession of some of which by an instance of its kind is necessary if the instance is to be a good instance. For example, the degree of bravery of a certain soldier, Private Smith, might be far greater than that of the typical good soldier, yet in all other respects he might be a much worse soldier than the typical soldier. Although his bravery far surpasses that of a typical soldier, he still is not a good soldier because he does not have to a sufficient degree various of the good-making properties or virtues of a soldier, the possession of which by a soldier is necessary if he is to be a good soldier.

If a thing is to be a good instance of its kind it must possess at least some of the good-making properties of the kind. It is not necessary, however, that it possess *all* the good-making properties of its kind. Indeed, some of these properties might be such that if an instance has one it cannot also have another. Sometimes certain of the good-making properties of a given kind are incompatible, so that although an instance of the kind can possess one of these properties it cannot possess both. Thus the properties f and g might be good-making properties of instances of the kind k, yet f and g might be incompatible properties, so that it is impossible that any instance of the kind k have both f and g. If it were necessary that an instance of the kind k have both these properties to be a good instance of that kind, then no instance of that kind could be a good instance of it. Although the possession of one of the two properties, f and g, might be a necessary condition that any instance of the kind k must satisfy if it is to be a good instance of that kind, the possession of both these properties cannot be such a necessary condition if they are in fact incompatible properties. One can, of course, arbitrarily specify that if any instance of a given kind is to be a good instance of the kind it must have both of two incompatible properties. The concept of a good instance of that kind that would be produced by such an arbitrary procedure, however, necessarily would fail to apply to anything at all. If, in order that something be a good instance of a given kind it must have both of two incompatible properties, then nothing can be a good instance of that kind.

Language such as the preceding concerning the necessary and sufficient conditions that must be satisfied if a thing of a given kind is to be a good instance of that kind might suggest that whenever we regard a given instance of a given kind as a good instance of that kind we have an exact concept of, and would encounter no difficulty in formulating with precision, the necessary and sufficient conditions that must be satisfied if anything is to be a good instance of the kind in question. In fact, however, almost all our concepts of the conditions that must be satisfied if any instance of a given kind is to be a good instance of that kind lack such exactness, and in the case of most such concepts we do encounter difficulty, frequently great difficulty, in attempting to specify with precision the necessary and sufficient conditions that must be satisfied by an instance of a given kind if it is to be a good instance of that kind. What, for example, are the necessary and sufficient conditions that must be satisfied if an apple is to be a good apple? Even though we have little or no difficulty, after seeing, grasping, biting into, and tasting a given apple, in deciding whether it is a good apple, we still, if asked, might find it quite hard to specify with precision the necessary and sufficient conditions that must be satisfied if an apple is to be a good apple. We might say that it must be firm and juicy and have a certain tart sweetness.

These might be necessary conditions of its being a good apple. But are they also the sufficient conditions, or are there also other necessary conditions? This example, I believe, suffices to show that even in those cases in which we have little or no difficulty in deciding whether an instance of a given kind is a good instance of that kind, we do frequently encounter difficulty in attempting to formulate precisely the necessary and sufficient conditions that must be satisfied by any instance of that kind if it is to be a good instance. Although we might have some idea of what these conditions are, we rarely have such a precise idea that we can formulate it adequately with no difficulty at all.

4. Good-Making Properties and Virtues

Earlier the good-making properties of a soldier were referred to as the virtues of a soldier. The term "virtue" is usually applied only to the virtues of persons, as though only persons can have virtues. There is, however, another use of the term, perhaps today a bit archaic, according to which the good-making properties of the instances of a given kind are the virtues of the kind. Thus we sometimes inquire about the virtues of a certain kind or make of automobile. Just as the good-making properties of the instances of a kind other than the human kind are the virtues of the kind, so also the virtues of a person are the good-making properties of a person. The virtues of a person are those good-making properties by virtue of the possession of which a person is a good person. An instance of a given non-human kind of thing can have certain of the good-making properties of the kind without having others. If it does, it is good in certain respects but not in others. So also, a person can have certain virtues proper to a person without having others. If he does, then he is good in certain respects but not in others.

The virtues of a person are essentially dispositional. To say that a person has a given virtue is to say that he is disposed to act or feel in certain ways in situations of certain sorts. Instances of various non-human kinds, especially instances of inanimate kinds, have various dispositional properties even though they never manifest them. Thus I might ascribe the dispositional property of brittleness, or being brittle, to a given glass windowpane even though it has never manifested this property and perhaps never will. This ascription is made on the basis of my knowledge of the brittleness of other glass windowpanes. Since many other glass windowpanes have proved to be brittle, i.e., have flown into fragments when struck sharply with a certain force, I take it for granted that this glass windowpane is also brittle, i.e., that it too would shatter into fragments if it were struck sharply with the force in question. Given my past experience of glass windowpanes, I regard my ascription of brittleness to this glass windowpane as justified, even though it has never manifested its brittleness and perhaps never will. To be brittle it need never manifest its brittleness.

The situation is radically different in the case of the virtues or good-making properties of persons. The reason, in part, is that various persons have various virtues. Although all, or nearly all, glass windowpanes are brittle, some persons have certain virtues that others do not have. In addition, those persons who have a given virtue might well have it in various degrees. Some people are courageous and some are not, and among those who are courageous some are more courageous than others. Thus although we can know that a given glass windowpane is brittle even though it has not and might never manifest its brittleness, we cannot know that a given person is courageous if he has never, or only rarely, manifested courage. Another difference between the dispositional properties of persons and those of inanimate things, such as the brittleness of a glass windowpane, is that some such properties might be possessed by a given inanimate thing constantly from the moment it comes into being until the moment it ceases to be, whereas a person who has a given virtue might later lose it and who does not have some other virtue might later acquire it. Given these differences between persons, we cannot know in advance which persons have which virtues, or the degree to which they have the virtues they have. We can know which persons have which virtues, and the degree to which they have the virtues they have, only through knowing how they act or feel in various situations. This applies to knowledge of one's own virtues as well as to knowledge of those of others. I can come to know which virtues I have, and the degree to which I have them, only through knowing how I act or feel in situations of certain sorts.

This means that I cannot know whether I or another person has a given virtue if neither he nor I is ever in a situation of the sort in which the virtue in question can be manifested. If neither he nor I is ever in a situation in which courage can be manifested, then I cannot know whether either of us is courageous. I might have a well-grounded belief, based on my knowledge of other virtues I know that he and I possess—

based, that is, on my knowledge of his character and of mine—that he or I would manifest courage if we were ever in a situation in which we could manifest it. But I cannot know with certainty that he or I is courageous if neither of us is ever in a situation in which we could manifest courage. From the fact, however, that a person is never in a situation in which he can manifest courage it does not follow that he is not courageous. Just as a glass windowpane can be brittle without ever manifesting its brittleness, so a person can be courageous without ever manifesting his courage. As we have seen, to say that a windowpane is brittle is to say that it *would* fly into fragments if it were struck sharply with a certain force. It is not to say that it ever is struck sharply with that force. Similarly, to say that a person is courageous is to say that he *would* act in certain ways in certain situations. It is not to say that he is ever in such situations. Nonetheless, even though a person can be courageous without ever manifesting his courage because he is never in a situation in which he can do so, we still cannot know with certainty that he is courageous if he is never in such situations.

Although it is at least abstractly possible that a person might never be in a situation in which he can manifest courage, most, if not indeed all, of the virtues are such that throughout the course of his life each of us is presented with a wide variety of situations in which we can manifest various of the virtues. One might never be, as sometimes soldiers are, in a life-and-death situation in which courage can be manifested only by risking one's life. But courage, like most of the other virtues, can be shown in small as well as in great ways. Although occasions calling for a magnificent manifestation of a given virtue rarely present themselves, each of us in the course of daily life confronts a host of situations of various sorts in which various of the virtues can be manifested in at least a small way. It is mainly through the knowledge we acquire in the course of living our daily lives about the ways in which we and others act in situations of various sorts that we come to know which of the virtues are possessed by ourselves and others, and the degree to which they are possessed. The better we come to know a person the better we come to know his virtues. To come to know another is to come to know his virtues, just as to come to know oneself is to come to know one's own virtues.

In one way it is easier for a person to come to know what his own virtues are and the degree to which he has them than it is to come to know what the virtues of others are and the degree to which they have them. Each of us has a more direct epistemological access than others can have to various of his thoughts, feelings, and desires. We have an immediate access to our silent thoughts, feelings, and desires that others cannot have. Others can come to know what they are only through coming to know their outward facial, bodily, and linguistic manifestations. Sometimes we come to know another person so well that, on the basis of our detecting certain subtle features of his facial expression, his bodily posture, or his speech, we ascribe to him various thoughts, feelings, or desires with such quickness and confidence that it is almost as if we had as direct an access to the inward phenomena we ascribe to him as to their outward manifestations. Even so, each of us has various inward thoughts, feelings, and desires that we do not reveal to others, either intentionally or inadvertently. To such inward phenomena only the person who has them has access. Not even the person who has them always has such access, since sometimes such inward phenomena go undetected even by the person who has them. To the degree, however, that each of us does have knowledge of his inward thoughts and experience, he is provided thereby a way of coming to know various of his virtues that others do not and cannot have. This is because various of the virtues are manifested not only outwardly in what we say and do but also inwardly in what we think, feel, and desire. Thus upon learning of some misfortune that has befallen others in some distant place I might feel compassion for them even though there is nothing I can say or do that would alleviate their plight in the least. Such an inward feeling of compassion would be an inward manifestation of the virtue of compassion, and anyone who feels compassion for others even though he can say or do nothing to help has at least to some slight degree the virtue of compassion. Such a person, however, would have this virtue only to a slight degree indeed if he is never moved by his compassion to render such aid as he can to those who need it.

5. Virtues and Vices

Although various of the virtues can be and sometimes are manifested inwardly without also being manifested outwardly, various of the vices or bad-making properties of a person are frequently more likely than the virtues to be manifested only inwardly. Thus I, upon hearing someone I regard as a rival being praised, might be displeased and envious of him even though such displeasure and envy remain entirely inward and receive no outward manifestation whatever. If so, then I am afflicted with the sin or vice of envy even though it has no outward manifestation at all. The fact that vice is frequently more likely than virtue to be manifested only inwardly is connected with the fact that people generally regard the virtues as good-making and the vices as bad-making properties of a person. They usually would not express the thought expressed by this language by using the latter but instead would probably express it, if they express it at all, by saying something to the effect that virtues and virtuous people are good, vices and vicious people bad. Regardless, however, of what language is used to express the thought, we generally tend to regard the virtues as good-making and the vices as bad-making properties of a person. We tend, that is, to think that people are good to the degree that they possess various of the virtues, bad to the degree that they are afflicted with various of the vices. We tend also to think that the respects in which a person is good are functions of the virtues he has and that the respects in which a person is bad are functions of the vices he has.

Given the preceding, and given also that people generally want others to regard them as good in various respects regardless of whether in fact they are, they have a motive for endeavoring to inhibit outward manifestations of various vices manifested inwardly in their secret thoughts, feelings, and desires. People generally want to seem to others to be good regardless of whether in fact they are. They want the approval and praise of others regardless of whether they merit it. The desire to be regarded by others as good and to be approved of and praised is independent of, although connected with, the desire not to suffer various of the consequences that might follow were they regarded by others as bad. People frequently want to be regarded as good by others regardless of whether they believe that they will suffer in some way if they are regarded as bad. This can be put by saying that frequently we want to be regarded as good by others as an end, not merely as a means of avoiding suffering in some way at the hands of others because they think us bad. It is as though in seeking to be regarded as good by others as an end we value being good, which is not something we should do were we to endeavor to be regarded by others as good merely as a means of avoiding suffering. That we do sometimes fear that others will inflict some form of suffering on us does, however, give us an additional motive for striving to be regarded as good regardless of whether in fact we are. From motives such as these vice seeks darkness, virtue sunlight. Wanting others to think us good, the motive we have for hiding our vices from others is not a motive for concealing from others our virtues. Because of this, our vices are frequently more likely than our virtues to manifest themselves only inwardly, unaccompanied by any outward manifestation.

We sometimes seek to hide our vices from ourselves as well as from others. In doing so we pay an even higher compliment to the virtues and to being good than we do in striving to hide our vices from others, since in endeavoring to hide them from ourselves our motive cannot be to avoid suffering at the hands of others. Nor will it do to say simply that our motive is to avoid suffering at our own hands in the form of remorse, a loss of self-respect, or the recognition that we are bad, since such forms of self-inflicted suffering can occur only if we regard as good the virtues we believe we lack and as bad the vices we believe we have. I cannot suffer remorse unless I believe that I have acted badly or wrongly, I cannot believe that I am bad unless I believe that I have various vices or do not have various virtues, and I cannot suffer a loss of self-respect unless I believe that the person I am does not merit respect.

The term "self-respect" can be misleading, since it might suggest that such respect consists simply of my respecting the person I believe I am. I cannot, however, respect the person I believe I am unless I believe that I am the kind of person who merits respect, nor can I lose my self-respect unless I believe that I am no longer the kind of person who merits respect. I can have self-respect only to the degree that I believe that I have various of the virtues to some acceptable degree, that I usually act rightly or well, and thus that I am a good person at least to some degree. And I cannot lose my self-respect unless I believe that I no longer have (or have never had) to an acceptable degree various of the virtues, that too frequently I act badly or wrongly, and thus that I am closer to being a bad person than a good one. Both self-respect and the loss of it therefore require that the person who has or loses it value something other than himself. He must value being a certain *kind* of person regardless of whether he believes that *he* is that kind of person. If he respects the *kind* of person he believes *he* is, he has (or at least can have) self-respect. If he comes to believe that he is not the *kind* of person he respects he thereby loses, at least to some degree, his self-respect.

Although, then, I can endeavor to hide my vices from others without believing that I am bad in the degree to which I have them or, indeed, without even believing that what I am attempting to hide from others are in fact vices, i.e., bad-making properties of a person, I cannot endeavor to hide them from myself unless I believe that they are such properties and that I am bad to the degree to which I have them. I can strive to hide from others my having what they regard as vices, regardless of whether I too regard them as such, because I fear the consequences of their coming to believe that I have them. But I cannot strive to hide them from myself for this reason. Nor can I endeavor to hide them from myself, in order to escape suffering the remorse or loss of self-respect that I believe would result from acknowledging that I have them, unless I believe that they are in fact bad-making properties of a person. I cannot, that is, suffer remorse or a loss of self-respect from admitting that I have certain defects of character unless I believe that they are indeed *defects* of character. Thus although I might not recognize that I am doing so, I pay an even higher compliment to the virtues in attempting to hide my vices from myself that I do in endeavoring to hide them from others. Such attempts at self-deception therefore necessarily honor various of the virtues, whereas attempts at deceiving others might or might not do so, depending upon the motives animating such attempts.

To say, however, that attempts at self-deception necessarily involve a kind of homage to the virtues, and that attempts to deceive others might also involve such homage, is to tell only one side of the story. There is another side, which is that such attempts manifest a certain contempt for the virtues one pretends to have. Even if it be true that I necessarily pay homage to a given virtue if I endeavor to deceive myself into believing that I have it, and even though it might also be true that I might also pay homage to a given virtue if I attempt to deceive others into believing that I have it, I do not in doing so pay as much homage to the virtue in question as I should do were I to endeavor to acquire it rather than to deceive myself or others into believing that I already have it. I can honor fully a given virtue, as distinguished from pretending that I already have it, only if I endeavor to acquire it, and this I can do only if I endeavor to do the sorts of things I must do if I am in fact to have it. To attempt to deceive myself or others into believing that I have a given virtue does mean, for reasons already given, that I pay a kind of homage to it. At least I honor it more than I should if I did not care in the least whether I have it and therefore made no attempt whatever to deceive myself or others into believing that I have it (except as a means of escaping unpleasant consequences that might occur if others believe that I do not have it). People who do not care in the least whether they have any of the virtues do not even do the virtues the honor of pretending to have them, except perhaps as a means to something else. To attempt, however, to deceive myself or others into believing that I have certain virtues that I do not in fact have is not only to pay a certain homage to them but is also to hold them in a certain contempt. I honor them in pretending to have them but also dishonor them in not endeavoring to acquire them. I honor them in wanting to seem to myself or others to have them but dishonor them in not wanting actually to have them. To the degree that I pretend to myself or others to have them when in fact I do not I am inauthentic. I can be fully authentic only if I do not attempt to deceive either myself or others into believing that I have virtues that in fact I do not have or that I do not have vices that in fact I do have. Such authenticity is itself one of the virtues, such inauthenticity one of the vices.

The degree to which deception, either of myself or others, is likely to succeed is a function of the degree to which I and others know myself. The better others know me, the less likely it is that attempts to deceive them will succeed. Others, such as my friends and relatives, who have knowledge of how I have acted in various situations in which various of the virtues can be outwardly manifested are less likely than those who do not have such knowledge to believe that I have virtues I pretend to have but in fact do not have. If so, then it might seem that it is even less likely that attempts at self-deception will succeed. This is the case, it might seem, for two reasons. The first is that each person is in a better position than others can ever be to know how he has acted in all the various situations in which he is involved. Unlike others, he is invariably present in all the situations that provide him an opportunity to act. The second reason is that each person, as was mentioned above, has a direct epistemological access that no one else can have to various inward manifestations of his virtues and vices. Others can come to know my virtues and vices only through coming to know how I have acted in situations of various sorts. I, however, can know not only how I have acted in situations of various sorts but also what my inward thoughts, feelings, and desires are regardless of whether they are out-wardly manifested. Thus whereas others have only one way of knowing what my virtues and vices are, I have two ways.

6. Loving and Hating

Because I have two ways whereas others have only one of knowing what my virtues and vices are, it might be thought that attempts at self-deception are less likely to succeed than are attempts to deceive others into believing that I have certain virtues and do not have certain vices. It seems true that attempts to deceive oneself are less likely to succeed than are attempts to deceive others who do not know us well or love us. From this, however, it does not follow that they are also less likely to succeed than are attempts to deceive those who do know us well and love us. It is easier for us to judge impartially the virtues and vices of those who do not stand in especially close relations to us than it is so to judge our own virtues and vices and those of the persons we love. Because of this it sometimes happens that those who know us best and love us most are worse judges of our character than are those who know us well but are not among those who love us most. Those who love us most, loving us as they do, are provided by their love for us with a motive for regarding us as good that those who do not love us do not have. It is hard, although not impossible, to love a person we regard as bad. Wanting those we love to be good, we are thereby provided a motive for ascribing to them various of the virtues the possession of which would make them good and for not ascribing to them various of the vices the possession of which would make them bad. Wanting those we love to be good, we are inclined to believe that they are indeed good. Being so inclined, we find it easy to overlook, to explain away, or even to fail to see in those we love various vices that those who do not love them as we do detect with an impartial eye and assess with an impartial accuracy. We also find it easy to see in those we love various virtues that remain invisible to an impartial eye. Love not only makes us blind to defects easily detectable by an impartial eye but also makes us see things utterly invisible to such an eye. Loving as we do those we love most, we can easily come to believe that they have various of the virtues that would make them worthy of our love and that they do not have various of the vices that would make them unworthy of it.

What has just been said applies also, with the necessary changes, to those who hate us most. Those who hate us most, hating us as they do, are provided by their hatred for us with a motive for regarding us as bad that others who do not hate us do not have. It is hard, although not impossible, to hate a person we regard as good. We want those we hate to be bad even though we believe them to be good and are thereby provided a motive for ascribing to them various of the vices the possession of which would make them bad and for not ascribing to them various of the virtues the possession of which would make them good. Wanting those we hate to be bad, we are inclined to believe that they are indeed bad. Being so inclined, we find it easy to explain away or even to fail to see in those we hate various virtues that those who do not hate them as we do detect with an impartial eye. We also find it easy to see in those we hate various vices that remain invisible to an impartial eye. Hate not only makes us blind to virtues easily detectable by an impartial eye but also makes us see things invisible to such an eye. Hating as we do those we hate most, we can easily come to believe that they have various vices that would make our hatred of them justified and that they do not have various virtues that would make it unjustified.

In the respects indicated, loving and hating are reverse images of one another. There is a kind of reverse phenomenological parallelism between the two. This, however, does not mean that the phenomena are equal in value. Instead, in the respects indicated the phenomenon of loving has positive value, that of hating negative value. One of the fundamental reasons this is so is that in hating someone we are inclined to want him to be bad rather than good, whereas in loving someone we are inclined to want him to be good rather than bad. Wanting the object of our hating to be bad, we are inclined to seek out and to emphasize defects in him that would make him bad and to ignore or explain away any virtues he might have that would make him good. If we fail to succeed fully in such an enterprise we might, hating the object of our hate as we do, ascribe to him various defects we have not detected and even come to believe that he does indeed have these defects. We might also seek ways of making him bad if we have not succeeded fully in convincing ourselves that he is bad or ways of making him even worse if we believe that he is already bad but not bad enough. The worse he becomes the greater our satisfaction becomes.

The central theme coursing through our little phenomenological dialectic of the development of hatred is the desire of the hater that the object of his hatred be bad and the satisfaction the hater derives from his belief that the object of his hatred is indeed bad. It is important to remember that the object of the hater's hatred is a person, not a vice or defect of character, much less a virtue. Indeed, there is a sense in which the hater may be said to regard various of the virtues as good-making properties and various of the vices as bad-making properties. The hater wants the object of his hatred to be bad, not good, since if the latter is good rather than bad the hater's hatred cannot be justified. The hater would doubtless be regarded as joking if he were to attempt to justify his hatred by saying that he hates the object of his hatred because the latter is good. I can be envious of another because he is good, or because of his goodness, and such envy can also lead me to hate him. If it does, then I not only envy but also hate him because he is good. My hating another person, however, can be justified, if indeed it can be justified at all, only if he is bad, and the degree to which I can justifiably hate him is determined, at least in part, by the degree to which he is bad. This is at least part of the reason I want the person I hate to be bad. My hatred can be justified only if the person I hate is bad, not if he is good.

A given person, John, might be loved by Peter and hated by Paul. Peter and Paul might be in complete agreement as to which properties of a person are virtues and as to which are vices. They might also agree that the virtues are good-making properties of a person, the vices bad-making properties. Paul, in hating John, also wants him to be bad regardless of whether he believes that he is, whereas Peter, in loving Johm, wants him to be good regardless of whether he believes that he is. In wanting John to be bad, Paul does not want virtues to be vices or vices to be virtues. Nor does Peter want this in wanting John to be good. Paul, in hating John, wants him to have bad-making properties suffi- cient to make him bad, and Peter, in loving John, wants him to have good-making properties sufficient to make him good. Thus Paul, in hating John, and in wanting him to be bad, wants him to have certain properties that Peter, in loving John and in wanting him to be good, wants him not to have. Paul would agree with Peter that John is good if he believed that John has the properties Peter wants him to have, and Peter would agree with Paul that John is bad if he believed that John has the properties Paul wants him to have. If they disagree as to whether John is good or bad it is because they disagree concerning which prop- erties he has. There is a difference between which properties each of the two wants John to have only because Paul hates and Peter loves John. It is also because Paul hates and Peter loves John that Paul would be pleased if he believed that John has certain bad-making properties and that Peter would be pleased if he believed that John has certain good-making properties.

The nature of the state of affairs consisting of John's being bad is such that its obtaining would be bad, and the nature of that consisting of his being good is such that its obtaining would be good. For the sake of economy of expression, let us say that Paul, in wanting John to be bad, wants a bad state of affairs to obtain and that Peter, in wanting John to be good, wants a good state of affairs to obtain. Such a way of speaking, although more economical, is elliptical because, as was argued earlier, to say that a state of affairs is good (or bad) is to say that its obtaining would be good (or bad). To say, however, that Paul wants a bad state of affairs, x, to obtain or that Peter wants a good state of affairs, y, to obtain is not to say that Paul regards the obtaining of x as bad or that Peter regards the obtaining of y as good. Paul might want x to obtain, and Peter y to obtain, while regarding the obtaining of x or of y as being neither good nor bad or without considering the question of whether the obtaining of either would be either good or bad. Similarly, Paul might believe and be pleased that x obtains, and Peter that y obtains, without regarding the obtaining of either as good or bad or without considering the question of whether the obtaining of either would be good or bad. Wanting a given state of affairs to obtain or being pleased that it obtains is neither identical with nor entails regarding its obtaining as being good. Conversely, regarding the obtaining of a given state of affairs as good is neither identical with nor entails either wanting it to obtain or being pleased that it obtains.

If the preceding is correct, the question of whether the obtaining of a given state of affairs would be good or bad is independent of the question of whether anyone who wants it to obtain regards its obtaining as good or bad. This is consistent with my earlier contention that the goodness or badness of the obtaining of a given state of affairs is determined by the nature of the state of affairs in question, taken in abstraction from any consideration of the question of whether it does or does not obtain. If the nature of a given state of affairs is such that its obtaining would be good (or bad), then anyone who wants that state of affairs to obtain thereby wants something that would be a good (or a bad) state of affairs to obtain even though he might not regard its obtaining as being good (or bad). Thus Paul, who wants John to be bad, thereby wants something that would be a bad state of affairs to obtain even though he might not regard its obtaining as being bad; and Peter, who wants John to be good, thereby wants something that would be a good state of affairs to obtain even though he might not regard its obtaining as being good.

Suppose, however, that Paul does believe that John's being bad would be bad. Could he then still want John to be bad or be pleased that he is? The answer, I believe, is that he could. He might hate John so profoundly that he wants him to be bad and is pleased that he is even though he regards his being bad as being itself bad. From the fact that a person regards the obtaining of a given state of affairs as good (or bad) it does not follow that he wants (or does not want) it to obtain. It is possible (1) to regard the obtaining of a given state of affairs x as good without wanting it to obtain and (2) to regard the obtaining of some state of affairs y as bad without wanting it not to obtain. This is consistent with my earlier contention that a person can like (or dislike) something even while also regarding it as bad (or good). People frequently, however, want a given state of affairs x to obtain because they believe that its obtaining would be good, yet rarely if ever want some state of affairs y to obtain because they believe that its obtaining would be bad. This is perhaps connected with the fact that the obtaining of a given state of affairs x would be good is a reason for wanting it to obtain, whereas the fact that the obtaining of some state of affairs y would be bad is not a reason for wanting it to obtain. Whereas it would not in the least be strange to say that I want x to obtain because I believe that its obtaining would be good, it would be strange to say that I want y to obtain because I believe that its obtaining would be bad. This perhaps in turn is connected with the fact that to want y to obtain because I believe it to be bad would be diabolical. Although it is at least abstractly possible for a person to be diabolical, people seem rarely if ever to actualize this possibility. Thus Paul, in wanting John to be bad because he hates John and not because he regards John's being bad as being itself bad, even though he does so regard it, is himself in that respect bad but not diabolical. Being bad is itself already bad enough without also being diabolical, which would be to be even worse.

If what has been said above is correct, to love a person is to be disposed to want him to have various virtues in a degree sufficient to make him good, whereas to hate him is to be disposed to want him to have various vices in a degree sufficient to make him bad. In this way the virtue of loving persons and the vice of hating persons are connected with other virtues and vices in such a way as to make such love one of the most central of the virtues and such hate one of the most central of the vices. From the fact, however, that to love a person is to be disposed to want him to be good and to hate him is to be disposed to want him to be bad it does not follow that a person who loves or hates another necessarily does in fact want the person loved or hated to be good or bad. His love or hatred might instead consist simply in wanting the person loved to have certain goods or in wanting the person hated not to have certain goods. Speaking very generally, such goods can be classified as the moral virtues on the one hand and all other goods on the other. We can therefore distinguish between being good, which consists in having various of the virtues, and having various other goods, such as health, wealth, intelligence, knowledge, and facial and bodily beauty. This can be put by saying that a distinction can be drawn between being good and having goods. One can be good without having various goods, and one can have various goods without being good. The obtaining of a state of affairs consisting of someone's being good is itself good, but the obtaining of a state of affairs consisting of someone's having various goods might or might not itself be good, depending upon circumstances. If, for example, a person is not a good person, his having certain goods might not itself be good. Or if a person has done or failed to do something, and if his doing or failing to do the thing in question makes it bad that he have certain goods, then his having the goods in question is itself bad.

Ordinarily, a person who hates another recognizes that being good and that having goods, except perhaps under certain conditions, are themselves good. Usually such a person does not regard being good itself or having goods itself as bad. Nor does he usually love being bad in itself or not having various goods in itself. Nor does he ordinarily hate being good in itself or having goods in itself. Instead, what he hates is that the person he hates is good or has certain goods. He hates the obtaining of the state of affairs consisting of the person he hates being good or having certain goods. He could not hate that person's being good or his having certain goods unless he believes that the obtaining of such states of affairs is good. His hatred is hatred of a person, not of being good in itself or having goods in itself, and it is because he hates the person in question that he hates that person's being good or having certain goods. Because he hates the person in question he does not want him to be what he recognizes as being a good person or to have certain goods he believes to be goods.

There are other phenomena, such as envy and dislike, that are kin to hate. I can envy a person without disliking or hating him, dislike him without envying or hating him, or hate him without envying or even disliking him. I might envy a given person because I believe that he is good or better in certain respects than I am or because he has certain goods I do not have. Envying him as I do, I also might not want him to be as good as he is or to be better in certain respects than I am or to have certain goods I do not have. I might even envy him so much that I want him to be bad, or at least worse than I am, and want not only that he not have certain goods he has but also that various positive evils befall him. And I might dislike a given person so much that I do not want him to be as good as he is or to have certain goods he has, or even so much that I want him to be bad or to be visited with various positive evils. Such phenomena, although not forms of hate, since I do not hate the person I envy or dislike, are certainly kin to it. And certainly also they have something in common, which is that in all three—envy, dislike, and hatred—there is a desire either that the person envied, disliked, or hated not be as good as he is or not have certain goods he has or else that he be bad or have certain positive evils befall him. Given that they have this is common, perhaps the difference between them is only one of degree and that between them there is a continuum ascending or, perhaps more accurately, descending from envy to dislike to hate.

If the preceding is correct, there are at least three reasons for regarding the love of persons as one of the most central of the virtues and the hatred of persons as one of the most central of the vices. The first, as we saw above, is that such love disposes us to want those we love to be good, such hatred to want those we hate to be bad. The second, as we have just seen, is that such love disposes us to want those we love to have various goods, such hatred to want those we hate not to have various goods and even to have various positive evils befall them. The third reason, related to the first two, is that such love disposes us to employ rightly various other virtues we might have, such hatred to employ them wrongly. Various other virtues, such as courage, resoluteness, and perseverance, can be put to either a good or a bad use. Such virtues, considered in themselves in abstraction from the use to which they are put, are good-making properties of a person. Other things being equal, a courageous person who is resolute in pursuing his goals and who perseveres when confronted with obstacles is more likely to achieve his ends than is a person who lacks these virtues. Thus a person who loves another and endeavors to contribute to the other's being good or to his having various goods is more likely, other things equal, to succeed in his endeavor if he has these virtues than if he does not. This applies also, however, to a person who hates another and endeavors to contribute to the other's being bad or to his not having certain goods or to his having certain positive evils befall him. Even though the possession of such virtues, taken in abstraction from the use to which they are put, be good in itself, it seems better, all things considered, that a person not have them at all, or at least that he have them to a lesser degree, if he uses them mainly in the pursuit of bad ends. Thus we sometimes wish that a person who frequently uses such virtues to pursue such ends were not quite as courageous, resolute, and persevering as he proves himself to be. All things considered, it would be better if he did not have these virtues to the degree to which he does, given that he uses them frequently in the pursuit of bad ends. Kant makes essentially the same point in his discussion of the relation of such virtues to the possession of a good or a bad will.[3] At least in part, to have a good will is to be disposed to use various of the virtues in the pursuit of good ends, to have a bad will to be disposed to use them in the pursuit of bad ends.

To some it will doubtless be evident that the love of which I have been speaking is kin to if not identical with what is sometimes referred to as Christian love. To some it might seem that such love would be too indiscriminate. It could, however, be too indiscriminate only if we can sometimes be justified either (1) in not caring about whether others are good persons or have various goods it would be good that they have or (2) in wanting others not to be good persons or not to have various goods it would be good that they have. It would seem, however, that we can never be justified either in (1) or in (2). We are, however, justified in not wanting others to have certain goods it would not be good that they have because of things thay have done or failed to do, the nature of which is such as to make them deserve not to have certain goods the having of which by them would otherwise be good. Regardless, however, of how badly anyone has acted and of how bad he has been or is, it would seem that we could never be justified in not wanting him to become and to be a better person than in the past he has been or in the present he is. Thus although loving another is compatible with not wanting him to have certain goods it would be bad that he have because of what he has done or failed to do, it is not compatible with not wanting him to be a good person or at least to become a better person than he has been or is.

Chapter 7

The Primacy of Practical Rationality

There is a difference between (1) conceiving of God as that than which no greater can be conceived, (2) believing that He exists, and (3) wanting Him to exist and hoping that He does. There is also a difference between (1) believing that He exists and wanting Him to exist and hoping that He does and (2) being justified in doing so. The question of whether we are justified in doing so is part of a larger question concerning (1) the value of knowledge, the attainment of which is the central object of theoretical reason, and of various other values, the attainment of which is the object of practical reason, and (2) which of these two types of value takes precedence over the other when they conflict in such a way that they cannot both be realized. It is this question that we shall consider in this chapter.

1. The Value of Religious Belief and Hope

Given that God is that than which no greater can be conceived, and given also that we ought to want and hope that the better rather than the worse exist, and that the best of the better exist, we ought to want and hope that God exist. Such want and hope, however, if we have them, can be authentic only to the degree to which we endeavor to act as that than which no greater can be conceived would act if He were in our place, although necessarily subject, of course, to our human limitations of knowledge and power. Such want and hope, that is, can be authentic only to the degree to which in our daily lives we endeavor to bring into being and to conserve the better rather than the worse and the best of the better. To the degree to which we do endeavor so to lead our lives we live as God Himself would live were he human and in our place, and His Divine and therefore Holy Spirit becomes incarnate and alive in each of us and animates and directs our daily lives. Through our endeavoring to live such lives, the Divine Holy Spirit of God becomes real and present and alive and active in us and, through us, in the world. To the degree to which we live such lives the Divine Holy Spirit becomes human as real, present, alive, and active in us, and our spirit becomes holy and divine. Because of this we may say literally that God becomes incarnate, real, present, alive and active in us and, through us, in the world, regardless of whether He also exists independently of us and the world.

It is one thing to believe that God exists independently of man and the world, another thing to want and hope that He does, and still another thing authentically to want and hope that He exist incarnate in man and in the human spirit and, through such incarnation, in the world. Each of these three things is distinct from and independent of the other two, and none of the three is reducible to either of the others, whether taken singly or in combination. I can believe that God exists independently of man and the world without wanting or hoping that He does and also without authentically wanting or hoping that He exist incarnate in man and, through man, in the world. Such belief has little or no intrinsic value and, like faith without works, may be said to be dead, regardless of whether it be arrived at through an act of faith or will or through seeing that the existence of God follows demonstratively from certain premises I see to be true and accordingly accept. I can also want and hope that God exist independently of man and the world without believing that He does and also without authentically wanting or hoping that He exist incarnate in man and, through man, in the world. Unlike believing that He exists independently of man and the world, such wanting and hoping does have some intrinsic value, especially if it arises from recognizing (1) that we ought to want and hope that whatever has an intrinsic goodness than which no greater can be conceived exists and (2) that it is God alone that can have such goodness. Yet such otherworldly wanting and hoping, if it may be so termed, like faith without works, may be said to be dead if it is unaccompanied by authentically wanting and hoping that God become incarnate in man and, through man, in the world. I can also authentically want and hope the latter without believing that God exists independently of man and the world and also without wanting or hoping that He do so. Such authentic wanting and hoping manifest themselves most fully in performing various of the acts or works of love that living faith issues in, and because of this they have not only great intrinsic value but also great instrumental and contributory value.

Insufficient attention has been paid by philosophers to the third person of the Christian Trinity—to God the Holy Spirit or the Holy Spirit of God, as this Spirit becomes incarnate in each of us in the degree to which each of us endeavors to live his life as that than which no greater can be conceived would live His life were He incarnate in human form. None of us, because of various of the frailties and limitations of our common human nature, can ever succeed fully in living our lives as God Himself would live His were He incarnate in human form. Nonetheless, the Holy Spirit of God may literally be said to be incarnate in and to be animating each of us in the degree to which we do endeavor so to live our lives. In doing so, we may be said authentically to want the Divine Holy Spirit to be real and present and alive and active in us and, through us, in the world, regardless of whether God also exists independently of us and the world. As was indicated above, an endeavor so to live our lives has greater intrinsic, instrumental, and contributory value than believing that God exists independently of man and the world and even than wanting and hoping that He so exist. This, however, does not mean that such an endeavor has greater intrinsic value than that which is believed, wanted, and hoped for in believing, wanting, and hoping that that than which no greater can be conceived does indeed exist independently of man and the world. Although endeavoring to live one's life as God Himself would live His life were He incarnate in human form might have greater intrinsic value than anything else in the created world could conceivably have, nothing conceivable could have an intrinsic value as great as that of the existence independently of man and the world of that than which no greater can be conceived.

From the preceding certain consequences follow. Just as nothing conceivable could have a positive value as great as that of the existence of that than which no greater can be conceived, so also nothing conceivable could have as great a negative value as the non-existence of God. Given that God is that than which no greater can be conceived, nothing conceivable can have an intrinsic goodness as great as that of the existence of God, and nothing conceivable could be as intrinsically bad as the non-existence of God. If, then, to use the language of Brentano, we love and hate correctly only if we love what is worthy of love and hate what is worthy of hate and also only if we love most what is most worthy of love and hate most what is most worthy of hate, we can love correctly only if what we want and hope for more than anything else is that God exist and also only if what we fear and dread more than anything else is the non-existence of God. Such loving and hating, wanting and hoping, fearing and dreading can be correct only if it is completely selfless. We ought, that is, to want God to exist and to hope that He does because the existence of nothing other than He can have an intrinsic goodness as great as that of His existence, and not simply because we believe that neither we nor the world could exist if He did not. This, however, is not to deny that the existence of God would have great instrumental value. If the existence of the world and of various of the things in it is intrinsically good, and if their coming into being and continuing to exist from moment to moment depend upon the creating and conserving activity of God, then His existence has not only an intrinsic but also an instrumental goodness greater than that of any other conceivable thing. And if God can be considered as part of a whole containing as parts Him and the created world, His existence also has greater contributory value than that of any other conceivable thing, since no other conceivable thing could contribute as much goodness to any whole of which it is a part as the existence of God would to the whole containing Him and the created world as parts.

It was said above that the belief that God exists independently of man and the world has little or no intrinsic value. At least its intrinsic value is less than that of wanting and hoping that He does so exist and that of endeavoring to live our lives as He would live His life were He incarnate in human form. Such belief, however, can, and frequently does, have great instrumental value. For countless numbers of people it has provided what they believe to be the central meaning of their lives, and for countless others it has moved them to endeavor to live their lives as they believe God would live His were He incarnate in human form. Such belief is sometimes so central to a person's life that were it lost his life would be irremediably broken into pieces. And although morality might be independent of such belief in the sense that some people who do not have such belief nonetheless live exemplary moral lives, for others morality is so tied to such belief that were the latter to be destroyed the central motive moving them to endeavor to lead morally good lives would also be destroyed.

The fact that such belief is frequently instrumentally good in the ways indicated does not mean that it is true. The possession of true belief and knowledge, however, if it be intrinsically good at all, is only one kind of intrinsic good among others, some of which in certain situations might have considerably greater intrinsic value. Philosophers, perhaps because of their theoretical interests, sometimes speak as though they believe true belief and knowledge to be the greatest of intrinsic goods, for the sake of which all other goods ought to be sacrificed in cases of conflict. Even if, however, the belief that God exists be false and the holding of that belief by someone be intrinsically bad, such belief might be so central to a person's life that its loss by him would have consequences the intrinsic badness of which would be incalculably greater than those of his continuing to hold it. If so, we must not treat lightly the loss of such belief by such persons and must take care not to cause its loss by what we say and do. The same point, or at least one similar, is made eloquently by J. N. Findlay in these words: "The whole security and moral progress of many persons is inwrought with the maintenance of their religion, and to subvert the latter is to menace the former. Respectful tolerance and abstinence from words and deeds that will cause religious shock or dismay, are plainly in most cases as obligatory as any abstinence from physical violence."[1]

It is perhaps important to emphasize that the preceding is in no way incompatible with the view that the possession of true belief and knowledge can, and sometimes does, have intrinsic value. This is the case even if we disagree with philosophers such as W. D. Ross, who seems to regard any instance of knowledge, regardless of however trivial it might be, as being intrinsically good,[2] and Brentano, who seems to regard even the having of an idea, regardless of however trivial it be, as being intrinsically good.[3] Whether having true belief and knowledge is intrinsically good depends upon what it is that is believed or known. If what is believed or known is trivial, believing or knowing it is also trivial and has no intrinsic value, regardless of how many trivial true beliefs and bits of knowledge one might accumulate.

One might go even further and maintain that the having of a given true belief or piece of knowledge can never be in itself intrinsically good but instead at best can be only extrinsically good as a means to or as contributing to increasing our understanding of some aspect of man, the world, or God. On such a view it is such understanding that is intrinsically good, not the having of true beliefs or pieces of knowledge. Although such understanding cannot be achieved unless one has various true beliefs and pieces of knowledge, it is only the having of such understanding that can be intrinsically good, not the having of the various true beliefs and pieces of knowledge, which can be only extrinsically good as a means to or as contributing to the acquisition of such understanding. If, however, we accept this view, the essential point I attempted to make above can still be made simply by changing slightly the language used to make it. Instead of saying that the having of true beliefs and of knowledge can be and sometimes is intrinsically good, we need only say that understanding can be and sometimes is intrinsically good. It is not, however, the only intrinsic good, and the acquisition and possession by certain persons of certain forms of understanding might have certain consequences the existence of which would have far greater negative intrinsic value than the absence of such forms of understanding on the part of such persons would have. Thus if God does not in fact exist, a person who believes that He does exist does not understand that He does not. Yet if that person came to understand that God does not exist his entire life might be shattered irreparably into pieces and lose whatever meaning it had previously had for him. If so, then the consequences of his losing his belief would be far worse than those of his continuing to hold it. And if this be so, then we who know such persons must take great care not to say or do those things that would cause them to lose their belief.

2. Theoretical and Practical Rationality

The preceding points are consonant with, if indeed they do not follow from, a certain general view of the difference between theoretical and practical rationality and their relationship to one another. What may perhaps be referred to as the traditional distinction between these two forms of rationality is that the proper object of theoretical reason is the acquisition of true belief, knowledge, and understanding, whereas the proper object of practical reason is the guidance of conduct or practice so that as much good and as little evil as possible will be produced. Given this traditional distinction, theoretical rationality consists in adopting and using those methods of inquiry that are most likely to lead to the acquisition of as much true belief, knowledge, and understanding as possible, whereas practical rationality consists in acting in those ways that are most likely to produce as much good and as little evil as possible. Given this traditional way of distinguishing between these forms of rationality, the primacy of practical over theoretical reason follows as a matter of course. This is the case because the scope of practical reason is wider than and includes that of theoretical reason. This can be put by saying that the object of theoretical reason is the acquisition and production of values of only one type, these being the values of true belief, knowledge, and understanding, whereas the object of practical reason is the acquisition and production of values of all types. The values of theoretical reason are therefore included among those of practical reason. Just as for Pascal *le coeur a ses raisons que la raison ne connait pas,* so also practical reason includes within its scope values that are not within the scope of theoretical reason. Because of this, practical reason has the right to assess the importance of and to pass judgment on the legitimacy of the pursuit of the values of theoretical reason.

The question of which of the two forms of reason takes precedence over the other perhaps would not arise, and certainly would not have the importance it does in fact have, if there were never any conflict between the values of theoretical reason and values of other kinds not included within the scope of theoretical reason. Such conflicts, however, do occur, just as they also sometimes occur between moral and aesthetic values. The claims of morality might require that a husband and father not desert his wife and children in order to devote his life to painting. Yet he might correctly believe that his art will suffer if he does not desert them. In such an unhappy situation he must choose between satisfying the claims of morality and those of art, if in fact he can produce paintings of considerable aesthetic value only if he does desert his wife and children. The best state of affairs would be one in which he could produce paintings having the same aesthetic value without deserting his wife and children. Since, however, this best state of affairs cannot obtain, he must choose between the two alternatives confronting him. He chooses correctly only if the choice he makes results in the realization of greater value than would otherwise be realized. Regardless, however, of which choice he makes, he sacrifices something of value for the sake of something he believes has even greater value.

Analogous conflicts can and sometimes do arise between satisfying the claims of theoretical reason and certain of the claims of practical reason. As before, the best state of affairs would doubtless be one in which no conflict occurs and no choice must be made. It might be the case that we ought to develop in ourselves, and also in others so far as we can, a character which is such that we can bear with equanimity to accept the results, whatever they might be, of inquiry conducted in accordance with the canons of theoretical reason. This, however, is more easily said than done, and it might well be the case that some people cannot do it at all. It is precisely because the character of many people is such that there are certain truths they cannot bear to face that conflicts between theoretical and practical rationality occur. In at least some such cases of conflict, practical rationality requires of others who know such truths that they not reveal them to those who cannot bear to know them, and it might also require of those who cannot bear to know them that they not undertake an inquiry conducted in accordance with the canons of theoretical reason in an effort to discover such truths. In such cases it is better that those who cannot bear the consequences refrain from eating of the fruit of the tree of theoretical knowledge. In such cases the requirements of practical reason overrule the claims of theoretical reason, and practical rationality consists in hiding from truths we cannot bear to know and in shielding others from truths we know, or believe we know, they cannot bear to know.

It is only narrow-minded and zealous partisans of the primacy of theoretical over practical reason who would reject such a position and proclaim "Let true belief, knowledge, and understanding be sought and revealed when attained even though the heavens fall." In practice, however, even the most zealous partisans of theoretical reason do not always comply with such a dictum. In a situation of the following sort, for example, it is doubtful that many such zealots would comply with such a dictum or advise others to do so. Suppose that a certain man is married and has six children. In all other respects he leaves nothing to be desired as a husband and father, but he is also a philanderer and has one affair after another with a series of various women and succeeds in concealing these affairs from his wife and children. There are others, however, who know of these affairs. Suppose also that if his wife and children learned of them disastrous consequences would ensue. His wife and children would be heartbroken, the marriage and the family would be destroyed, and the happy life of the family would be gone forever. Ought those who know of his philandering to enlighten his wife and children? By doing so we reveal to them certain truths of some importance. Even if their coming to know such truths has a certain intrinsic value, the consequences of their coming to know them would have a negative intrinsic value incalculably greater than any positive intrinsic value their coming to know them could have. Confronted with such a situation, it is unlikely that many of even the most zealous partisans of the primacy of theoretical reason would advise that our philanderer's wife and children be enlightened. Despite their philosophical espousal of the primacy of theoretical reason, it is unlikely that many among them would practice what they preach when confronted with concrete existential situations of the sort in question. In such situations their hearts would overrule, and rightly so, the dictates of their heads, and their practice would manifest a practical wisdom far greater than any theoretical wisdom their abstract philosophical pronouncements might possess.

In the example above we considered only the value, or the lack thereof, of the enlightenment by others of the philanderer's wife and children. Similar considerations apply to attempts at self-enlightenment on the part of the wife or children. Suppose that the wife suspects her husband of philandering but neither believes nor knows that he is doing so. In such a situation she might or might not want to know the truth. If she does not want to know, the reason she does not might well be that she fears the consequences that might ensue were she to come to know. She might, however, want to know the truth even though she fears these consequences. Let us suppose that the consequences of her coming to know would be those indicated above and that it is these she fears. Suppose also, as before, that the negative intrinsic value of these consequences would be inestimably greater than the positive intrinsic value of her coming to know. Given all this, ought she to undertake the investigations that would enable her to come to know? Ought she, simply for the sake of coming to know the truth about her husband, take steps which, if taken, would lead to the destruction of the happy life she and her husband have lived with each other and with their children? Or ought she instead to endeavor to dismiss her suspicions and to avoid discovering anything that would confirm them? Here too practical wisdom would seem to counsel that she choose the latter alternative, even though by choosing it she does not come to know the truth about her husband, as she would if she chose the former alternative. By choosing the former alternative she learns a truth about her husband that she would not learn if she chose the latter alternative, yet if she is wise she will nonetheless choose the latter. Sometimes ignorance is bliss, and sometimes the positive intrinsic value of the bliss ignorance brings is incalculably greater than the negative intrinsic value of the ignorance that brings bliss.

3. Silence and Deception

Let us call the husband John. Those who know of his philandering and refrain from informing his wife and children of it do not thereby deceive them. To deceive others it is necessary either that I do something or that I do not do something, the doing or the not doing of which by me leads others to believe something. But in remaining silent about John's philandering I do not lead his wife and children to believe anything. The thought that he is a philanderer might never have occurred to them, and if they believe that he is not it is not my silence that leads them to believe this. This is the case even though I could lead them to believe that he is a philanderer by informing them that he is. From the fact, that is, that by breaking my silence I could lead them to believe something true, it does not follow that by remaining silent I lead them to believe something false. By my silence I lead them to believe something false only if they and I are in a situation that is such that my silence could reasonably be taken by them as indicating that something is the case when in fact it is not the case, regardless of whether they believe prior to my silence either that it is or that it is not the case. In our example they and I are not in such a situation. If, however, John's wife, who suspects that he is philandering, asks me whether her suspicion is true, then I do deceive her if I tell her that it is not and if, by telling her this, I lead her no longer to suspect him of philandering. If, however, I tell her that John is not philandering when I know that he is, I attempt to deceive her but do not succeed in doing so if she continues, despite what I tell her, to suspect that he is. To deceive a person it is not sufficient to attempt to do so; instead, it is also necessary that I succeed in leading her to believe whatever it is that I am endeavoring to lead her to believe.

From the fact, however, that there is a difference between remaining silent and attempting to deceive, and that the former is sometimes justified, it does not follow that so also is the latter. The fundamental difference between the two, at least in situations such as the one we have been considering, would seem to be that in remaining silent I do not attempt to lead another person to believe something he does not already believe, whereas in attempting to deceive him I do attempt to do this. There are other sorts of situations, however, in which, by lying to someone, I do not attempt to lead him to believe something he does not already believe. Thus if John's wife, believing that he is not philandering but also suspecting that he might be, asks me whether he is, and if I, knowing both what she believes and suspects and also that he is philandering, tell her that he is not, I do thereby attempt to deceive her even though I do not attempt to lead her to believe anything she does not already believe. In such a situation I no more, by lying, attempt to lead her to believe anything she does not already believe than I do by remaining silent, as in the other situation. But if by lying I attempt to deceive her, and if by remaining silent I do not attempt to do so, then the fundamental difference between attempting to deceive and remaining silent cannot in all cases be that in the former but not the latter I attempt to lead her to believe something she does not already believe. Just as by remaining silent I do not attempt to lead John's wife to believe anything she does not already believe, neither do I do so if I tell her that her husband is not philandering if she already believes, and I know that she does, that he is not doing so.

What, then, is the difference between remaining silent and attempting to deceive? It might be thought that the difference is that in remaining silent I do not do anything, whereas in attempting to deceive I am doing something. This, however, is not acceptable just as it stands. It requires a certain modification specifying that my remaining silent is not the consequence of my agreeing with others to do so. This is the case because if I have agreed with others to remain silent, and if I remain silent because I have entered into such an agreement, then my remaining silent constitutes my doing something, namely my complying with the terms of the agreement. If, however, I remain silent independently of any agreement I have made with others, my remaining silent does not constitute my doing anything, except in a very loose sense of the expression "doing something," according to which keeping a resolution I have silently made or doing what I believe to be right constitutes doing something. In this very loose sense of the expression, I do something if I remain silent because I have silently resolved to do so or because I believe it to be the right thing to do.

This sense of the expression, however, is very loose indeed. In the case of a resolution to keep silent, what it seems to involve is treating something as doing something because something else has been done.

I do something if I silently resolve to remain silent, and it is because I do something in doing this that my remaining silent is also regarded as doing something. What, however, I have resolved to do in silently resolving to remain silent is not to inform John's wife that he is philandering. My remaining silent is my *not* informing her of his philandering. I remain silent, that is, by *not* doing something—by *not* informing her of his philandering. Similarly, if I remain silent because I believe it to be the right thing to do, my silence consists of my *not* doing something. To say that I believe that remaining silent is the right thing to do is to say that I believe that the right thing to do is *not* to inform her of his philandering. If so, then I do what I believe to be the right thing to do by *not* doing something—by *not* informing her of his philandering. If these considerations are acceptable, then my remaining silent can be regarded as my doing something only in an extremely loose and tenuous sense of "doing something". This sense of the expression, however, is so tenuous that doing something amounts to *not* doing something.

It was maintained above that from the fact that remaining silent is sometimes justified it does not follow that so also is attempting to deceive. If so, then one can consistently contend that remaining silent is sometimes justified and that attempting to deceive is never justified. Since, however, the justification for remaining silent would seem to be the same as that for attempting to deceive, it is hard to see how the former but not the latter can sometimes be justified. In each case the justification would be that the positive intrinsic value of the probable consequences of remaining silent and of attempting to deceive would be greater than that of the probable consequences of not remaining silent and of not attempting to deceive. If this is correct, then the most that those who believe that there is a significant moral difference between remaining silent and attempting to deceive can hope to establish is that any instance of the latter is intrinsically worse than any instance of the former. On such a view, both remaining silent and attempting to deceive can sometimes be justified, but more is required to justify the latter than is required to justify the former. Thus if the positive intrinsic value of the probable consequences of a given instance of remaining silent is the same as those of a given instance of attempting to deceive, it might suffice to justify remaining silent but not to justify attempting to deceive. Since, that is, any instance of attempting to deceive is intrinsically worse than any instance of remaining silent, anything that justifies the former justifies the latter, but something can justify remaining silent without also justifying attempting to deceive.

It seems, however, to be false that any instance of attempting to deceive is intrinsically worse than any instance of remaining silent. Whether a given instance of either is intrinsically worse than a given instance of the other depends upon the importance of whatever it is that one is remaining silent about or that one is attempting to deceive another into believing. If the negative intrinsic value of the probable consequences of remaining silent about something is much greater than that of those of attempting to deceive another, then remaining silent is intrinsically worse than attempting to deceive. To some it might seem that in such a case remaining silent would be only extrinsically, not intrinsically, worse than attempting to deceive. This would perhaps be true if the person who remains silent or who attempts to deceive neither knows nor could reasonably be expected to know either (a) what the probable consequences are of his remaining silent or attempting to deceive or (b) what the value of those consequences is if he does know or could reasonably be expected to know them. If, however, he does know both (a) and (b), then his remaining silent or his attempting to deceive does have an intrinsic value that otherwise it would not have.

This is the case because the intrinsic value of an act is determined, at least in part, by the nature of the agent's intention in acting. It will be convenient here, despite what was said above, to treat not only attempting to deceive but also remaining silent as acts. If I intend by acting to bring about certain consequences that I know, or could reasonably be expected to know, to be bad, then my act is intrinsically as well as extrinsically bad. Indeed, the act itself can still be intrinsically bad even though it be extrinsically good. This would happen if the act, rather than issuing in the bad consequences I intended to bring about, has instead good consequences unintended and unforeseen by me. If this were to happen, my act would be extrinsically good but intrinsically bad. Suppose now that I attempt to deceive another person about some utterly trivial matter. If so, then my act is intrinsically bad, although only slightly so, regardless of whether my attempt at deception succeeds, and thus regardless of whether it is also extrinsically bad. Suppose also that on another occasion I remain silent about some matter of great importance to another, that my remaining silent has consequences having great negative intrinsic value, and that I know it will have such consequences. If so, then my remaining silent is both intrinsically and extrinsically bad. As before, however, it is still intrinsically bad regardless of whether it is also extrinsically bad, as it would not be if it has neither the consequences in question nor any other bad consequences. Its negative intrinsic value would also be considerably greater than that of my attempting to deceive another about some utterly trivial matter.

4. Positive, Negative, and Conflicting Duties

If the preceding is correct, then attempting to deceive is not always intrinsically worse than remaining silent, and some instances of remaining silent can be intrinsically worse than some instances of attempting to deceive. The issue at stake here is similar to two other issues. One is the issue of whether any duty not to perform an act of a certain type is always weightier than a duty to perform an act of a certain other type. Duties of the first type are sometimes called negative duties, those of the second type positive duties. If the duty not to deceive is a negative duty and the duty to remain silent a positive duty, then negative duties are not always weightier than positive duties, since the duty not to deceive, taken as a negative duty, is not always more stringent than the duty to remain silent, taken as a positive duty. It might, however, seem strange to regard the duty to remain silent as a positive duty, since, being a duty *not* to speak, it is a duty *not* to do something. There are nonetheless other duties that seem clearly to show that negative duties are not always weightier than positive duties. Thus the negative duty not to deceive is overridden by the positive duty to save human life in a situation in which I can save a human life only by deceiving another intent upon wrongly taking that life.

The second issue referred to above is the issue of whether an order of stringency of specific duties can be established in which all duties can be ranked in terms of their stringency in such a way that any given duty is either more stringent or less stringent than any other duty in any conceivable situation that might arise, so that if duty b is less stringent than duty a but more stringent than duty c in some given situation, x, it is also less stringent than a and more stringent than c in any other conceivable situation, y. What has been said above suggests that this cannot be done, and a simple example might serve to show that this is indeed the case. Are the duties of keeping promises and of rendering aid to those in need of aid whom we can aid such that in any conceivable situation one is more stringent than the other, so that in any conceivable situation in which they might conflict the more stringent of the two overrides the other? I believe the following examples show that the answer is "no".

Suppose that I have promised a friend that I will meet him at his house at 8:00 P.M. so that he and I can go together to a movie. Suppose also that at 7:55, as I am walking toward his house near a secluded lake, I hear a cry for help coming from someone thrashing about in the water on the verge of drowning. No one else is about, and I am an excellent swimmer. The drowning person clearly needs my aid, and I can render him the aid he needs. But if I do I cannot keep my promise to meet my friend at 8:00. In this situation my duty to render aid conflicts with my duty to keep my promise. I cannot fulfill both. It seems obvious that in this situation my duty to render aid overrides my duty to keep my promise, so that I act rightly only if I attempt to render aid. Consider now a second situation. Suppose that I have borrowed a hundred dollars from a very rich friend and have promised to repay him by a certain date. That date has now arrived, and as I am about to enter the building in which he works to repay him in cash I see a crippled blind beggar who needs aid. I can aid him by giving him the cash I have, but if I do I cannot repay my rich friend who, let us suppose, does not need the money I owe him and has even forgotten that I have borrowed it. In this situation which duty takes precedence—that of keeping my promise or that of rendering aid? Most of us, I believe, would think that the former does, and let us suppose that in fact it does. If so, then whereas in the first example the duty of rendering aid overrides the duty to keep my promise, in the second the duty to keep my promise overrides the duty of rendering aid.

If the preceding examples, and many others that could also be adduced, show what I think they do, then there can be no hierarchy of specific duties descending from the most stringent to the least stringent in such a way that any given duty is either more stringent or less stringent than any other in every conceivable situation. Instead, in one situation duty *a* might override duty *b*, so that we act rightly in that situation only by doing *a*, and in another situation duty *b* might override duty *a*, so that we act rightly in this situation only by doing *b*. It is also conceivable that there be situations such that in them we have a duty to do something, *a*, and also a duty to do something, *b*, that *a* and *b* cannot both be done, and that neither takes precedence over the other. Most of us tend, I believe, to regard such dilemmatic situations as uncomfortable. If we do, part of the reason we do is perhaps that we like to have decisive reasons for doing *a* rather than *b,* or for doing *b* rather than *a,* and in such situations there are no such decisive reasons, so that the choice we make, whether it be to do *a* or to do *b,* seems arbitrary. Part of the reason might sometimes also be that we want something to guide and justify our choice, and in such situations there is nothing that counts decisively from a moral point of view in favor of doing *a* or in favor of doing *b.* It is sometimes uncomfortable to be in a situation in which we must do either *a* or *b,* cannot do both, and have no better reason for doing *a* rather than *b* or *b* rather than *a.* If only we had some decisive reason for doing one rather than the other we should be freed from the need to choose between the two. At the same time, however, there is also a comfortable side to such situations, which is that we act rightly whether we do *a* or do *b* and are therefore morally free to do either and even to choose the alternative we are more inclined to choose independently of any need to attempt to justify on moral grounds the choice we make. Given that we act rightly by doing either *a* or *b,* we are morally free to choose whichever alternative we believe would please us most or displease us least.

The preceding position is realistic in that it recognizes that there are genuine conflicts between competing values and duties that cannot be resolved by an appeal to abstract universal principles that would enable us in any conceivable situation that might arise, regardless of its complexity, to determine definitively that one value or duty takes precedence over another. Despite the animadversions and easy cavils of various of their critics, some of whom seem not to have taken the trouble to read them with care, it is "intuitionists" such as Prichard, Ross, and Carritt who, among twentieth-century moral philosophers, seem most clearly and fully to have recognized and appreciated the complexities of moral and value questions that require an acceptance of the kind of realistic position presented above.

Such a realistic position does not deny that certain duties are generally weightier than others or that certain sorts of things generally have greater value than other sorts of things, nor does it deny that we can sometimes know which duties are generally weightier than others and which sorts of things generally have greater value than other sorts of things. Nor does it deny that such knowledge is frequently helpful, and sometimes indispensable, in endeavoring in concrete existential situations to divine which of two or more conflicting duties overrides the others in such situations or which of two or more competing values in such situations takes precedence over the others when it is impossible that they all be realized. It does, however, deny that such abstract and general knowledge is always sufficient, in any conceivable concrete situation in which we might find ourselves, to enable us to determine, in the situation in which we find ourselves, which of the conflicting duties applicable to us in that situation overrides the others in *that* situation and which of the competing values realizable by us in that situation takes precedence over the others in *that* situation. In such situations the best we can reasonably hope to do is to reflect as carefully as we can, given the limited amount of time available for reflection in the situation in which we find ourselves, upon the circumstances of the situation, upon the varying weights of the various duties applicable to us in the situation, and upon the probable consequences of the various courses of action available to us in the situation. It is on the basis of such reflection, which in certain situations must be very hasty indeed, that we must decide on which among the various courses of action available to us in the situation is the one we ought to take, while recognizing that what seems to us on reflection to be the right thing to do might very well *not* be the right thing to do. In general, the more complex the situation in which we find ourselves, and the less the amount of time we have for reflection, the greater the chances are that we might make some mistake in reflection and thereby do what might well turn out not to be the right thing to do. All the same, the most that can reasonably be expected of us is that, despite our susceptibility to error, we do that which, on reflection, seems to us to be the right thing to do.

Such a realistic position therefore recognizes not only that in existential situations there are frequently conflicts between duties and between competing values, not all of which can be realized, but also that human reflection and judgment are fallible. The human condition and the condition of the world in which we live are therefore such that the realization of certain values inevitably involves the sacrifice of certain others. They also seem to be such that the inescapable fallibility of human reflection and judgment will inevitably continue from time to time to lead to the choice of things of lesser value over things of greater value.

To some, such an assessment of the human condition and of the world in which we live might seem pessimistic. That it might seem so is especially so in the case of those who believe that there is a single systematic comprehensive hierarchy of specific duties and values of the sort indicated above, that we can acquire knowledge of such a system, and that in concrete situations we can discover what the right thing to do is, and which of the various values possible in such situations we ought to attempt to realize, simply by applying our knowledge of this system to our own existential situation. If, however, the considerations presented above are acceptable, such beliefs are unrealistically optimistic. The opposite of such an unrealistically optimistic position would be the pessimistic skeptical view that denies not only the possibility of the existence of a single systematic hierarchy of duties and values, and thus also the possibility of our acquiring any knowledge of such a system, but also the possibility of our acquiring even the more modest sort of knowledge indicated above. If the considerations advanced above are acceptable, these two extreme positions are unacceptable, the first because it is unrealistically optimistic, the second because it is unrealistically pessimistic.

5. Self-Deception

Thus far we have considered only attempts to deceive others and have not considered attempts to deceive oneself. It might be thought that attempts to deceive oneself are morally worse than attempts to deceive others. One argument that might be advanced in support of such a view goes as follows. It would be good if everyone were so constituted that each person could bear to face with equanimity any truth that might confront him. In point of fact, however, some people cannot bear to face certain truths. Some cannot bear to face certain truths about themselves, some cannot bear to face certain truths about certain of the persons they love, and some cannot bear to face certain truths about the existence or non-existence of God and/or about human mortality. If they came to believe various of the truths they cannot bear to face, or if they came even to doubt various of their beliefs that conflict with such truths, their lives would be hopelessly shattered. Compassion for their condition therefore requires that we refrain from saying or doing anything that might cause them to lose or even to doubt the beliefs they are happy in holding, and even that we attempt to deceive them into believing that we too believe what they believe if we believe that such deception is necessary to avoid the unhappy consequences that would issue from their losing or coming to doubt their beliefs. They, however, cannot rightly attempt to deceive themselves, nor could we were we in their situation. Although I can justifiably attempt to hide certain truths from others, either by remaining silent or by resorting to deception, if I believe correctly that their lives would be shattered if they were to lose or to come to doubt certain of their beliefs that conflict with these truths, I can never justifiably attempt to deceive myself even though it be necessary that I do so to avoid facing certain truths I cannot bear to face. What reasons, if any, can be given in support of such a position?

One reason that might be given is that the consequences for others if they lost or came to doubt certain of their beliefs would be worse than the consequences for me if I lost or came to doubt certain of my beliefs. This, however, is not a good reason, since the consequences for me if I lost or came to doubt certain of my beliefs might well be as bad as the consequences for others if they lost or came to doubt certain of their beliefs. Just as their lives would be shattered, so also might mine. Another reason that might be given is that attempts to deceive oneself are intrinsically worse than attempts to deceive others. This too is not a good reason, since whether an attempt to deceive oneself is intrinsically worse than an attempt to deceive others depends upon the importance, either for oneself or for others, of whatever it is that one is attempting to deceive oneself or others into believing. An attempt to deceive oneself about some utterly trivial matter would be far less serious and require far less in the way of justification than an attempt to deceive others about some matter of the utmost importance to them. If so, then an attempt to deceive oneself is not always intrinsically worse than an attempt to deceive others.

A third reason that might be given in support of the view that attempts at self-deception are always worse than attempts to deceive others is somewhat more subtle than the first two. It goes as follows. Each of us has a duty to endeavor to develop a character which is such that we can bear to face any truth that confronts us, regardless of how unpleasant we might find it. Each of us has such a duty because of the intrinsic goodness of understanding oneself, others, and the world, and we are more likely to acquire such understanding if we develop such a character than if we resort to self-deception in an effort to escape various truths we find distasteful. Each of us also has a duty to do what we can to assist others to develop such a character, especially those, such as our children, with whom we have some influence. Since, however, there are some people who have not in fact developed such a character, and whose lives would be shattered were they to lose or to come to doubt certain beliefs they hold, we have a duty not to do or to say anything that would lead them to lose or to come to doubt these beliefs. We may therefore resort to deception, and indeed might even have a duty so to do, if such deception is necessary to avoid the unhappy consequences that very likely would follow upon their losing or coming to doubt the beliefs in question. Since, however, each of us has a duty to develop the kind of character in question, and since self-deception is incompatible with the development of such a character, none of us can ever rightly resort to such deception.

Such a position manifests a certain compassion for others that is missing in the view that we can never rightly deceive others, even in those situations in which our not doing so has profoundly unhappy consequences for those we decline to deceive. It seems, however, to be less compassionate than the position that each person may also resort to self-deception if doing so is necessary to prevent deeply unhappy consequences for himself. It might well be true that each of us does indeed have a duty to develop in himself the kind of character mentioned above and also to do what he can to assist others in the development of such a character. But just as others, despite our having such a duty, might still be unable to face certain truths, so also I might equally be unable to face certain truths. Just as the lives of others might be shattered if they were to lose or to come to doubt certain of their beliefs, so also might mine were I to lose or to come to doubt certain of my beliefs. If so, and if I can rightly resort to deception to prevent the shattering of the lives of others, then why cannot I also rightly resort to self-deception to prevent the shattering of my own life? If in such cases I can rightly resort to deception, and indeed have a duty to do so, for the sake of others, then why cannot I resort to self-deception, and even have a duty to do so, for my own sake? The answer would seem to be that if I can rightly do, and indeed have a duty to do, the former, then I can also rightly do, and even have a duty to do, the latter. Just as I can rightly deceive others from compassion for them, so also I can rightly deceive myself from concern for my own happiness.

The position advocated here is compatible with the view that each of us has a duty to develop in himself, and to assist others in developing in themselves, the kind of character mentioned above. It is compatible also with the view that the possession of such a character is a good-making property or virtue of a person, and thus with the view that, other things equal, a person is a better person if he has this virtue than he would be if he did not have it. It is compatible further with the view than an understanding of oneself, of others, and of the world is a great intrinsic good. But it also recognizes that this is not the only intrinsic good and that there are situations in which its sacrifice in some degree is justified for the sake of an even greater intrinsic good such as the prevention of the shattering of a person's life, whether one's own or that of another. It recognizes, that is, that the prevention of the shattering of a person's life can be, and sometimes is, a far greater intrinsic good than some increase in his understanding of himself, of others, or of the world would be. It also recognizes that the duty to develop in oneself, and to assist others to develop in themselves, the kind of character mentioned above is not the only duty and that the duty of compassion and concern for one's own happiness at times requires of us that we suspend for a time the attempt to develop such a character in ourselves in order that we practice those deceptions, whether of others or of ourselves, required by compassion for others and concern for oneself. It recognizes further that the possession of the kind of character in question is not the only virtue and that there are other virtues, especially the virtue of compassion, the practice of which in certain situations takes precedence over attempting in such situations to develop the kind of character in question.

6. The Possibility of Self-Deception

To some it might seem that in concrete existential situations the question of the justifiability of self-deception can never arise, since instances of self-deception can never occur. Although we can deceive and attempt to deceive others, on such a view we can never deceive ourselves and perhaps never even endeavor to do so. One reason that might be presented in support of such a view is connected with what may be referred to as the alleged intentionality and self-consciousness of deception. On such a view of deception, in order that I attempt to deceive, and therefore in order that my attempt succeed, I must intend to deceive, and in order that I intend to deceive I must know or be conscious of my intention to deceive. I cannot, that is, attempt to deceive unless I know or am conscious that I am attempting to do so. But although I can succeed in deceiving another even though I know that I am attempting to do so, I cannot succeed in deceiving myself, since my knowing that I am attempting to do so necessarily precludes any possibility of the success of such an endeavor. This, it might be argued, is the case for the following reasons.

To attempt to deceive is to attempt to lead the person I am endeavoring to deceive to believe either (1) that some proposition I believe to be false is true or (2) that some proposition I believe to be true is false. To do this, however, I must know that I believe that the proposition I am endeavoring to deceive someone into believing is (1) true if I am attempting to deceive him into believing it to be false or (2) false if I am attempting to deceive him into believing it to be true. I can successfully attempt to lead another to believe either (1) that a given proposition is true while I know that I believe it to be false or (2) that a given proposition is false while I know that I believe it to be true. But I cannot successfully attempt to lead myself to believe either (1) or (2). It might be possible for me to *attempt* to deceive myself into believing either (1) or (2). But it is not possible for me to *succeed* in such an endeavor. To do so I must come either (1) to believe that a given proposition is true while I also know that I believe it to be false or (2) to believe that a given proposition is false while I also know that I believe it to be true. If, however, I am to know that I believe that a given proposition is true (or false) I must believe that it is, since if I do not believe that it is true (or false) I cannot know that I believe that it is. In order, then, that I succeed in deceiving myself into believing that a given proposition is true or that a given proposition is false, I must come to believe both that it is false and also that it is true. I cannot, however, believe of any given proposition both that it is true and also that it is false. I therefore cannot deceive myself, and self-deception is therefore impossible.

I think we must agree that a person cannot at the same time believe of a given proposition both that it is true and also that it is false. This is not to deny that it is possible for a person to believe what are in fact contradictory propositions without recognizing that he is doing so. Thus I might believe both of two propositions that are in fact contradictories because one entails some proposition that is the contradictory of some proposition entailed by the other, provided that I do not recognize that the two propositions entail contradictory propositions or that the entailed propositions are in fact contradictories. Thus I might believe both p and q, which in fact are contradictories because p entails that r is true and q that r is false. I can, however, believe that p and q are both true only if I do not recognize or believe that p entails that r is true and q that r is false. If I believe that p entails that r is true and q that r is false and recognize or believe that if this is the case p and q cannot both be true, then I cannot believe that both are true. Indeed, it is hard to understand what could be meant by saying that it is possible for a person to believe both of two propositions he believes or recognizes to be contradictories. If so, then it is also hard to see what could be meant by saying that it is possible for a person to believe of a given proposition both that it is true and also that it is false. From the fact, however, that a person cannot believe this of any given proposition, it does not follow that self-deception is impossible.

Perhaps the major flaw in the argument outlined above against the possibility of self-deception is the assumption that a necessary condition of anyone's attempting to deceive anyone, either himself or others, is that he know that or be conscious that he is attempting to do so. Such an assumption has things backwards. The truth of the matter is that a necessary condition of one's knowing that or being conscious that he is endeavoring to deceive someone, whether himself or others, is that he in fact be attempting to do so. Just as a necessary condition of one's knowing that a given proposition is true is that it be true, so also a necessary condition of my knowing that I am attempting to deceive someone is that in fact I be doing so. If I am not attempting to do so, then I cannot know that I am attempting to do so. And just as a given proposition can be true regardless of whether I believe or know that it is, so also I can endeavor to deceive someone, whether myself or others, regardless of whether I believe or know that I am endeavoring to do so. What holds here for attempts to deceive holds generally for other endeavors, acts, and mental states. In general, a necessary but not a sufficient condition of my knowing that I am doing or attempting to do something or that I am in a certain mental state is that I am in fact doing or attempting to do the thing in question or that I am in fact in the mental state in question. If so, then although I cannot know that I am endeavoring to deceive someone, either myself or others, unless in fact I am attempting to do so, I can endeavor to deceive myself or others without knowing that I am attempting to do so.

A second major flaw in the argument outlined above against the possibility of self-deception is the assumption that to endeavor to deceive someone, whether myself or others, is to attempt to lead him to believe either (1) that some proposition I believe to be true is false or (2) that some proposition I believe to be false is true. This assumption is false for at least two reasons. One reason is that I can attempt to deceive a person into believing that some proposition I believe to be true is in fact true, not false, by giving him reasons for believing it to be true that I know or believe are not good reasons for his believing it to be true. This type of attempt at deception is perhaps most likely to occur in situations in which someone who believes that a given proposition is true (1) wants another person also to believe that it is true, (2) believes that he knows of no good reason for the other person's believing it to be true, and (3) therefore gives the other person reasons for believing it to be true that he believes are not in fact good reasons for the other person's doing so. Even if the reasons given the other person are in fact good reasons for his believing the proposition in question to be true, the person who gives the other person these reasons for accepting the given proposition is still endeavoring to deceive the other person if he believes that these reasons are not good reasons for the other person's accepting the given proposition. Moreover, even if the other person accepts the given proposition because he sees that the reasons given him for accepting it are good reasons, the person who gives him these reasons is still endeavoring to deceive him if he believes that the reasons he gives are not good reasons. In such a case the person who gives what he mistakenly believes to be bad reasons for accepting the given proposition attempts to deceive the other person but does not succeed in doing so because the other sees that the reasons given him are good reasons for accepting the given proposition. If the person who gives the reasons in question is to succeed in deceiving the other person, the latter must accept the proposition in question because he is given the reasons in question but does not see that they are in fact good reasons. Although he might *believe* that the reasons in question are good reasons, he is still deceived by the other person if he does not *see* that the reasons given him are good reasons.

Since attempts at the kind of deception in question do in fact occur, attempting to deceive does not always consist of endeavoring to lead someone, whether oneself or others, to believe either (1) that some proposition one believes to be true is false or (2) that some proposition one believes to be false is true. It might, however, be objected that the argument presented, if it establishes anything at all, establishes only that attempts to deceive *others* do not always consist in endeavoring to lead them to accept as true some proposition one believes to be false or to reject as false some proposition one believes to be true. Since I cannot endeavor to deceive *myself* into accepting some proposition I believe to be true or into rejecting some proposition I believe to be false, endeavoring to deceive myself does consist in attempting to lead myself to believe either (1) that some proposition I believe to be true is false or (2) that some proposition I believe to be false is true.

This brings us to the second reason for rejecting the view that to endeavor to deceive someone, whether oneself or others, is to attempt to lead him to believe (1) that some proposition one believes to be true is false or (2) that some proposition one believes to be false is true. The second reason for rejecting this view is based on the fact that a person can attempt to deceive someone, either himself or others, into believing that some proposition he neither believes to be true nor believes to be false is (1) true or (2) false. Such attempts at deception are perhaps most likely to occur when I neither believe that a given proposition, p, is true nor believe that it is false, yet want either myself or others to believe either that p is true or that p is false. If I want to believe myself that p is true, the reason is likely to be that I want p to be true. It is because I want p to be true that I want to believe that it is true. If, however, I want others to believe that p is true, the reason might well be, not that I want p to be true, but that I want something else, the attainment or acquisition of which by myself or others I believe will be facilitated if others believe that p is true. Indeed, in certain situations I might well want others to believe that p is true while wanting that p be false. It is unlikely, however, that I will want myself to believe that p is true if I want p to be false. Such a combination of wants, however, does seem to be possible. Thus I might want p to be false but want myself to believe that p is true because I believe that p is more likely to be false if I believe it to be true than if I believe it to be false. This combination of wants might occur because in the past so many of my beliefs I have wanted to be false have turned out to be true that I have come to believe that it is more likely that a proposition I want to be true will in fact be false if I believe it to be true than if I believe it to be false. Although such a belief might be irrational or superstitious, people have held irrational or superstitious beliefs, and the belief in question is one such belief that might be held by someone. Thus wanting p to be false, and believing that p is more likely to be false if I believe it to be true than if I believe it to be false, I come to want not only that p be false but also that I believe it to be true.

If the preceding is correct, then endeavors to deceive do not always consist in attempting to lead someone, either myself or others, to believe (1) that some proposition I believe to be true is false or (2) that some proposition I believe to be false is true. Instead, I can endeavor to deceive someone, myself or others, into believing that some proposition I neither believe to be true nor believe to be false is (1) true or (2) false. Everyone will agree that attempts to deceive others are frequently successful, and there is also no difficulty in understanding what must be done in situations of various sorts if one is to succeed in deceiving others. Many will also agree that attempts at self-deception are also sometimes successful. How they succeed, however, is not always easily understandable, and it is perhaps the difficulty of understanding how they succeed that inclines some people to deny, or at least to doubt, that they ever do succeed. Yet they do sometimes seem to succeed, even though how some such attempts succeed might well seem to be ultimately incomprehensible. One can, however, give certain simple general rules that, if followed faithfully, might be of some slight assistance in helping those who want to deceive themselves to succeed in doing so.

Thus if you want to believe that a certain proposition p is true, and if you want so much to believe that it is true that you are willing to endeavor to deceive yourself into believing that it is, then (1) do your best to discover whatever evidence there might be, regardless of however slight its evidential value might be, for the truth of p, (2) do your best to avoid whatever evidence there might be that might lead you to doubt the truth of p, and (3) do your best to ignore whatever evidence you might happen to come across, regardless of however great its evidential value might be, that might lead you to doubt the truth of p. There are doubtless other rules of self-deception that would be of some assistance. Perhaps, however, all such more or less specific rules would be covered by the general rule directing that you violate as much as you can those rules that have generally been helpful in directing inquiry aimed at the acquisition of knowledge and understanding. Since, however, you do not want to deceive yourself about everything, violate these rules only when you do want to deceive yourself about something and observe them when what you seek is knowledge and understanding.

7. The Value of Knowledge

This long (perhaps overly long) discussion of deception was occasioned by our earlier discussion of the relation of practical to theoretical reason and of the primacy of practical over theoretical reason. Such primacy means that attempts at deception, whether of oneself or others, are sometimes justified because necessary for the realization of certain goals the attainment of which has greater value than the realization of certain of the aims of theoretical reason would have. It must, however, be remembered and indeed emphasized that something of value, sometimes something of great value, is frequently lost when the claims of theoretical reason are overridden, regardless of however justified their sacrifice might be. It must also be remembered and emphasized that any sacrifice of the ends of theoretical reason requires justification precisely because of the loss, sometimes small but sometimes great, of the values of knowledge and understanding. We must also remember and emphasize that attempting to deceive others imperils something else of great value. This is the trust and friendship between persons that relies upon honesty and truthfulness. The possible loss of such trust and friendship is something that must carefully be taken into account when endeavoring in a concrete existential situation to determine the cost of deception. If the attempt to deceive another fails, we have a duty to explain to him why we believed the attempt to be justified. And if, having succeeded in deceiving another, our situation changes so that our continued deception is no longer justified, we have a duty to cease the deception and explain why we believe our deception was justified. The fact that people do not like to be deceived indicates, I believe, not only that they do not like to be treated merely as things to be used for our attaining whatever ends we might set ourselves, but also that they place some value on such goals of theoretical reason as knowledge and understanding. People generally want their beliefs to be true and prefer understanding to ignorance.

The fact that we generally do value knowledge and understanding also explains, I believe, at least in part, our uneasiness when confronted with skeptical hypotheses to the effect that we are only brains in vats or that we are constantly being deceived by Cartesian-like evil demons or scientists (in the seventeenth century by evil demons, in the twentieth by evil scientists).[4] Why, one might ask, ought we to be troubled by the fact that our ordinary commonsensical beliefs about the existence of the material world, other minds, and the past might be false, given that we continue to be able in the future to satisfy our desires as well as we have in the past? The answer, I believe, is that one of our desires is to have true rather than false beliefs and understanding rather than ignorance.

We want our commonsensical beliefs about the existence of the material world, other minds, and the past to be true not because their truth is necessary if we are to satisfy various of our non-theoretical or practical interests, but rather because their truth is necessary, given the difficulty if not indeed the impossibility of abandoning such beliefs, for the sake of our theoretical concern for knowledge and understanding. We want our intellect or understanding to be informed or well formed, not mis-informed or badly formed. Our concern for knowledge and under-standing also explains why James Rachels' conceited scientist, whose colleagues feed his conceit by concocting a gigantic hoax, never discov-ered by him, involving the conferring of various high honors on him, is such a pathetic figure.[5] Regardless of how contented and happy he might be in his conceited ignorance, he is pathetic precisely because of his false beliefs about and his ignorance and lack of understanding of himself and his importance. Had we no concern for the values of theo-retical reason it would be hard to understand why we regard him as such a pathetic figure, regardless of how contented and happy he in his conceited ignorance might be.

There is perhaps no harm in regarding the advocacy of the primacy of practical over theoretical reason as a form of pragmatism, provided that it is recognized that such a form of pragmatism would be a very attenuated form indeed. Although such a form of pragmatism would have certain affinities with the position advocated by William James in "The Will to Believe," it would have few if any with the views advanced in his book *Pragmatism*. As is evident from what was said above, such a form of pragmatism in no way requires an acceptance of a pragmatic theory of truth and in fact is incompatible with such a theory. Although deception, whether of others or of oneself, might work in the sense that it makes possible the attainment of certain non-theoretical values the realization of which would otherwise be impossible, and the attainment of which has greater value than the realization of the sacrificed theoret-ical values would have, it by no means follows that the propositions the deceived are deceived into accepting are true. Deception might work, in the sense of contributing to the realization of certain non-theoretical values, regardless of whether the proposition the deceived person accepts is true or false. It is true if the state of affairs believed to obtain in accepting the proposition does in fact obtain, false if it does not in fact obtain. Such a view of truth is not pragmatic.

Indeed, one can even conceive of circumstances in which even the acceptance of contradictory propositions might work, in the sense of contributing to the realization of certain non-theoretical values that otherwise would not be realizable. Although, as was indicated above, one cannot believe both of two contradictory propositions if one recognizes that they are contradictories, since to recognize that they are contradictories is to see that if one is true the other is false, one can accept both of two propositions, p and q, even though p entails that r is true and q that r is false, provided that one does not recognize that p entails the truth of r and q the falsity of r. Thus the acceptance of the conjunctive proposition, p and q, might well work, in the sense in question, even though it is impossible that such a proposition be true. Moreover, the acceptance of such a self-inconsistent proposition might also be perfectly rational from the standpoint of practical reason, since it would work in the sense in question, even though it cannot be rational from the standpoint of theoretical reason, since the proposition in question, being self-inconsistent, necessarily is false.

Although from the standpoint of practical reason it is sometimes rational to accept a proposition even though we have no more evidence for believing it to be true than for believing it to be false, and indeed even though we have more evidence for believing it to be false than for believing it to be true, to do so cannot be rational from the standpoint of theoretical reason. Instead, from the latter standpoint it is rational to accept a given proposition only if we have more evidence for believing it to be true than we have for believing it to be false. This difference between the two standpoints concerning what it is rational for us to believe could not arise if the interest of each standpoint were identical with that of the other. It is because the goal of theoretical reason is the acquisition of knowledge that we ought, from the standpoint of theoretical reason, to accept a proposition only if the evidence we have for its truth is greater than the evidence we have for its falsity. And it is because the goal of practical reason is the attainment of something other than knowledge that sometimes we ought, from this standpoint, to accept a proposition even though we have no more evidence for believing it to be true than for believing it to be false, and sometimes even though we have more evidence for believing it to be false than for believing it to be true.

Some doubtless will dislike talk about the end, goal, or purpose of practical and theoretical reason. If so, such dislike is likely to issue from a belief that such talk implies, or at least suggests, that practical and theoretical reason have an end, goal, or purpose independently of, and not reducible to, various of the ends, goals, or purposes of human beings. No such implication or suggestion is intended. Instead, to say that the goal of theoretical reason is the acquisition of knowledge is to say nothing more than that human beings sometimes desire to acquire knowledge as an end. Given such a desire, it is an empirical fact that we are likely to satisfy it more completely if we accept propositions only if we have more evidence for believing them to be true than we have for believing them to be false. It is because of the existence of such a desire, coupled with the empirical fact just indicated, that it is rational, from the standpoint of theoretical reason, to accept propositions only if we have more evidence for believing them to be true than for believing them to be false. Theoretical rationality consists in our doing this only because we are more likely to increase our knowledge if we do than if we do not. Similarly, to say that the goal of practical rationality is the attainment as an end of something other than knowledge is to say nothing more than that human beings sometimes desire as an end the attainment of something other than knowledge. Given such a desire, it is an empirical fact that sometimes we are more likely to satisfy it if we accept certain propositions even though we have no more evidence for believing them to be true than for believing them to be false. It is because of the existence of such a desire, coupled with the empirical fact just indicated, that it is sometimes rational, from the standpoint of practical reason, to accept certain propositions even though we have as much evidence for believing them to be false as for believing them to be true. Practical rationality sometimes consists in our doing this only because we are sometimes more likely to satisfy certain of our non-theoretical desires if we do than if we do not.

Conflicts between practical and theoretical reason can occur only because we sometimes desire as an end something other than the acquisition of knowledge. As was indicated above, if the end of each were identical with that of the other, no such conflicts could occur. But the end of each is not identical with that of the other, and sometimes conflicts do occur. When they do, sometimes an increase in knowledge has greater value than, and therefore takes precedence over, the attainment of whatever else it is that such an increase conflicts with, and sometimes the reverse is the case. Sometimes it is very hard indeed, and sometimes impossible, to decide in particular cases of conflict which of the conflicting claims—that of practical or that of theoretical reason—takes precedence over the other. Nonetheless, practical wisdom consists in part in the ability to determine in particular cases which of the conflicting claims takes precedence over the other. Such wisdom is practical rather than theoretical because the determination of which of the conflicting claims takes precedence over the other can be made correctly only by considering carefully the degree of value that would probably be realized, and the degree that would probably be lost, by choosing one of the competing alternatives rather than the other. Since, that is, an increase in knowledge, although often a value, is not the only value, and since reason functions practically rather than theoretically when we endeavor to determine which among competing values has greater value, it is the function of practical rather than theoretical reason to determine in particular cases whether some increase in knowledge would have greater value than the attainment of something else would have when the two cannot both be had. It is because of this that practical reason has primacy over theoretical reason.

Throughout much of this chapter I have used the terminology of practical and theoretical rationality. This I have done primarily because such terminology is familiar and has a long history going back at least to Aristotle. I believe, however, that a better terminology, at least for the purposes of value theory, would be that of axiological and epistemic rationality. The concept of axiological rationality corresponds more or less to the concept of practical rationality, that of epistemic rationality more or less to that of theoretical rationality. Just as practical rationality has primacy over theoretical rationality, so also, for much the same reasons, axiological rationality has primacy over epistemic rationality.

Chapter 8

Morality and Rationality

In the last chapter we examined some aspects of the difference between practical and theoretical reason and their relationship to one another. We turn now to consider in somewhat more detail various views of what practical rationality consists in and of its relationship to morality.

1. Acting Morally and Acting Rationally

Different philosophers have taken different positions concerning the nature of practical rationality. Two widely held positions may be stated roughly, but with sufficient precision for our purposes here, as follows. On one view practical rationality consists of using whatever means happen to be appropriate for the attainment of whatever end one happens to have, regardless of what it might happen to be. The adoption of any end, however, regardless of whatever it might be, is no more nor any less rational than the adoption of any other end. On this view, to take an example from Hume, it is not irrational for me to prefer the destruction of the world to the scratching of my finger.[1] If I do have such a preference, then practical rationality in my case consists of taking appropriate means to prevent the scratching of my finger even if doing so requires the destruction of the world. Despite Hume, however, there does seem to be something irrational about preferring the destruction of the world to the scratching of my finger. The first would clearly seem to be worse than the second, and if such a preference would not be irrational it is hard to know what would be. Should the Humean retort that it is hard to know what would be because no end is either more rational or more irrational than any other, the appropriate response would appear to be that some ends are more irrational than others, if for no other reason than that preferring the destruction of the world to the scratching of my finger is irrational.

A second widely held position is the view that practical rationality consists of adopting appropriate means to the promotion of one's own long-term interests, welfare, happiness, or good. Each person acts rationally if and only if, and only to the degree that, he acts compatibly with the promotion of his own long-term interests. Whereas on the first view no end is either more rational or more irrational than any other end, on this view the only ultimate end it is rational for anyone to adopt is the promotion of his own long-term welfare. Thus whereas on the first view it would not be irrational to prefer the destruction of the world to the scratching of one's finger, on the second view it would be, provided that the destruction of the world, but not the scratching of one's finger, would be incompatible with the promotion of one's own long-term happiness. If, however, the promotion of my own long-term good were to require that I take steps that would lead to the destruction of the world after my death, then practical rationality would require that I take such steps. Fortunately for others, the promotion of my own long-term interests does not in fact require that I take such steps. It is also fortunate for others that I could not bring about the destruction of the world even if I tried.

It might, however, on behalf of the view in question, be objected that it is also fortunate for me that the promotion of my own long-term welfare requires neither the destruction of the world nor my taking steps to bring about its destruction, since if it did, then, given that I cannot bring about its destruction or even take steps to do so, I would not be able to promote my own long-term happiness. On the view in question, the reason it is fortunate for me cannot be the reason it is also fortunate for others. This is so because on the view in question it would not be unfortunate for me if the promotion of my long-term interests required the destruction of the world shortly after my death if I could in fact succeed in bringing about its destruction. But it would be unfortunate for others if I, believing that the promotion of my long-term welfare required the destruction of the world, and knowing that I have the power to bring about its destruction shortly after my death, chose to do so and also succeeded in so doing. The fact, however, that it would be unfortunate for others would not give me a reason not to destroy the world, and in such an unlikely situation I would act rationally only if I did endeavor to destroy it. If, that is, I can act rationally only by acting compatibly with the promotion of my long-term happiness, if the promotion of the latter requires the destruction of the world, and if I have the power to destroy it, then I act rationally only if I do endeavor to destroy it.

Whether such an egoistic view of practical rationality conflicts with morality depends upon what morality requires of us. There are two conflicting views of morality, one of which is compatible with such a view of practical rationality, the other of which is not, or at least seems not to be. The first view of morality is the position that a person acts rightly only if he acts compatibly with the promotion of his own long-term good. On such an egoistic view of morality, a person acts rightly only if he acts as the egoistic view of practical rationality requires. The content of egoistic morality is therefore identical with the content of what may be referred to as egoistic rationality. Since what egoistic morality requires of us is identical with what egoistic rationality requires of us, a person acts rightly if and only if he acts rationally.

On such a view of morality and rationality, the expressions "right action" and "rational action" are not only extensionally but also intensionally equivalent. Each applies to all and only those acts to which the other does, and each does so because of the meaning of the expressions "right action" and "rational action". Given the meaning of these expressions, it is impossible that one apply to any act unless the other also applies. Thus the question "Is it rational to act morally?" has precisely the same meaning as the question "Is it moral to act rationally?". If, that is, "acting morally" or "acting rightly" has exactly the same meaning as "acting rationally," there is no difference between asking whether it is rational to act morally and asking whether it is moral to act rationally. Indeed, given an identity of meaning between "acting morally" or "acting rightly" on the one hand and "acting rationally" on the other, to ask whether it is rational to act morally is to ask whether it is rational to act rationally, and to ask whether it is moral to act rationally is to ask whether it is moral to act morally. Given such an identity of meaning, the sentences "It is rational to act morally" and "It is moral to act rationally" are analytically true, and the sentences "Sometimes it is not rational to act morally" and "Sometimes it is not moral to act rationally" are self-inconsistent and therefore necessarily false.

Perhaps the major difficulty confronting such a view is that the question "Is it rational to act morally?" and the sentence "It is rational to act morally" lose much, if not indeed all, the significance they appear to have for practice. Ordinarily when we ask such a question or make such a statement we do not intend to be asking whether it is rational to act rationally or to be saying that it is rational to act rationally. Instead, by asking such a question or by making such a statement we intend to raise a question or to make a statement that has some significance for practice. Such a question and such a statement can have such significance only if "acting morally" does not have the same meaning as "acting rationally". It might be true that one cannot act morally without acting rationally and that one cannot act rationally without acting morally. But if it is, one cannot show that it is simply by using "acting morally" in such a way that it has precisely the same meaning as "acting rationally". Instead, what one must show is that it is rational to act morally even though the concept of acting rationally is a different concept from the concept of acting morally. The question of whether it is rational to act morally and the claim that it is rational to do so can have significance for practice only if the concepts in question are distinct and not identical concepts.

There are two ways in which one might attempt to show that the concepts in question are distinct. One way is to develop an egoistic concept of rationality and a non-egoistic concept of morality. The other is to develop an egoistic concept of morality and a non-egoistic concept of rationality. Few, if indeed any, philosophers who have dealt with the problem have taken the second alternative. Perhaps the major reason this is so is that the conjunction of concepts it would require would be somewhat strange. The view it would involve is that although each person acts rightly if and only if he acts compatibly with the promotion of his interests, a person can act in this way without thereby acting rationally. On such a view a person could act rationally only by endeavoring to bring about something other than the promotion of his own interests, perhaps something such as the promotion of the interests of others, yet he could act rightly if and only if he acts compatibly with the promotion of his own interests. Such a view would seem to have acting rationally and acting rightly confused with one another. This is perhaps because we are more accustomed to thinking of rationality in egoistic terms and of acting rightly in non-egoistic terms. We are more accustomed, that is, to thinking that a person acts rationally only if he acts compatibly with the promotion of his own interests, rightly or morally only if he seeks to bring about something else, such as the promotion of the interests of others. This is perhaps reflected in the fact that we frequently hear the question "Is it rational to act morally or to be moral?" but rarely, if ever, hear the question "Is it moral to act rationally or to be rational?"

The fact that we frequently hear the first question but rarely, if ever, hear the second indicates, I believe, that those who raise the first question but rarely, if ever, raise the second assume that it is more important to act rationally than it is to act morally. If this is true, then since many philosophers have raised the first question and few have raised the second, it would seem that most philosophers think it more important to be rational than to be moral. Perhaps this is only to be expected, given that their prevailing professional concern is with rationality and being rational. If one does place greater value on being rational than on being moral, then one is more likely to be concerned (1) to justify acting morally by showing that it is required by, or at least compatible with, acting rationally than (2) to justify being rational by showing that it is required by, or at least compatible with, being moral. If, that is, one places greater value on acting rationally than on acting morally, one might well assume that the latter but not the former requires justification. Indeed, one might well assume that being rational neither needs to be nor can be justified rationally, on the ground that any attempt at such justification would suffer from a self-defeating circularity, given that any proposed justification must itself be rational if it is to be rationally acceptable. And if one does place greater value on acting rationally than on acting morally, one might also believe that the latter not only requires a rational justification in terms of the former but also that it can be given such a justification in a non-circular way, since there is nothing circular about justifying acting morally by showing that it is rational so to act.

Such a view, however, although it has been the prevailing view among philosophers who have discussed the relationship to one another of morality and rationality, is by no means the only possible view. Although such an answer has rarely been given by philosophers to the question "Is it rational to be moral?," one might well answer it by responding as follows. "No, it is not, but we nonetheless still ought to be moral and to act morally. Although acting rationally might be important, it is more important to act morally, and if one cannot be both fully rational and fully moral it is more important to be moral than to be rational. Moreover, if either of the two, acting morally and acting rationally, requires justification in terms of the other, it is the latter that requires justification in terms of the former, since it is more important that we act morally than it is that we act rationally. Instead, then, of asking and attempting to answer the question 'Is it rational to be moral?' which implies, or at least suggests, that it is more important that we be rational than that we be moral and that we can be justified in acting morally only if it can be shown that it is rational so to act, we ought instead to raise the question of whether it is moral to be rational. If it is, then we ought to be rational. If it is not, then, since being moral has greater value than being rational, we ought not to be rational. It would be good if there were never any conflict between the two, so that every morally right act is also a rational act and every rational act a morally right act. But if conflicts between acting morally and acting rationally ever do occur, and they do sometimes seem to occur, we ought always to sacrifice acting rationally for the sake of acting morally. If, therefore, we ask ourselves the question 'What, after all has been said and done, is so important about being rational?' we must answer that it is not very important at all when we compare the value of being rational with the value of being moral. It can be good to be rational only if our being rational does not prevent us from being moral."

Such a position, since it places greater value on being moral than on being rational, may be labeled the "moralist" position. The other position, since it places greater value on acting rationally than on acting morally, may be labeled the "rationalist" position. For the moralist we are justified in acting rationally only if doing so is compatible with acting rightly. For the rationalist we are justified in acting rightly only if doing so is compatible with acting rationally. Each position, however, assumes an egoistic view of rationality and a non-egoistic view of morality. It is because of this that for each position what seem to be conflicts between acting rationally and acting morally, between being rational and being moral, can and do occur. As these positions were characterized above, however, such conflicts cause less distress for the moralist than for the rationalist. This is because the moralist, in openly and unequivocally proclaiming that morality has greater value than rationality, is under less pressure to resolve such conflicts by attempting to show that they are only apparent and not real. Indeed, what may be referred to as the "extreme" moralist places little or no value on rationality and might even regard it with contempt when its claims seem to him to conflict with the claims of morality. He takes a kind of Kierkegaardian either/or attitude when such conflicts occur and might also even take a certain delight in their occurrence. By contrast, the more moderate moralist and the rationalist take a kind of Hegelian both/and attitude when such conflicts occur and endeavor to resolve them either by attempting to show, as the more moderate moralist does, that it is moral to be rational or by attempting to establish, as the rationalist does, that it is rational to be moral. Even so, the occurrence of at least apparent conflicts between acting morally and acting rationally is likely to cause greater discomfort for the rationalist than for even the moderate moralist. This is because one who openly places greater value on morality than on rationality is under less pressure to show that it is moral to be rational than one is under to show that it is rational to be moral if one, perhaps not so openly, places greater value on rationality than on morality.

2. Morality and Self-Interest

The rationalist is under the pressure in question because (1) he accepts an egoistic view of rationality and a non-egoistic view of morality and (2) wants to show that it is nonetheless rational, in an egoistic sense of "rationality," to act morally or to be moral, in a non-egoistic sense of "morality". What he must show is that each person can succeed in promoting his own long-term interests if and only if he acts in accordance with the requirements of a non-egoistic morality. He need not, however, show that one can promote one's long-term interests only by acting compatibly with all the requirements of any and every non-egoistic system. This would be an impossible task, since various of the requirements of any given non-egoistic system inevitably will conflict with certain of the requirements of any other such system. Indeed, a necessary condition of there being more than one such system is that at least some of the requirements of one system conflict with some of those of any other system. This is the case because if all the requirements of one system were identical with all those of another system, we should have only one system rather than two. A necessary condition, however, of any moral system's being non-egoistic is that it require either (1) that we do certain things, such as keeping promises, regardless of whether anyone's interests are thereby promoted or (2) that we act compatibly with the promotion of at least some of the interests of at least some of the people affected by our acts and omissions, regardless of whether our doing so is compatible with the promotion of various of our own interests, and even regardless of whether in certain cases our doing so requires us to sacrifice certain of our own interests.

The preceding characterization of non-egoistic moral systems makes the task of the rationalist most difficult indeed, if not in fact hopeless. What he must show is that the requirements of any acceptable non-egoistic moral system are such that each person can succeed in promoting his long-term interests if and only if, and only to the degree that, he acts in accordance with these requirements. Since, however, the requirements of such a system are such that from time to time conflicts can arise between complying with them and promoting certain of one's own interests, a high level of moral luck, indeed an impossibly high level of such luck, is required if each person is to avoid such conflicts in any situation in which he might find himself. Although the rationalist can admit that it is abstractly possible that such conflicts occur, he must nonetheless insist that in actuality each person can unfailingly avoid them. Such insistence is necessary because each person can in fact always succeed both in promoting his own long-term interests and in complying with the requirements of an acceptable non-egoistic moral system only if such conflicts can always be avoided. Since, however, they cannot, the task the rationalist sets himself is hopelessly unrealistic.

To some it might seem that the position of the rationalist is also inconsistent, since one cannot consistently hold both an egoistic view of rationality and a non-egoistic view of morality. He would, however, be inconsistent only if he took a position somewhat different from the one ascribed to him above. He would, that is, be inconsistent if he held both (1) that each person ought always to seek as an end the promotion of his own long-term interests and (2) that each person ought always to seek as an end to comply with the requirements of an acceptable non-egoistic moral system. Such a position would be inconsistent because the two ends to be sought sometimes conflict, and one cannot continue to seek both once one recognizes that the attainment of one would preclude the attainment of the other. I can, however, consistently (1) seek as an end the promotion of my own long-term interests and (2) seek, as a means to the attainment of this end, to comply with the requirements of an acceptable non-egoistic moral system. In this case no conflict between ends occurs because I would have only one end, not two. Instead, the conflict that occurs is between the end I seek and the means I seek in order to attain the end I have set myself. I am mistaken, but not inconsistent, in thinking that the attainment of my end requires that I employ the means I choose.

Given that conflicts do inevitably arise from time to time between promoting one's own long-term interests and complying with the requirements of an acceptable non-egoistic morality, the moderate moralist is confronted with the same difficulty that confronts the rationalist. This difficulty confronts them both because (1) each operates with an egoistic concept of rationality and a non-egoistic concept of morality and (2) each attempts to reconcile the two by showing that one can promote one's own long-term interests only by acting in accordance with the requirements of an acceptable non-egoistic moral system. The moderate moralist has no better chance than the rationalist of escaping the difficulty that confronts them both. In fact, the moderate moralist is in an even more uncomfortable position than the rationalist. This is so for the following reason. The rationalist places greater emphasis on rationality than on morality and regards the former as being more important than the latter. It is because of this that he endeavors to show that we are rationally justified in acting morally by arguing that we can promote our own long-term interests only by complying with the requirements of an acceptable non-egoistic morality. For the rationalist such compliance is required not as an end but rather as a means of promoting our long-term interests. Such an approach is not available to the moralist. As a moralist, he places greater emphasis and importance on morality than on rationality and therefore cannot consistently attempt to show that we ought to comply with the requirements of an acceptable non-egoistic morality because doing so is necessary as a means to an end consisting of the promotion of our long-term interests. Nor can the moralist plausibly argue that we ought to attempt to promote our long-term interests because doing so is necessary as a means to the end of complying with the requirements of an acceptable non-egoistic morality. Such an argument would treat as an end what the rationalist treats as a means and would treat as a means what the rationalist treats as an end and would have even less plausibility than the opposing rationalist position.

If the preceding is correct, both the position of the rationalist and that of the moderate moralist are unacceptable. Indeed, to some who see the difficulty confronting them both it might seem incomprehensible that they could also themselves see it and also believe that they can resolve it satisfactorily while continuing to accept an egoistic view of rationality and a non-egoistic view of morality. To some, in fact, it might seem that the difficulty in question is so manifest that the belief of the rationalist and the moderate moralist that they can resolve it satisfactorily without rejecting either their egoistic view of rationality or their non-egoistic view of morality can be accounted for only in either of two ways. On one account the belief in question is only an apparent and not an actual belief. On such an account the rationalist and the moderate moralist do not themselves believe that the difficulty in question can be resolved satisfactorily but want so much that others believe that it can be that they present what they secretly know to be spurious arguments in an effort to deceive others into believing that it can be resolved. On such an account, the rationalist and the moderate moralist believe that it is so important that others believe that the requirements of an egoistic view of rationality are completely compatible with, and indeed even coincide with, those of a non-egoistic view of morality that they are justified in resorting to spurious arguments in an effort to deceive others into holding the belief in question. On a second, perhaps more charitable, account the rationalist and the moderate moralist want so much themselves to believe in the truth of what they espouse that in some way they have succeeding in deceiving themselves into believing in the truth of what they say. Having succeeded in deceiving themselves into believing that the requirements of an egoistic view of rationality are compatible or coincide with those of a non-egoistic view of morality, they are perfectly sincere in their endeavor to lead others to believe what they themselves have succeeded in deceiving themselves into believing.

The insuperable difficulty confronting the rationalist and the moderate moralist is escaped by the extreme moralist. He, like the rationalist and the moderate moralist, accepts an egoistic view of rationality and a non-egoistic view of morality. Unlike, however, the rationalist and the moderate moralist, the extreme moralist recognizes that at times the requirements of an egoistic view of rationality conflict with those of a non-egoistic view of morality in such a way that it is impossible that both sets of requirements be satisfied. This, however, presents no serious problem for the extreme moralist, since he unequivocally maintains that in such cases of conflict the satisfaction of the requirements of an acceptable non-egoistic morality always takes precedence over the satisfaction of the requirements of egoistic rationality. For him it is more important to act rightly and to be moral than it is to be rational, so that if at times it is not rational to act rightly or to be moral we ought always to sacrifice acting rationally for the sake of acting rightly and being moral. Thus for the extreme moralist the existence of conflicts between the claims of rationality and those of morality does not even present a serious problem, much less an insuperable difficulty.

The rationalist, the moderate moralist, and the extreme moralist all hold an egoistic view of rationality and a non-egoistic view of morality. Another possible position, mentioned above, takes a non-egoistic view of rationality and an egoistic view of morality. Although this is a possible position, I do not know of anyone who has held it. All the same, it might be worthwhile to compare it with the first three positions. Whereas each of the first three positions holds that practical rationality consists in acting compatibly with the promotion of one's own long-term interests, the fourth position holds that it is morality, not rationality, that requires that we act in this way. And whereas each of the first three positions holds that morality requires, at least in certain situations, that we seek as an end something other than the promotion of our long-term interests, the fourth position holds that it is rationality, not morality, that requires this of us. Thus what rationality requires of us on the first three positions is what morality requires of us on the fourth position, and what morality requires of us on the first three positions is what rationality requires of us on the fourth position. This is the source of what was referred to above as the "strangeness" of the fourth position. It seems to confuse rationality with morality and morality with rationality. What each of the first three positions refers to as "rationality" the fourth refers to as "morality," and what the first three label "morality" the fourth labels "rationality".

The fact that the fourth position is a possible position, despite the fact that no one, as far as I know, has ever held it, suggests that the terms "rationality" and "morality" can be used in significantly different ways. This suggestion is supported by the existence of two other possible positions. One of these positions, since it holds both an egoistic view of practical rationality and an egoistic view of morality, may be labeled "unmitigated egoism". The other, since it holds both a non-egoistic view of practical rationality and a non-egoistic view of morality, may be labeled "unmitigated non-egoism". The unmitigated egoist maintains not only that practical rationality but also morality require that each person act compatibly with the promotion of his own long-term interests. The unmitigated non-egoist, on the other hand, maintains not only that morality but also practical rationality require that each person, at least at times, seek as an end something other than the promotion of his long-term interests, such as the promotion of the long-term interests of others affected by his acts and omissions. Thus although the unmitigated egoist and the unmitigated non-egoist disagree on what practical rationality and morality require of us, they agree that what one requires of us is identical with what the other requires. They both therefore escape the difficulty confronting those, whether they be rationalists or moralists, who hold an egoistic view of rationality and a non-egoistic view of morality (and also any who might hold an egoistic view of morality and a non-egoistic view of rationality). This difficulty, it will be recalled, is that what an egoistic (or a non-egoistic) view of rationality requires of us sometimes conflicts with what a non-egoistic (or egoistic) view of morality requires, so that at times it is impossible to act both rationally and morally. No such conflicts, however, can occur if what practical rationality requires of us is identical with what morality requires of us.

At least a partial recognition that this is so has perhaps been at least one of the considerations moving rationalists who hold an egoistic view of rationality and a non-egoistic view of morality to endeavor to show that it is rational to be moral or to act morally by attempting to establish that it is in our long-term interests so to be or to act. On such a view, acting in accordance with the requirements of non-egoistic morality is regarded as a means to an end consisting of the promotion of one's long-term interests. The difficulty, however, is that although such action might generally or usually be a means to the attainment of such an end, it is not always, and there are times when such an end can best be attained only by rejecting such a means. This the unmitigated egoist recognizes. He therefore recommends that we comply with the requirements of non-egoistic morality when it is in our interests to do so and that we ignore or violate these requirements when it is in our interests not to comply with them. Sometimes it might be in our long-term interests to deceive others into believing that we are complying with such requirements when in fact we are not, and sometimes it might not be. When it is we ought to engage in such deceit; when it is not we need not bother. In this way the unmitigated egoist, who recognizes that compliance with the requirements of non-egoistic morality is only sometimes, not always, necessary as a means to the promotion of one's long-term interests, escapes the difficulty in question.

This difficulty is also escaped by the unmitigated non-egoist. Since he holds a non-egoistic view of both rationality and morality, no conflict can occur between what rationality requires and what morality requires. Instead, those acts that satisfy the requirements of rationality also satisfy the requirements of morality and vice versa. Thus both unmitigated egoism and unmitigated non-egoism escape the difficulty confronting those, whether they be rationalists or moderate moralists, who hold an egoistic view of rationality and a non-egoistic view of morality. They also escape a certain difficulty confronting not only the rationalist and the moderate moralist but also the extreme moralist and the position that takes an egoistic view of morality and a non-egoistic view of rationality. The difficulty in question arises from the fact that each of these positions holds either (1) an egoistic view of rationality and a non-egoistic view of morality or (2) a non-egoistic view of rationality and an egoistic view of morality. By holding either (1) or (2), advocates of any of these positions must finally admit, once the implications of such positions are recognized, that certain acts can be rational without being morally right and that certain other acts can be morally right without being rational. Consistency therefore requires them to regard certain acts as being rational but morally wrong and certain other acts as being morally right but irrational. Confronted with such a consequence, they will also be confronted at times with situations in which they must choose between (1) acting rationally but wrongly and (2) acting rightly but irrationally. Regardless of which alternative we choose, in such situations we shall either act rationally but wrongly or rightly but irrationally. Thus regardless of how in such situations we act we must either (1) sacrifice morality for the sake of rationality or (2) sacrifice rationality for the sake of morality. Those who value both morality and rationality will find such situations uncomfortable and will also doubtless desire some means of escaping them.

If the argument presented above is sound, no such means is available as long as one continues to hold either (1) an egoistic view of rationality and a non-egoistic view of morality or (2) an egoistic view of morality and a non-egoistic view of rationality. Such a means, however, is readily provided by accepting either (1) an egoistic view both of rationality and of morality or (2) a non-egoistic view of both. One cannot, however, consistently accept both (1) and (2), which is to say that one cannot consistently accept both unmitigated egoism and unmitigated non-egoism. One or the other of these two positions might be acceptable, but it is impossible that both be. The question therefore arises of which of the two we ought to adopt. This question cannot be answered satisfactorily simply by assuming that rationality requires us to accept unmitigated egoism. Such an answer would beg the question at issue by assuming that an egoistic view of rationality is the only acceptable view. We would be no more justified in making this assumption than we would be in assuming that the only acceptable view of rationality is some non-egoistic view. Nor is there any antecedent impartial concept of practical rationality that is neither egoistic nor non-egoistic to which we can make an appeal.

If, however, we cannot assume either an egoistic or a non-egoistic view of rationality without begging the question at issue between unmitigated egoism and unmitigated non-egoism, and if there is no antecedent impartial concept of practical rationality that is neither egoistic nor non-egoistic, then it might seem that the issue at stake between these two positions cannot be settled by showing that one is rational and the other irrational. Such a conclusion, however, would be reached too quickly and would seem to assume that there is no other way in which one of the contending positions can be shown to be rational and the other irrational. There is, I shall seek to show, another way. It consists essentially in reversing the order assumed by many who have raised and endeavored to answer the question, "Is it rational to be moral?" Instead of attempting to show that practical rationality requires that we accept either (1) an egoistic moral position or (2) a non-egoistic moral position, the procedure to be employed is to endeavor to show that morality requires that we accept either (1) an egoistic view of practical rationality or (2) a non-egoistic view of such rationality. Instead, that is, of antecedently assuming either an egoistic or a non-egoistic view of practical rationality and tailoring our view of morality to fit the view of rationality we antecedently assume, the procedure we ought instead to follow is to tailor our view of practical rationality to fit the view of morality we adopt. Since, however, the issue at stake is that of whether we ought to accept an egoistic or a non-egoistic view of morality, we cannot begin by assuming without argument that one of these views is acceptable and the other unacceptable. Such a procedure would amount to begging the question against the position we antecedently reject in advance of any argument. What we must instead endeavor to do is to give non-question-begging arguments for accepting one of these views of morality and rejecting the other.

If by means of moral argument we can establish that some kind of egoistic morality is morally preferable to any kind of non-egoistic morality, we can thereby show that an egoistic view of practical rationality is preferable to a non-egoistic view. But if by means of moral argument we can establish that some sort of non-egoistic morality is morally preferable to any sort of egoistic morality, we can thereby show that a non-egoistic view of practical rationality is preferable to an egoistic view. If this is correct, then the question of whether we ought to accept some egoistic or instead some non-egoistic view of morality cannot properly be answered by arguing that practical rationality requires that we adopt one view rather than the other. Instead, we can properly determine what practical rationality requires of us only by determining first, by means of moral argument, whether we ought to adopt an egoistic or a non-egoistic view of morality. It is only by means of such moral argument that the abstract and relatively empty concept of practical rationality can be given adequate content.

3. The Inadequacy of Egoism

Let us begin by asking whether there are any good reasons for accepting an egoistic morality. If what was said above is correct, it will not do to say that we ought to do so because it is rational so to do. Nor will it do to say that it is so evident that we ought to do so that there is no need to supply reasons for so doing. This, I think, will be evident if we put the question in a more explicit way. Why ought each person to seek as an ultimate end only the promotion of his own interests, regardless of the effect on others? Why, that is, does a person act rightly if and only if, and only to the degree that, he acts compatibly with the promotion of his own welfare, regardless of the effect on others? The phrase "regardless of the effect on others" is important. It indicates that the fundamental contention of the egoist is that each person ought to seek as an ultimate end nothing other than the promotion of his own good and that each person acts rightly if and only if he acts compatibly with the attainment of this end. The egoist recognizes that there are situations in which a person can act compatibly with the promotion of his own interests only if he acts compatibly with the promotion of the interests of certain other people and that in such situations a person acts rightly only if he does the latter. The promotion of the interests of others, however, can never for the egoist be morally required as an end but instead can be required only as a means to the promotion of one's own interests.

There are two kinds of reasons the egoist might supply in support of his position, one of which may be labeled, perhaps somewhat misleadingly, "deontological," and the other, again perhaps somewhat misleadingly, "teleological". According to the deontological reason, acting in the way the egoist recommends is simply right in itself, regardless of whether such action does in fact succeed in promoting one's own long-term interests and regardless also of the effect on others. To say, however, that acting in the way the egoist recommends is simply right in itself, independently of its consequences, would seem to amount only to saying that the rightness of such action is evident in itself. The rightness of such action does not, however, in fact seem to be evident. Indeed, there are acts of other specific sorts, such as keeping a promise or rendering aid, the performance of which in certain situations might not contribute to the promotion of one's own interests, yet the performance of which in such situations would be more evidently right than the omission of such acts for the sake of promoting one's own interests. If so, then it seems that the egoist cannot supply adequate support for his position by giving "deontological" reasons, which in any event would not be reasons in any acceptable sense of "reason".

We turn now to the question of whether the egoist would fare any better by giving "teleological" reasons in support of his position. This he would do if he were to argue that each person ought to seek as an ultimate end only the promotion of his own long-term interests because the attainment of one's long-term interests is intrinsically good. It is because the attainment of my long-term interests would be intrinsically good that I ought to act compatibly with their promotion, and it is because the attainment of your long-term interests would be intrinsically good that you ought to act compatibly with their promotion. It would seem, however, that if the fact that the attainment of my long-term interests would be intrinsically good gives me a reason for acting compatibly with their promotion, then, as Moore argued long ago, it also gives you a reason for doing so if you can.[2] Similarly, if the fact that the attainment of your long-term interests would be intrinsically good gives you a reason for acting compatibly with their promotion, then it also gives me a reason for doing so if I can. If, in short, the fact that the existence of something, x, would be intrinsically good gives one person a reason for acting compatibly with its existence, then it also gives any other person in a position to do so a reason for doing so.

The "teleological" egoist might attempt to evade this argument by assuming something akin to a solipsistic or quasi-solipsistic position and maintaining that it is only the attainment of *his* long-term interests, not those of any other person, that would be intrinsically good. If, however, the fact that the attainment of his long-term interests would be intrinsically good gives him a reason for acting compatibly with their attainment, then, as before, it also provides anyone else capable of promoting his interests a reason for doing so. This would mean that not only the egoist but anyone else who has any dealings with him acts rightly only if they act compatibly with the promotion of *his* interests. It is hard, however, to say the least, to see why only the attainment of the interests of the egoist, and not also the attainment of the interests of others, would be intrinsically good. Thus suppose that I am the egoist in question, that I believe that my long-term interests consist in my having pleasant experiences and not having unpleasant experiences, and that I believe that my pleasant experiences, and only *my* pleasant experiences, are intrinsically good and that my painful experiences, and only *my* painful experiences, are intrinsically bad. The pleasant and painful experiences of others, I believe, are neither intrinsically good nor intrinsically bad.

Such beliefs could not possibly be true. For one thing, just as my pleasant experiences are not pleasant because they are mine, so also they are not good because they are mine. Similarly, just as my painful experiences are not painful because they are mine, so also they are not bad because they are mine. If it were their being mine that makes my pleasant experiences pleasant, then their being mine would also make my painful experiences pleasant, since they too are mine. But my painful experiences are not pleasant. Similarly, if my painful experiences were painful because they are mine, then my pleasant experiences would also be painful, since they too are mine. Yet my pleasant experiences are not painful. Nor can my pleasant experiences be good and my painful experiences be bad because they are mine. If my pleasant experiences were good because they are mine, then my painful experiences would also be good, since they too are mine. Similarly, if my painful experiences were bad because they are mine, then my pleasant experiences would also be bad, since they too are mine. If my pleasant experiences are good it is not because they are mine that they are good but rather because they are pleasant, and if my painful experiences are bad it is not because they are mine that they are bad but rather because they are painful. But if my pleasant experiences are good not because they are mine but because they are pleasant, and if my painful experiences are bad not because they are mine but because they are painful, then the pleasant experiences of anyone, and not only mine, are good, and the painful experiences of anyone, and not only mine, are bad. If, that is, their pleasantness makes pleasant experiences good, and if their painfulness makes painful experiences bad, then pleasant experiences are good and painful experiences bad regardless of whose experiences they are. This, however, does not mean that every pleasant experience necessarily is good or that every painful experience necessarily is bad. Whether a pleasant or a painful experience is good or bad depends upon the nature of whatever it is that the person who has the experience finds pleasant or painful. It is intrinsically bad to be pleased that something intrinsically bad, such as unmerited suffering, exists, and intrinsically good to be pained or displeased that something intrinsically bad exists.

Confronted with such objections, the "teleological" egoist might respond in the following way. "It is true that neither my pleasant nor my painful experiences are good or bad simply because they are mine. Nor are my pleasant experiences good simply because they are pleasant and my painful experiences bad simply because they are painful. Instead, the pleasantness of my pleasant experiences is only a necessary, not a sufficient, condition of their being good. Similarly, the painfulness of my painful experiences is only a necessary, not a sufficient, condition of their being bad. Likewise, although their being mine is not a sufficient condition of their being good or bad, it is a necessary condition, since if they were not mine they would be neither good nor bad. There are thus two conditions that must be satisfied if my pleasant experiences are to be good. One is that they be pleasant; the other is that they be mine. Although neither of these conditions taken by itself is sufficient to make my pleasant experiences good, each is nonetheless necessary, and the two, taken together, suffice to make my pleasant experiences good. Precisely similar considerations, with of course the obvious necessary changes, apply to the badness of my painful experiences."

Such a response would not be of much help to the "teleological" egoist. He might by his use of "my" and "mine" mean only that a necessary condition of the goodness or badness of his experiences is that they be his. This would be unobjectionable, since a necessary condition of the goodness or badness of his experiences is indeed that they be his. If, that is, the experiences in question were not his but instead experiences of some other person, the goodness or badness of the experiences in question would not be the goodness or badness of his experiences but instead would be the goodness or badness of experiences of some other person. If, however, by his use of "my" and "mine" he intends to say that a necessary condition of the goodness or badness of *any* experience is that it be his, then what he says is objectionable, since it would amount to saying that no experiences of any other person can be good or bad. If, however, a necessary condition of the goodness or badness of *any* experience is that it be his experience, then he must have some feature no one else has by virtue of which only his experiences, not those of anyone else, can be good or bad. It is hard, however, to see what such a feature would be. It cannot be simply his being himself, since every other person, also being himself, has the property of being himself or of being identical with himself.

Another way in which the "teleological" egoist might attempt to defend his position consists in or involves a rejection of the concepts of intrinsic goodness and badness. On such a view nothing is or can be good or bad in itself. Instead, to be good or bad is to be good or bad for someone. Thus the promotion of my interests is neither good nor bad in itself but instead is good for me, and the promotion of your interests also is neither good nor bad in itself but rather is good for you. At least two things are wrong with such a view. The first is that it provides no support of the position of the egoist. This is because the promotion of your interests as well as the promotion of mine can be good both for me and also for you in the sense that I as well as you take an interest in or desire the promotion both of your interests and also of mine. This leads to the second thing wrong with the view in question. To say that something, *x*, is good for someone can mean only either of two things. It might mean that it is beneficial for him. In this sense of the expression, an injection of insulin can be good for a diabetic person but bad for someone who is not diabetic. The fact, however, that something can be good for someone in this sense of the expression provides no support for the egoist, since the admission that various things are good for various people in the sense in question is compatible with a rejection of egoism. The second thing that might be meant by saying that something is good for someone is that he regards it as being or believes it to be good. Something can be good for someone in this sense without being good for him in the previous sense and vice versa. Thus someone who is not diabetic can believe that injections of insulin are good for diabetic people but not good for himself, and injections of insulin can be good for a diabetic person even though he does not believe that they are. If I am diabetic and you are not, injections of insulin can be good for me and bad for you in the sense that they would be beneficial for me but harmful for you, yet also good for you and bad for me in the sense that you believe them to be beneficial for me and I believe them to be harmful for me (and perhaps also for anyone else, regardless of whether he be diabetic). The fact, however, that various things can be good or bad for various people in either or both of these senses is compatible with the view that various things are intrinsically good or bad regardless of whether they are good or bad for anyone in either of the senses in question. From the fact, therefore, that various things are good or bad in either or both of the senses in question it does not follow that nothing is intrinsically good or bad.[3]

Still another way in which the egoist might attempt to eliminate the concepts of intrinsic goodness and badness is to replace them with the concepts of liking and disliking. One need not be an egoist if one is to replace the first pair of concepts with the second pair. If, however, the first pair of concepts can in fact be successfully replaced by the second, then arguments against egoism that use the concept of intrinsic goodness and badness cannot succeed. The question therefore arises of whether the first pair of concepts can in fact be replaced successfully by the second.

On the view in question, no liking or disliking, and nothing liked or disliked, is intrinsically good or bad, so that no liking or disliking, and nothing liked or disliked, can be intrinsically better or worse than any other liking or disliking and than anything else liked or disliked. Instead, each liking and disliking, and each thing liked or disliked, is in itself indifferent. On such a view likings and dislikings, and things liked and disliked, take the place of, and have the same function as, intrinsically good and bad things. Rather than things being extrinsically good or bad because of their relationships to intrinsically good and bad things, they are extrinsically good or bad because of their relationships to likings and dislikings and to things liked or disliked. And rather than preferences, choices, and acts being rational or irrational because of their relationships to intrinsically good and bad things, they are rational or irrational because of their relationships to likings and dislikings and to things like or disliked.

One of the major difficulties confronting such a view, as was suggested in the first chapter, is that not only things liked and disliked, but also likings and dislikings, can be intrinsically good or bad, depending upon the nature of whatever it is that is liked or disliked. If the nature of something liked is such that the thing liked is intrinsically good, then liking it is also intrinsically good and disliking it intrinsically bad; and if the nature of something disliked is such that the thing disliked is intrinsically bad, then disliking it is intrinsically good and liking it intrinsically bad. Now if anything at all is intrinsically good or bad, unmerited suffering is certainly so, regardless of whose suffering it happens to be. If anyone understands the meaning of the expressions "intrinsically good," "intrinsically bad," and "unmerited suffering," yet denies or doubts that unmerited suffering is intrinsically bad, I do not know what would convince him that it is indeed bad other than, perhaps, his undergoing such suffering himself. It is because such suffering is intrinsically bad that anyone's liking another's undergoing it is itself intrinsically bad and that anyone's disliking another's undergoing it is itself intrinsically good. Although someone's liking or disliking another's undergoing such suffering might also be extrinsically good or bad, depending upon what the consequences of such liking and disliking are, such liking and disliking are still intrinsically good or bad regardless of what their consequences might be. Since, then, likings and dislikings can themselves be intrinsically good or bad, the concepts of intrinsically good and intrinsically bad cannot be replaced with the concepts of liking and disliking.

4. Unmitigated Non-Egoism

If the argument of the previous section is acceptable, then unmitigated egoism is unacceptable. And since the positions referred to above as rationalism, moderate moralism, and extreme moralism, and the position that holds an egoistic view of morality and a non-egotistic view of rationality, are all confronted with various of the difficulties indicated above, unmitigated non-egoism remains as the only acceptable alternative. The difficulties confronting the other positions issue from the fact that they all accept either an egoistic view of practical rationality and a non-egoistic view of morality or an egoistic view of morality and a non-egoistic view of such rationality. Unmitigated non-egoism escapes these difficulties precisely because it holds a non-egoistic view of both practical rationality and morality. It recognizes that there is no antecedent impartial concept of practical rationality that is neither egoistic nor non-egoistic, that the relatively empty concept of practical rationality can be given adequate content only by adopting an egoistic or a non-egoistic view of morality, and that an egoistic morality is unacceptable. This means that the concept of practical rationality can be given adequate content only by adopting a non-egoistic view of morality, so that the only acceptable concept of practical rationality must also be non-egoistic.

I have given the position for which I have argued the ugly negative name "unmitigated non-egoism" rather than "unmitigated altruism" for the following reason. The latter name might suggest that each person acts rightly only if he acts compatibly with the promotion of the interests of others affected by his action, regardless of how his own interests are affected. Such a view, however, would ignore the fact that the agent who acts as well as those affected by his actions is a person and that the promotion of his interests as well as those of others has value. Because of this each person may rightly have as much concern for the promotion of his own interests as for the promotion of those of others. Just as each of us ought not to treat others as things to be used and manipulated solely for the sake of the promotion of one's own interests, so also no one ought to regard himself as a thing to be used by himself solely for the sake of the promotion of the interests of others. Just as others are persons the promotion of whose interests has value, so also I am a person the promotion of whose interests has value. Just as I would act wrongly by ignoring the interests of others, so also I would act wrongly by ignoring the promotion of my own interests. Thus just as practical rationality and morality require that I act compatibly with the promotion of the interests of others, so also they require that I act compatibly with the promotion of my own interests. Sometimes, of course, the promotion of the interests of others conflicts with the promotion of one's own interests. In such cases of conflict the interests of others sometimes have greater weight than mine have, and sometimes mine have greater weight. Sometimes it is hard to know which interests have greater weight—those of others or mine—and sometimes it might seem or indeed in fact be impossible to reach an impartial decision. Nonetheless, practical rationality and morality require that I seek, as far as possible, to promote my own interests only in those ways compatible with the promotion of the interests of those affected by my action. For the unmitigated non-egoist the promotion of each person's rational self-interest consists precisely in acting in this way.

Those who hold an egoistic view of practical rationality or of morality usually regard a person's interests as consisting in having various goods such as health, bodily beauty, intelligence, wealth, power, and pleasant experiences. But, as was indicated in chapter 6, it is possible that a person have various of these goods without being a good person. Yet, as was also indicated there, most of us also have some concern about whether we are good persons, as is evidenced by the fact that we do not like to regard ourselves as or to acknowledge that we are bad persons. This indicates that most of us are concerned not only to have goods of various sorts but also to be good. This perhaps can be put by saying that most of us regard our good as consisting not only of having goods of various sorts but also in being good. We can, however, be good persons only by having various of the moral virtues and using them to act as we are required by unmitigated non-egoism to act. If so, then the promotion of what may be referred to as one's complete good requires not only that one act compatibly with one's having various goods but also with one's being a good person. For the unmitigated non-egoist it is in one's interest not only to have goods but also to be a good person.

The position that a person's good consists not only in his having goods of various sorts but also in his having various of the moral virtues in a degree sufficient to make him a good person is by no means original. It can be found in Plato and Aristotle, in the biblical view that it profits a man nothing to gain the world at the cost of losing his soul, and in Kant's view that the complete good is blessedness, which is a union of happiness and good will. Although the man who gains the world at the cost of losing his soul does thereby come to have a certain good, namely the world, the cost he pays to gain it, namely his being a bad person, is so great that he profits nothing. Although a happy bad person does have a certain good, namely happiness, he lacks another good, namely being a good person. Moreover, the non-egoistic view of practical rationality advanced here, though at odds with egoistic views of such rationality prevalent in much recent moral philosophy, is also by no means original. Although not identical with Kant's view of practical rationality, it nonetheless, like his, is non-egoistic and tailored to meet the requirements of a non-egoistic view of morality. That it is so tailored cannot reasonably be found objectionable, given the argument by means of which it has been arrived at and given also that there is no antecedent impartial concept of practical rationality that is neither egoistic nor non-egoistic.

Chapter 9

Attitudes toward the Indifferent

In this chapter we turn to treat a topic that has not received the attention it merits. This is the topic of the value of different attitudes that might be taken toward things that are neither intrinsically good nor intrinsically bad but rather intrinsically indifferent. If, as subjectivists in value theory hold, nothing is either intrinsically good or intrinsically bad, then everything is indifferent, including all likings, dislikings, and indifferences, so that no liking or disliking of or being indifferent toward something, regardless of what it might be, would be either good or bad but instead would be indifferent. On the other hand, the view prevalent among late medieval scholastics to the effect that the concept of good, like that of being, is a transcendental concept and thus is applicable to everything that has being, would seem to imply that there are no indifferent things. If there were none, the question of which attitudes that might be taken toward the indifferent are appropriate would not arise or at least would have little or no importance for practice. Some things, however, do seem to be intrinsically good, others intrinsically bad, and others intrinsically indifferent. To avoid such repeated uses of "intrinsically," in the remainder of this chapter the terms "good," "bad," and "indifferent," unless otherwise indicated, will be used to indicate intrinsic rather than extrinsic goodness, badness, and indifference.

1. Likings and Dislikings of Good and Bad Objects

We begin with a brief review of some points that are at least implicit in what was said earlier. A first-order liking is good if its object is good, bad if its object is bad. A first-order disliking, on the other hand, is good if its object is bad, bad if its object is good. Precisely similar considerations apply to second-order likings and dislikings. Such a liking is good if the first-order liking or disliking that is its object is good, bad if the corresponding first-order liking or disliking is bad. Thus my liking my liking of something good is itself good, as is also my liking your disliking something bad; and your liking my liking something bad is itself bad, as is also your liking your disliking something good. Similarly, a second-order disliking is good if the first-order liking or disliking that is its object is bad, bad if the corresponding first-order liking or disliking is good. Thus your disliking your liking something bad is good, as is also your disliking my disliking something good; and my disliking your liking something good is bad, as is also my disliking my disliking something bad. Thus just as to like a good and to dislike a bad thing is good and to like a bad and to dislike a good thing is bad, so also to like a good and to dislike a bad liking or disliking is good and to like a bad and to dislike a good liking or disliking is bad.[1]

To some it might seem that the goodness or badness of an object, whether it be the object of a first-order or a second-order liking or disliking, does not suffice to make the liking of a good and the disliking of a bad object good. Instead, it might be thought, the liking of a good and the disliking of a bad object is good only if the good object is liked to the degree to which it is good and the bad disliked to the degree to which it is bad. On such a view, the liking of a good object is bad if the degree to which it is liked is greater or less than the degree to which it merits being liked, and, similarly, the disliking of a bad object is bad if the degree to which it is disliked is greater or less than the degree to which it merits being disliked. Thus on such a view it is not sufficient that the object liked be good or that the object disliked be bad if the liking and the disliking are themselves to be good. Instead, it is also necessary that the good object be liked to the precise degree to which it is good, neither more nor less, and, similarly, that the bad object be disliked to the precise degree to which it is bad, neither more nor less.

If such a view were correct, the symmetry suggested above between the goodness of liking good and disliking bad objects on the one hand and the badness of liking bad and disliking good objects on the other would not exist. This is the case because the view in question does not deny that it is bad to like bad and to dislike good objects, regardless of the degree to which bad objects are liked and good objects disliked. It does not deny, that is, that the badness of an object suffices to make liking it bad or that the goodness of an object suffices to make disliking it bad, regardless of the degree to which a bad object is liked or a good object disliked. It would, however, if correct, make it much harder for likings of good objects and dislikings of bad objects to be good. Indeed, given the great difficulty of liking good and disliking bad objects to the precise degree to which they merit being liked or disliked, very few indeed of such likings and dislikings would be good. Although they would not be as bad as likings of bad and dislikings of good objects, few would be good because few are proportioned precisely to the goodness or badness of their objects. It is hard enough for most of us to like only good and to dislike only bad objects, and to require of us not only that we like only good and dislike only bad objects but also that we like and dislike them neither more nor less than they merit being liked or disliked is to impose upon us a requirement that few, if any, of us have much chance of satisfying.

Fortunately, however, the view in question does not seem to be correct. We can agree that it is better to like good and to dislike bad objects neither more nor less than they merit being liked or disliked than it is to like the good and to dislike the bad either more or less than they merit. From this, however, it does not follow that liking good and disliking bad objects either more or less than they merit are not good. Instead, all that follows is that such likings and dislikings are not as good as those that are proportioned precisely to the goodness or badness of their objects. This is only an instance of the principle, if it may be called such, that from the fact that something, a, is better than something else, b, it does not follow that b is not good. Something, b, can still be good even though it is not as good as, and is therefore worse than, something else, a. Similarly, from the fact that something, a, is better than something else, b, it does not follow that a is good. Instead, a and b might both be bad, with a not being as bad as b. If a is better than b, it is good to like a more than b, or to dislike a less than b, regardless of whether a and b are both good, both bad, or a good and b bad. Given that a is better than b and that a and b are both good, liking each is still good even though liking b more than a is bad. Given, however, that a is better than b and that a and b are both bad, liking either is still bad even though liking a more than b, or disliking a less than b, is good. But if a is good and b bad, liking a and disliking b is good, disliking a and liking b bad, regardless of whether they are liked or disliked to the precise degree to which they merit being liked or disliked.

It is possible, however, that a good object be liked far more than it merits being liked and that a bad object be disliked far more than it merits being disliked. Although such excessive liking and disliking would be bad, the liking of the good object, taken simply as a liking of a good object completely in abstraction from the fact that it is an excessive liking, would be good, as would the disliking of the bad object, taken simply as a disliking of a bad object completely in abstraction from the fact that it is an excessive disliking. Thus liking good and disliking bad objects, insofar as they are simply the liking of good and the disliking of bad objects, are both good, even though the excessive liking of a good or disliking of a bad object are both bad, taken as excessive. They are bad because they are excessive, not because one is simply the liking of a good object, the other a disliking of a bad object. To say, however, that a good object is liked excessively or that a bad object is disliked excessively is not equivalent to saying simply that they are not liked or disliked to the precise degree to which they merit being liked or disliked. It is instead to say that they are liked or disliked far more than they merit being liked or disliked. Even though an object be liked or disliked somewhat more or less than it merits being liked or disliked, such liking or disliking is not necessarily excessive. The line between (1) simply liking or disliking an object somewhat more or less than it merits being liked or disliked and (2) liking or disliking an object excessively, however, is a line that it is by no means always easy to draw.[2]

If the preceding is correct, liking good and disliking bad objects are good, disliking good and liking bad objects bad, regardless of whether the object is liked or disliked to the precise degree to which it merits being liked or disliked. Although to like a good or to dislike a bad object to the precise degree to which it merits being liked or disliked is better than liking or disliking it either more or less than it merits, the latter liking or disliking is still good. Similarly, although to like a bad object, a, more than an even worse object, b, is better than liking b more than a, and although to dislike a good object, x, more than a better object, y, is better than disliking y more than x, liking a and disliking x are still bad. In the case of good and bad objects, whether a liking or a disliking is good or bad is determined by whether the object liked or disliked is itself good or bad, not by whether it is better or worse than some other object that might be liked or disliked either more or less than it. Indeed, whether one object, a, is better than another, b, is determined by the nature each has independently of the other. Their independent nature, that is, determines not only whether they are good or bad but also whether one is better than the other. Thus if either is good or bad, it is because of the nature each has independently of the other, not because one is better or worse than the other. If either is good then liking it is also good and disliking it bad even though it not be as good as the other, and if either is bad then liking it is also bad and disliking it good even though it not be as bad as the other.

2. Extreme Views of Attitudes toward the Indifferent

In addition to first-order likings and dislikings, there are also what may be referred to as first-order "indifferences". Just as the object of a first-order liking or disliking is something liked or disliked that is not itself a liking, a disliking, or a being indifferent, so also the object of a first-order indifference is something toward which one is indifferent that is not itself a liking, a disliking, or a being indifferent. Thus just as first-order likings and dislikings require intentional objects that are liked or disliked, so also first-order indifferences require intentional objects toward which one is indifferent. Given that it is good to like good and to dislike bad objects and bad to like bad and to dislike good objects, a first-order indifference is bad if the object toward which one is indifferent is either good or bad. If, however, the object is neither good nor bad it is indifferent. Three possible attitudes might be taken toward an indifferent object. One might like it, one might dislike it, or one might be indifferent toward it. The question confronting us is this: Are such attitudes toward indifferent things themselves good, bad, or indifferent?

There are various possible answers to our question. Some may be labeled "extreme," others "moderate". The extreme answers maintain that any instance of liking, disliking, or being indifferent toward an indifferent thing is itself one, but only one, of the three—good, bad, or indifferent. On this view (1) any instance of liking an indifferent things is one, but only one, of the three—good, bad, or indifferent; (2) any instance of disliking an indifferent thing is one, but only one, of the three—good, bad, or indifferent; and (3) any instance of being indifferent to an indifferent thing is one, but only one, of the three—good, bad, or indifferent. The moderate answers, on the other hand, maintain (1) that some instances of liking an indifferent thing are good, some bad, and some indifferent; (2) that some instances of disliking an indifferent thing are good, some bad, and some indifferent; and (3) that some instances of being indifferent toward an indifferent thing are good, some bad, and some indifferent. Thus on the moderate answer some instances of liking, some instances of disliking, and some instances of being indifferent toward indifferent things are good, some bad, and some indifferent. We turn first to consider the extreme answers.

The extreme answer that most will perhaps find to have the greatest initial plausibility is the view (1) that any instance of being indifferent toward an indifferent thing is good and (2) that any instance of liking or disliking an indifferent thing is either bad or indifferent. In support of such a view one might argue that if a thing is indifferent the appropriate attitude to take toward it is to be indifferent toward it and thus neither to like nor to dislike it. If so, then being indifferent toward it is good and liking or disliking it bad or at least indifferent. A proponent of this view might also argue that if the appropriate attitude to take toward an indifferent thing is an attitude of indifference, then liking or disliking such a thing, rather than being indifferent, must instead be bad. If, that is, the appropriate attitude to take toward such a thing is one of indifference, then liking or disliking it would be inappropriate and therefore bad.

A second possible extreme answer to our question is that an attitude of indifference toward an indifferent thing is itself indifferent, liking or disliking it both bad. Although liking or disliking an indifferent thing are both bad, being indifferent toward it can be neither good nor bad but instead must itself be indifferent. This answer, however, does not have much plausibility and would seem to rest on the assumption that if a thing is indifferent indifference toward it is also indifferent. From the fact, however, that something is indifferent it does not follow that indifference toward it must also be indifferent. If, then, we had to choose between the first and second answers, the first would seem to be preferable. It would seem, that is, to be more plausible, at least initially, to hold that a thing's being indifferent makes an attitude of indifference toward it good rather than indifferent.

A third possible extreme answer is that an attitude of indifference toward an indifferent thing, rather than being good or indifferent, is instead bad. There would, however, seem to be little, if anything, to recommend such a view. The view that an attitude of indifference toward an indifferent thing is good, given that the thing toward which one is indifferent is itself indifferent, does have at least some initial plausibility. But the view that such an attitude would be bad seems to have no plausibility whatever. If such an attitude would be bad, then, given that there are only three possible attitudes one can take toward an indifferent thing—one of liking, one of disliking, or one of indifference—any attitude one could take toward an indifferent thing would be bad unless either liking or disliking it were either good or indifferent. If, however, neither liking nor disliking an indifferent thing can be either good or indifferent, and if being indifferent toward such a thing is bad, then any possible attitude one could take would be bad. Although one of these attitudes might be better and one worse than the other two, all would be bad. Given that there are indifferent things, this would be a bad, or at least an undesirable, outcome. Given also that it is appropriate or good to dislike bad things, it would then be appropriate or good to dislike any of the possible attitudes one could or does take toward indifferent things.

A fourth possible extreme answer is that the appropriate attitude to take toward indifferent things is to like them all. On such a view liking indifferent things is good, disliking or being indifferent to them bad. The proponent of such a view could readily admit that it is better to like good than to like indifferent things and also that it is inappropriate or bad to like indifferent things as much as or more than good things. But, as we have seen, from the fact that *a* is better than *b* it does not follow that *b* is bad or indifferent. The present view, despite what probably will seem to most to be its initial implausibility, does have a certain attractiveness. For one thing, a person who likes all the indifferent things of which he has experience or knowledge would appear thereby to manifest a greater generosity of spirit than does the person who likes only good things and remains indifferent to all indifferent things. Such generosity would be especially evident in the attitude such a person would adopt toward other persons, who by no means would always merit the love (if we may move from liking to loving) he, through his magnanimity, would bear them. Unlike the person who endeavors to love others only to the precise degree to which they merit being loved, the magnanimous person, rather than calculatingly attempting to apportion his love to others so that he loves them neither more nor less than they merit being loved, would love them more than he would doubtless do were he to engage in such precise calculations of the merits of others. The love he bears others, rather than being the result of something like a precise mathematical calculation, would instead be or at least resemble what is sometimes referred to as Christian love.

A second source of the attractiveness of the present view is that, given that there seem to be more indifferent than good or bad things, the person who likes all the indifferent as well as all the good things of which he has experience or knowledge would probably lead a happier life than the person who likes only good things. If, that is, a person is likely to lead a happier life if more rather than less of the things he likes exist, a person who likes indifferent as well as good things is likelier to lead a happier life than a person who likes only good things. To this one might respond that a person who likes bad as well as good and indifferent things would be even more likely to lead a happier life, given that the number of good, bad, and indifferent things is greater than the number of good and indifferent things. To this the reply is that although such a person might be likely to lead a happier life he would not lead a better life, given that it is bad to like bad things.

Being happy and having a happy life is one thing, being good and having a good life another. Other things being equal, a person is happy and has a happy life (1) to the degree to which the things of which he has experience or knowledge are things he likes and are not things he is either indifferent toward or dislikes and (2) the more he likes the things he likes and the less he dislikes the things he dislikes. But a person is good and leads a good life, other things being equal, not only to the degree to which he is happy and has a happy life but also to the degree to which he does not like bad and dislike good things. Although one person, Peter, who likes many bad and dislikes many good things, might be happier and have a happier life than another, Paul, who likes far fewer bad and dislikes far fewer good things, Paul is a better person and has a better life than Peter. If this be so, then a happy person can be a good person and a happy life a good life only to the degree to which the person in question, who is any person, does not like bad and dislike good things and who acts accordingly. Given, however, that two persons and their lives are otherwise equally good but one is happier, the happier life but not the happier person is better than the other. This means that a distinction must be drawn between a person and his life. Although being happier makes one of two otherwise equally good lives better than the other, it does not make one of two equally good persons better than the other.

If the preceding is correct, then although the person who likes all the things of which he has experience or knowledge, regardless of whether they be good, bad, or indifferent, might be likelier to be happier and to have a happier life than the person who likes only good and indifferent things, he has his happier life only at the cost of being a worse person and leading a worse life than the other person. This is the case even though liking all the indifferent things of which one has experience or knowledge is not itself good, since even if such liking is not good it still would not seem to be bad, as is the liking of bad things. But even if liking all indifferent things is not intrinsically good, it still would be extrinsically good if it led to greater happiness than would liking only good things and had no other consequences the negative value of which would be greater than the positive value of the increased happiness to which it leads. Given that such liking would be likely to be extrinsically good in the way indicated, endeavoring to develop it would also seem to be extrinsically good. If so, then the fourth possible extreme answer to our question is perhaps not as implausible as it might initially appear to be.

A fifth possible extreme answer to our question is that it is good to dislike all the indifferent things of which one has experience or knowledge. Given that many, perhaps most, of the things of which we have experience or knowledge are indifferent, disliking all such indifferent things would lead to far greater unhappiness for the person who succeeded in doing so than would be likely to result if he disliked only the bad things of which he has experience or knowledge. "Sufficient unto the day is the evil thereof," and the unhappiness issuing upon our disliking the bad things of which we have experience or knowledge would seem to exist in a quantity sufficiently great without the addition of the unhappiness that would result from our disliking indifferent as well as bad things. Moreover, the unhappiness issuing from a person's disliking the existence of bad things does not seem to be completely bad, whereas that issuing from one's disliking the existence of indifferent things would seem to be. If it is good to dislike the existence of bad things (and such dislike does seem to be good), and if the natural issue of such dislike is some degree of unhappiness over the existence of such things, then such unhappiness is fitting or appropriate and, as such, is itself good or at least, if not good, is not as bad as it would be if it were not appropriate. Rather, however, than its seeming to be good to dislike the existence of indifferent things, it seems instead to be bad, or at least to be indifferent. If so, then the unhappiness that would naturally issue from the existence of the indifferent things one dislikes would not be appropriate and therefore would lack the goodness it would have were it appropriate. Lacking such goodness, it would seem not to be good at all and, indeed, to be intrinsically bad.

We have examined briefly five extreme answers to the question of whether it is good, bad, or neither good nor bad to like, to dislike, or to be indifferent toward indifferent things. Stated in a summary way, these answers are: (1) that it is good to be indifferent toward them and either bad or indifferent to like or dislike them; (2) that being indifferent toward them is neither good nor bad, liking or disliking them both bad; (3) that it is bad to be indifferent toward them; (4) that it is good to like them; and (5) that it is good to dislike them. The second, third, and fifth answers seem to have little or no plausibility. And although the first and fourth answers do seem to have some plausibility, they both suffer from being extreme answers to our question. As such, they both hold that it is good to take the same attitude toward any and all of the indifferent things of which we have experience or knowledge—the first that it is good to be indifferent toward them all, the fourth that it is good to like them all. It is because of this that neither, despite its plausibility, seems finally to be satisfactory. If, however, it is because of this that neither is ultimately satisfactory, then it is good to take different attitudes toward different indifferent things or kinds of things—to be indifferent toward some, to like others, and perhaps also to dislike still others. This is the view espoused by those who give what I have termed a "moderate" answer to our question.

3. Moderate Views of Attitudes toward the Indifferent

Such an answer is more congenial than any of the extreme answers to various of the attitudes we do in fact take toward various of the indifferent things of which we have experience or knowledge, since we do in fact like some, dislike others, and remain indifferent to still others. If it were good to be indifferent toward them all and bad or indifferent to like or dislike any, or if it were good to like them all and bad to dislike or to be indifferent toward any, then many of our attitudes toward them would be bad or at least indifferent, given that we do like or dislike some and are indifferent toward others. And if to claim that it is good to be indifferent toward them all or that it is good to like them all is to imply that we have a duty or that we ought, in the first case, to be indifferent toward them all and, in the second, to like them all, and if such claims be true, then each of us has a duty that few, if any, of us do or can succeed in fulfilling, given that each of us does in fact like some indifferent things, dislike others, and is indifferent toward still others and would find it difficult in the extreme, if not in fact impossible, to adopt an attitude of indifference toward them all or to like them all. Regardless, however, of whether such claims do have such implications, all our likings and dislikings of indifferent things would be bad if the only appropriate attitude to take toward them all is one of indifference, and all our dislikings of and indifferences toward indifferent things would be bad if the only appropriate attitude to take toward them is to like them all. The number of our bad likings, dislikings, and indifferences is already sufficiently great without adding needlessly to their number. It is because what I have labeled the "moderate" view does not do this but instead holds that it is good to like some indifferent things, to be indifferent toward others, and perhaps also to dislike still others, that it is more congenial to our actual likings, dislikings, and indifferences.

There are, however, two versions of the moderate view, one of which may be referred to as the "uniform" version, the other the "individualistic" version. According to the uniform version, all indifferent things fall into at least two and perhaps three classes. One class consists of those indifferent things it is good for anyone to like and bad for anyone to dislike or to be indifferent toward. Anyone's liking any member of this class is good, and anyone's disliking or indifference toward any member of it is bad. A second class consists of those indifferent things it is good for anyone to be indifferent toward and bad for anyone to like or dislike. Anyone's being indifferent toward any member of this class is good, and anyone's liking or disliking any member of it is bad. A third class, if a third is recognized, would consist of those indifferent things it would be good for anyone to dislike and bad for anyone to like or to be indifferent toward. Anyone's disliking any member of this class would be good, and anyone's liking or being indifferent toward any member of it would be bad. Let us call the first class *a*, the second *b*, the third *c*.

There seems to be little, if anything, to recommend this version. If the members of class *a* are such that anyone's liking any of them would be good and anyone's disliking or being indifferent toward any of them would be bad, then it would seem that there must be some property possessed by each member of class *a* by virtue of the possession of which it is good to like it and bad to dislike or to be indifferent toward it. Similar considerations, with of course the obvious necessary changes, would apply to the members of class *b*, the members of which are such that it would be good that anyone be indifferent toward them, and to the members of class *c,* if such a class is recognized, the members of which are such that it would be good that anyone dislike them. If, however, these considerations are acceptable, then it is hard to see how all three classes can be classes of indifferent things. If, that is, there is something about the members of class *a* that makes it good for anyone to like any of them and bad to dislike or to be indifferent toward any, and if there is something about the members of class *c* that makes it good for anyone to dislike any of them and bad to like or to be indifferent toward any, then the members of class *a* would seem to be good rather than indifferent and those of class *c* bad rather than indifferent. It is hard, that is, to see how all the members of any class can be indifferent if it is good for anyone to like any of them and bad to dislike or to be indifferent toward any if there is also another class all the members of which are such that it would be good for anyone to dislike any of them and bad for anyone to like or to be indifferent toward any. Indeed, perhaps part of what is meant by saying that all the members of a given class are good is that it would be good for anyone to like any of them and bad for anyone to dislike or to be indifferent toward any, just as perhaps part of what is meant by saying that all the members of a given class are bad is that it would be good for anyone to dislike any of them and bad to like or to be indifferent toward any.[3] If so, then class *a* above would be a class whose members are good, class *c* a class whose members are bad. It is only the members of class *b* that would be indifferent.

The individualistic version of the moderate view avoids this difficulty. This it does by denying that there are classes of the kind posited by the uniform version. Instead, it maintains, if a class consists entirely of indifferent things, then each of its members is such that it can be good that one person like it, that a second be indifferent toward it, and perhaps also that a third person dislike it. It holds, that is, that any indifferent thing, by virtue of its being indifferent, is such that one person's liking it can be good, a second person's being indifferent toward it can be good, and perhaps also that a third person's disliking it can be good. Just as the goodness of a good thing supervenes upon its nature and the badness of a bad thing upon its nature, so also the indifference of an indifferent thing supervenes upon its nature. And just as the nature of a good thing makes liking it good and disliking or being indifferent to it bad and the nature of a bad thing makes disliking it good and liking or being indifferent to it bad, so also the nature of an indifferent thing is such that one person's liking it, another's being indifferent to it, and perhaps also another's disliking it can all be good.

If, however, it can be good to like, to dislike, or to be indifferent toward an indifferent thing, a person who takes one of these attitudes toward a given indifferent thing cannot rightly condemn another for taking some contrary attitude toward it nor can he rightly expect that everyone else who has experience or knowledge of it take toward it the same attitude he takes. This is one of the major respects in which indifferent things differ from good and bad things. If a thing is good, then those who have experience of it can rightly be expected to like it and not to dislike or to be indifferent toward it; and if a thing is bad, then those who have experience or knowledge of it can rightly be expected to dislike it and not to like or to be indifferent toward it. If, however, a thing is indifferent, those who take any of the three possible attitudes toward it are required to take an attitude of tolerance toward those who take some contrary attitude toward it. Such an attitude consists of neither expecting others to take the same attitude toward it nor condemning them for taking a different attitude. Thus if, as subjectivists in value theory claim, nothing were intrinsically good or bad, far greater tolerance would be required of us than if some things are intrinsically good and others bad. If, however, the tolerance that would be required of us if nothing were intrinsically good or bad is itself intrinsically good and its absence bad, then it would be false that nothing is intrinsically good or bad, since then such tolerance would itself be intrinsically good and its absence bad.

The proponent of the individualistic version of the moderate view might also go further and maintain not only that it can be good to like some indifferent things and dislike others but also that it can be better to like some indifferent things even more than one likes some good things and to dislike other indifferent things even more than one dislikes some bad things. The advocate of such a view might well admit that some things are so greatly good and others so greatly bad that it would be bad if one who had experience or knowledge of them were to like some indifferent thing more than he likes any of these greatly good things or to dislike some indifferent thing more than he dislikes any of these greatly bad things. He might also readily admit that it is difficult in the extreme, if not in fact impossible, to distinguish precisely and unerringly between those things that fall within the classes of greatly good or greatly bad things and those that do not. Such admissions, however, are consistent with the view that it can be good to like some indifferent things more than some good things and to dislike other indifferent things more than some bad things. Thus on such a view it can be good that a widow like and treasure more some indifferent bauble given her long ago by her now dead husband than some exquisite diamond necklace willed her by some distant relative. She might well recognize that as pieces of jewelry the necklace has far greater aesthetic value than the bauble she cherishes, as she also might well recognize that it would be unreasonable of her to expect others to like the bauble more than the necklace. She might well realize, that is, that as a piece of jewelry the necklace is exquisitely good, the bauble indifferent. Yet despite this she cherishes the bauble more than the necklace because the former and not the latter was given her long ago by her now dead husband, and on the view in question it is or can be good that she do so.

The proponent of the view in question might go further and maintain that it would also be good if our widow liked the necklace more than the bauble. On such a view each of two conflicting attitudes on her part would be good. Her liking the bauble more than the necklace would be good but so also would her liking the necklace more than the bauble. Although she cannot like each more than the other, she can like either more than the other, and, regardless of which of the two she likes more than the other, her liking it more than the other would be good. If so, then not only can one person's preferring a good thing, *a,* to an indifferent thing, *b,* and another person's preferring *b* to *a* both be good, but also one and the same person's preferring *a* to *b* and also his preferring *b* to *a,* whichever of the two is the case, can both be good. Moreover, each of the two persons can like the liking or preference of the other even though it is contrary to his own. Thus the person who likes *a* more than *b* can like the other's liking *b* more than *a,* and the person who likes *b* more than *a* can like the other's liking *a* more than *b.* Indeed, given that each knows of the other's liking or preference, and given also that the liking or preference of each is good, the liking by each of the liking of the other is also good. In fact, given that the liking or preference of each is good, either's indifference toward or disliking the liking of the other would be bad. To like a good liking of another that is contrary to one's own liking is good, to dislike or to be indifferent toward

it bad, even though one's own contrary disliking is also good. It is therefore good not only to tolerate but also to like the contrary good likings
of others and bad not only to dislike or to be indifferent toward them
but also to be intolerant toward them. Such tolerance is the natural
issue of such liking, such intolerance the natural issue of such disliking.
Such liking and tolerance manifest a generous disposition, such disliking and intolerance a narrow mind.

It might be objected that the bauble of our example is not in fact
indifferent and thus that our example is not an instance of someone's
liking something indifferent more than something good. Such an objection might be based on either or both of two considerations. One is that
the widow is not herself indifferent toward the bauble, the other that
she likes it more than the necklace because it, not the necklace, was
given her by her husband. Neither of these considerations, however,
suffices to show that the bauble is not in fact indifferent. First, the fact
that the widow is not indifferent toward it but rather likes it does not
mean that it is not indifferent, since one can like or dislike a thing even
though the thing itself, taken completely in abstraction from one's
liking or disliking of it, in fact be indifferent. Second, even though she
likes the bauble only because it was given her by her husband, it is still
the bauble itself that she likes. Its having been given her by her husband
is the cause of her liking it or the reason she likes it, and even though she
would not like it had it not been given her by him, it is still it that she
likes. Even though she might also like his having given it to her, perhaps
because she takes his having done so as a little early sign of his love for
her, such a liking would be a different liking in addition to her liking of
it. Nor does the fact that she likes it only as a token of his love mean
that it is not it that she likes, any more than the fact that she also likes
the necklace as an aesthetic object means that it is not the necklace itself
that she likes. Although many, perhaps most, of the things we like are
liked as being instances of some kind, it is still the things themselves that
we like even though we like them only as instances of certain kinds.
Even though the widow likes the necklace only as an aesthetic object
and the bauble only as a token of her husband's love, it is still the necklace and the bauble that she likes. Not everything we like, however,
seems to be liked only as being an instance of some kind. Thus the
widow might like her husband's having loved her, not as its being or
having been an instance of some kind, but simply for itself alone.

4. Instances, Kinds, and Value

The preceding means that it is possible for a person (1) to like something, *a,* more than something else, *b,* as an instance of one kind, (2) to like *b* but not *a* as an instance of another kind, and (3) to like *b* on the whole or *simpliciter* more than *a* regardless of their being instances of certain kinds. Thus the widow might like the necklace more than the bauble as an aesthetic object, like the bauble but not the necklace as a token of her husband's love, and like the bauble on the whole more than the necklace. It is also possible (1) for one thing, *a,* to have greater value of one kind than another, *b,* (2) for *b* but not *a* to have value of another kind, and (3) for either of the two, *a* or *b,* to have greater value on the whole than the other. Thus (1) the necklace might have greater aesthetic value than the bauble, (2) the bauble but not the necklace might have what may be referred to as "sentimental" value, at least for the widow, and (3) either of the two, the necklace or the bauble, might have greater value on the whole than the other. It is possible also for a person (1) to like one thing, *a,* more than another, *b,* as an instance of one kind, (2) to like *b* but not *a* as an instance of another kind, (3) to like something else, *c,* simply for itself alone and not as being an instance of some kind, and (4) to like *c* more than *a* or *b.* Thus the widow might (1) like the necklace more than the bauble as an aesthetic object, (2) like the bauble but not the necklace as a token of her husband's love, (3) like her husband's having loved her for itself alone and not as being an instance of some kind, and (4) like her husband's having loved her more than either the necklace or the bauble.

From the preceding several consequences follow. One is that in order that one of two things have greater value than the other it is not necessary that they both be instances of the same kind. Thus although *a* might have greater value than *b* as an instance of the kind, *k, c,* which is not an instance of that kind, might have greater value than either *a* or *b.* If so, then an instance of one kind can have greater value than an instance of some other kind. This, however, does not mean that *c* has greater value than any instance of the kind, *k,* nor does it mean that any other instance of the same kind as *c* has greater value than any instance of the kind *k.* Instead, some instances of one kind can have greater value than some instances of a second kind and vice versa. Moreover, in order that this be the case it is not necessary that the value of the instances of these different kinds differ in kind. Thus the aesthetic value of a musical performance of one kind, such as a country, jazz, or rock performance, might be greater than that of another kind, such as a performance of a classical symphony, even though most performances of the latter kind have greater aesthetic value than most of the former kinds. This, however, does not mean that one kind cannot have greater value than another. Thus the kind having performances of classical symphonies as its instances might have greater aesthetic value than any of the kinds having country, jazz, or rock performances as their instances. The first kind, however, can have greater aesthetic value than any of the latter kinds only if most performances of classical symphonies have greater value than most country, jazz, or rock performances. It is the value of the instances of a kind that determines the value of their kind, not vice versa.

A second consequence, connected with the first, is that the value of an instance of a kind is not determined simply by the kind of which it is an instance. If it were, then two instances of the same kind would have the same or equal value, so that neither could have greater value than the other. Instead, the value of an instance of a kind, as an instance of that kind, is determined by the degree to which it has various of the good-making properties of the kind, and this can be discovered, not simply by knowing that it is an instance of the kind in question, but only by knowing also what the good-making properties of instances of that kind are and by discovering the degree to which the instance in question has these properties. Moreover, if the value of an instance of a kind were determined simply by the kind of which it is an instance, then no instance of a less valuable kind could have greater value than some instance of a more valuable kind. Yet if what was said above is correct, some instances of a less valuable kind can have greater value than some instances of a more valuable kind. Indeed, if what was said above is true, one kind can have greater value than another only because most of its instances have greater value than most of the instances of the other kind. In order, however, that an instance, *a,* of one kind have greater value than an instance, *b,* of another kind, it is not necessary, and indeed might not even be possible, that *a* have various of the good-making properties of instances of the latter kind to a greater degree than *b* does.

A third consequence, connected with the first two, is that in order that a thing have value it is not always necessary that it have its value as an instance of some kind. Or if this be too strong a claim, let us say instead that in order that a thing be valued it is not necessary that it be valued as an instance of some kind. Instead, a person can value a thing even though he finds it most difficult or even impossible to determine some kind of which it is an instance. He might believe that it is an instance of some kind, but if he has no belief as to which kind it is an instance of, he does not, indeed cannot, value it as an instance of some specific kind as opposed to others. He simply values it as what it presents itself as uniquely being. Thus the widow of our example likes and regards as good her dead husband's love for her, and good indeed it might be. But is it good as an instance of some kind and because it has to a sufficient degree various of the good-making properties of instances of that kind? If it is and if it does have such properties, the widow might neither know what kind it is an instance of nor what these good-making properties are that it has to a sufficient degree. Perhaps it is an instance of the kind consisting of a husband's love for his wife, and perhaps it is good because it is an instance of that kind. This, however, would seem to have things backwards. It would seem to imply that any instance of the kind consisting of a husband's loving his wife is good because the kind itself is good, whereas in fact if there is such a kind and if it is good it would seem to be good only because instances of husbands loving their wives are good. Kinds, that is, if good, are good because their typical instances are good, not vice versa.

A fourth consequence, or at least something suggested by the preceding, is that when a person likes some indifferent thing it is frequently, perhaps usually, because of some special relation in which he stands to it, not because it is an instance of some kind or a member of some class. Each of us has experience or knowledge of many indifferent things to which we stand in no special relation, and ordinarily we are indifferent to them and neither like nor dislike them. If what was said earlier is correct, such indifference cannot be bad but is either good or indifferent. Had the bauble not been given her by her dead husband, and were she to stand in no other special relation to it, the widow doubtless would be indifferent toward it, and such indifference would not be bad. Moreover, the special relation in which a person stands to an indifferent thing that leads to his liking it need not be direct, as is that in which the widow stands to the bauble. It might instead be indirect. Thus a son of the widow, who knows that she cherishes the bauble because it was given her by his father, might also come to cherish it. In such a case the special relation in which he stands to it that leads to his treasuring it is indirect, since he treasures it because she treasures it. If, however, he were to cherish it because it was given her by his father, and not because she treasures it, the special relation in which he stands to it would be direct. This relation would be even more obviously direct if he were to treasure it because his father gave it to her even though she does not cherish it and he knows that she does not. This can be put more generally by saying that the special relation in which a person stands to an indifferent thing he likes is (1) direct if he likes it independently of its being liked by anyone else, (2) indirect if he likes it because someone else who stands in a special relation to it likes it.

5. Egocentrism, Anthropocentrism, and Magnanimity

We are more likely to like an indifferent thing liked by another and to like his liking it if we stand in some special relation to him, such as friendship or kinship, than if we do not. In order, however, that we like another's liking an indifferent thing it is not necessary that we also like the thing he likes. Indeed, we might well like another's liking some indifferent thing even though we dislike the thing he likes. One of the marks of a generous disposition is that we like not only another's liking the things we like but also another's liking various indifferent things we are indifferent toward or dislike. Other things being equal, we are more magnanimous if we like the latter likings of others as well as the former than if we like the former but not also the latter. We are more magnanimous still if we like not only the likings of indifferent things by our friends and relatives but also such likings by anyone, regardless of whether we like the things they like.

Our magnanimity is even greater if we like in addition the likings of dumb animals even though we are indifferent toward or dislike various of the things they like. Other things equal, the person who likes a dog's, whether his own or a stranger's, liking to play with a rubber toy is more generous than the person who does not. More magnanimous still is the person who likes maggots' liking to eat garbage and who likes in advance the future liking of worms to eat the flesh of his cadaver as it lies moldering in its grave. Much modern moral philosophy and value theory has suffered from egocentrism, and most moral philosophy and value theory in the western tradition has suffered from anthropocentrism. Just as the satisfaction of various of the desires of other human beings as well as those of one's own has value, so also the satisfaction of various of the wants of non-human as well as those of human animals is good. Unbounded magnanimity of spirit consists, at least in part, in recognizing this and in liking the likings and the satisfaction of the wants of even such seemingly insignificant creatures as maggots and worms even though we do not like what they like or want what they want.

What has been said about liking the likings of indifferent things by others even though we do not like what they like also applies, with the necessary changes, to liking the indifferences, but I think not the dislikings, of others when the things they are indifferent toward are indifferent. Other things equal, a person is more generous if he likes rather than dislikes another's indifference toward some indifferent thing he likes. It is important, however, to keep in mind that to like another's indifference toward or disliking something good, rather than manifesting a magnanimous spirit, is instead bad. Liking or indifference toward another's disliking or indifference toward something good is bad, as is also disliking or indifference toward another's liking or indifference toward something good. Since, that is, both (1) liking or indifference toward something bad is bad and (2) disliking or indifference toward something good is bad, so also is liking or indifference toward such likings, dislikings, and indifferences.

6. Disliking Indifferent Things

The individualistic version of the moderate view was characterized above as holding that it can be good not only to like or to be indifferent toward indifferent things but also as maintaining that perhaps it can also be good to dislike such things. From the fact, however, that it can be good to like or to be indifferent toward some such things it does not follow that it can also be good to dislike any. Just as most of us who like various indifferent things usually do so because we stand in some direct or indirect special relation to them, so also indifferent things are usually disliked because those who dislike them stand in some such relation to them. If, that is, a person stands in no such relation to a given indifferent thing of which he has experience or knowledge, he is more likely to be indifferent toward it than to like or dislike it. Given, however, that there are indifferent things and that some such things are sometimes disliked by some people, can such dislikings be good? That they can be extrinsically good seems undeniable, since disliking some such things can have better consequences than liking or being indifferent toward them would have. From this, however, it does not follow that they can also sometimes be intrinsically good.

In considering this question it is important to remember that the existence of a given indifferent thing might prevent the existence of something good, in the sense that were the indifferent thing not to exist something good would exist in its place, and that because of this the indifferent thing might be disliked. In such a case, however, the existence of the indifferent thing would be extrinsically rather than intrinsically bad, just as the existence of some other indifferent thing might be extrinsically good because its existence prevents the existence of something bad in its place. And just as the knowledge that the existence of a given indifferent thing prevents the existence of something bad might lead one to like its existence, so also the knowledge that the existence of another indifferent thing prevents the existence of something good might lead one to dislike its existence. If, however, the first is liked and the second disliked only because the existence of the first prevents the existence of something bad and that of the second the existence of something good, then the first is liked only because it is extrinsically good and the second disliked only because it is extrinsically bad.

In order, then, to consider properly the question of whether it can be good to dislike an indifferent thing, we must abstract completely from the question of whether its existence is extrinsically good or bad and consider instead only the thing itself and the disliking of it. To achieve such an abstraction, we must also put aside the fact, indicated earlier, that disliking an indifferent thing is more likely than liking or indifference toward it to lead to unhappiness on the part of the person who dislikes it, since this means only that such disliking is likely to be extrinsically bad and not that it is intrinsically bad. Leaving aside, then, the question of whether the existence of a given indifferent thing and of whether disliking such a thing is extrinsically good or bad, we are left with the question of whether disliking such a thing can be intrinsically good. The correct answer would seem to be that it cannot be.

It was maintained above that liking various indifferent things, especially those to which we stand in no direct or indirect special relation, is sometimes a manifestation of a magnanimous disposition on the part of the person who likes them. I want now to suggest that it is because some such likings are manifestations of such a disposition that they are intrinsically good. This, however, can be the case only if manifestations of such a disposition are intrinsically good. If they are, and they do clearly seem to be, then those likings of indifferent things that are manifestations of such a disposition are themselves also intrinsically good. Indeed, given that magnanimity consists, at least in part, in liking various indifferent things, a person has this virtue, other things being equal, only if and only to the extent to which he does in fact like various such things.

If the preceding is correct, then, again other things equal, the person who likes few, if any, and is indifferent toward most, if not all, of the indifferent things of which he has experience or knowledge is not as magnanimous as the person who likes many such things. And since magnanimity is a virtue or good-making property of a person, an indifferent person, again other things equal, is not as good a person as a magnanimous person. Indeed, a person, if such were possible, who is indifferent toward all the indifferent things of which he has experience or knowledge, including even all those things to which he stands in some special relation, would not in that respect be a very good person at all. From this, however, it does not follow that anyone can reasonably be expected to like all the indifferent things of which he has experience or knowledge. Although such a person, for reasons given above, might be more likely to lead a good and happy life than one who does not, such supererogatory liking, if it may be called such, is too much to ask, much less to require, of anyone. The most we can reasonably expect of people is that they have sufficient magnanimity to like various of the indifferent things of which they have experience of knowledge, especially those to which they stand in some special relation.

The opposite of such magnanimity is manifested by the person who dislikes indifferent things, and it is because of this that such dislike is intrinsically bad. Dislike of indifferent things is a manifestation of a vice opposed to magnanimity, which perhaps may be called "mean-spiritedness". Other things equal, a person subject to this vice is a worse person than a person who is not so subject. Just as, however, few, if any, people do or can like all the indifferent things of which they have experience or knowledge, so also few, if any, dislike all such things. Perhaps the type of person who comes closest to doing so is the type of aesthete who dislikes, or who pretends to dislike, anything and everything other than a pleasing aesthetic object. Such people are hard to please. Because of this they are less likely to lead happy lives than are those who like various indifferent things and are thus easier to please.

Although a pervasive dislike of indifferent things is intrinsically bad and makes a person a worse person than he would otherwise be, an occasional dislike of something indifferent, though intrinsically bad, does not necessarily manifest the vice opposed to magnanimity and is sometimes understandable and forgivable and sometimes even lovable. Thus the widow of our example might dislike a certain indifferent make of automobile because it was a car of that make that struck and killed her husband. Such dislike, though intrinsically bad and doubtless also irrational, is understandable and forgivable, and few, if any, would take it as a manifestation of an absence of magnanimity on her part if they know that she is magnanimous in various other ways. And some old codger's intense dislike of a given indifferent thing or kind of thing, though irrational and intrinsically bad (although not greatly so), even though not understandable, might nonetheless have significant contributory value as contributing to making him the delightful and lovable old character he is. Indeed, his intense dislike of the thing in question might well on the whole be good, as it would be if its positive contributory value is greater than its negative intrinsic value. Such occasional dislikings of indifferent things, though doubtless intrinsically bad at least to some slight degree, need not and frequently do not manifest a lack of magnanimity. But the person who pervasively dislikes indifferent things does thereby manifest a lamentable lack of magnanimity concerning such things even though he be quite magnanimous in various other respects, and it is because of this that such dislike is intrinsically bad.

It is because the nature of magnanimity is such that its instances are intrinsically good and therefore that the nature of the vice opposed to magnanimity is such that its instances are intrinsically bad, coupled with the fact that the pervasive dislike of indifferent things is a specific form of the vice opposed to magnanimity, that such pervasive dislike is also intrinsically bad. If, that is, the nature of a given genus is such that all its instances are intrinsically bad, then so also are all the instances of any of the species comprehended by that genus. But if a pervasive dislike of indifferent things is intrinsically bad, then so also are particular instances of such dislike on the part of a person who does not generally dislike such things. Although particular occasional instances of such dislike, taken singly, are not as bad as a pervasive dislike of such things, they are still at least slightly bad, if for no other reason than that a person who occasionally dislikes particular indifferent things, even though he does not pervasively dislike them, is less magnanimous than he would otherwise be. As such slightly bad instances of such dislike on the part of a given person become increasingly frequent, his magnanimity correspondingly diminishes, and he becomes in that respect a worse person than he would otherwise be even though he remains magnanimous in other respects and continues to like good things and good likings and dislikings of others and to dislike bad things and bad likings and dislikings of others.

Chapter 10

The Complete Human Good and Higher Education

In this concluding chapter we turn to discuss some of the implications for higher education of what was said above concerning the complete human good.[1] This will require a brief discussion of the distinction between civilization and morality and their relation to one another. Our discussion in this chapter will be somewhat less abstruse than various parts of earlier chapters. Because of this, and because relevant points made in earlier chapters will be reiterated, this chapter might be intelligible to those who have not read what has gone before.

1. Civilization and Morality

I take it that almost everyone will agree that higher education has a duty to contribute to the welfare of the wider society of which colleges and universities are but a part. This is the case, it might be argued, if for no other reason than that colleges and universities depend for their continued existence upon public and private financial support from those who are not themselves faculty or students of such institutions at the time they render their support, whether willingly through private contributions or unwillingly through being required to pay taxes they might not always like to pay. Yet, it might by some be thought, colleges and universities can fulfill the duty in question simply by educating and training their students in the various arts and sciences and have no duty beyond this to help their students become morally good persons. Such a view seems to me to be perniciously one-sided. That it is in fact so is what I hope to show.

In 1750 the Academy at Dijon in France offered a prize for the best essay on the question of whether the restoration of the arts and sciences in Europe since the Renaissance had tended to the purification of morals. The prize was won by an essay submitted by Jean-Jacques Rousseau, who had previously published nothing. This essay was his *Discourse on the Arts and Sciences.* The announced topic of the competition had already distinguished, at least implicitly, between the arts and sciences on the one hand and morality on the other, since the restoration of the arts and sciences necessarily would amount to the purification of morals if there were no difference between the two. Rousseau accepted the distinction between the two and argued unequivocally that the restoration of the arts and sciences, rather than tending to the purification of morals, had instead contributed to their corruption. In the process of doing so, he raised and essayed to answer a wider question concerning the relationship between civilization on the one hand and morality and justice on the other at any time and at any place, not just in Europe during the period in question.

The distinction between civilization on the one hand and morality and justice on the other implicit in the question raised by the Academy at Dijon and made explicit by Rousseau can be explicated in the following way. The distinction applies both to societies and to individuals. A society is civilized to the degree to which the various arts and sciences are developed in it, morally good and just to the degree to which its customs, institutions, and laws are such that each person within it, by acting in accordance with the latter, can promote his own welfare and become morally good. An individual person, on the other hand, is civilized to the degree to which he is knowledgeable about the various arts and sciences, morally good and just to the degree to which he acts in accordance with the requirements of morality.

Given the preceding distinction between civilization and morality, there are various possible relationships between the two. It is possible that a society and an individual person be (a) both civilized and morally good, (b) neither civilized nor morally good, (c) civilized but not morally good, or (d) morally good but not civilized. To some it might seem that the last two are not in fact possibilities—that in fact it is impossible that any person or society be at once both civilized and morally corrupt or both uncivilized and morally good. This view is perhaps more widespread than at first one might think. People frequently refer to behavior they regard as grossly immoral as being uncivilized or barbaric, as though to be civilized is identical with being morally good. Such language, however, would seem to rest upon a confusion of being immoral with being uncivilized or barbaric. The opposite of being morally good is being morally corrupt, not being uncivilized or barbaric, just as the opposite of being civilized is not being morally corrupt but rather being uncivilized or barbaric. If this is correct, to be civilized is one thing, to be morally good another, and a society and an individual person can be one without being the other.

Just a little reflection should suffice to show that this is in fact the case. Since the Renaissance, European nations, and for the past two centuries also the United States, have contributed more to the development of the various arts and sciences, and thus to the development of civilization, than all other nations and societies taken together throughout the entire rest of the world. Yet throughout much of this historical period the internal social, political, and economic structure of these highly civilized nations has left much to be desired from a moral point of view. So also have their relations with one another and their treatment of people in other parts of the world who, within this historical period, have contributed far less to the development of the arts and sciences. To take one example, from the first third of the eighteenth century to the first third of the twentieth, the German people contributed as much to the development of the arts and sciences as those of any other nation. Yet we all know something of what happened in Germany and the rest of Europe as a consequence of the rise to power of German National Socialism. Certainly the use of their power by National Socialists, both in their treatment of certain members of the German state and in their treatment of certain other peoples, left something to be desired from a moral point of view. This example is just one of many that could be given in support of the claim that the development to a high degree of the arts and sciences in a society is by itself no guarantee that it will unfailingly use its high civilization in morally acceptable ways. One need only think of the ways in which in the past, and to some extent also in the present, many of the black people of Africa and many of the Indians of the Americas were treated by more highly civilized Europeans and white Americans.

The preceding does not mean, as Rousseau perhaps tended at times to think, that uncivilized societies and individuals are without exception morally good and just. It is instead intended only to illustrate, by means of a few historical examples, that there is no necessary connection between being civilized and being morally good that precludes a civilized society conducting itself in morally unacceptable ways. It is intended, in short, to show that it is indeed possible for a society to be at once highly civilized and morally corrupt. From this it does not follow that uncivilized or less civilized societies without exception are morally good and just. Yet civilized societies, because in them the arts and sciences are more highly developed, can and in point of historical fact have caused more evil to exist in the world than uncivilized societies could bring about even if they tried. The power that the development of the arts and sciences brings in its wake can be used for good or ill, and because of this it is more important that civilized societies be morally good and just than it is that less civilized societies be so. This, of course, does not imply that it is not important that the latter also be good and just.

Just as civilized societies can be morally corrupt and unjust and uncivilized societies can be morally good and just, so too an individual person who has great knowledge of various of the arts and sciences can be a worse person from a moral point of view than another person who knows little or nothing of the arts and sciences. Let us call a person of the first type an educated person, a person of the second type an uneducated person. An educated person can be morally corrupt, an uneducated person morally good. This does not mean that an educated person necessarily is morally corrupt or that an uneducated person necessarily is morally good. Some educated people are morally good, some uneducated people morally bad. There is, however, no necessary connection between being educated and being morally good, nor is there one between being uneducated and being morally bad. As suggested above, a person is educated to the degree to which he is knowledgeable about various of the arts and sciences, uneducated to the degree to which he is not.

Some aesthetes, for example, who are very knowledgeable indeed about various of the arts and who live, or at least pretend to live, for literature, music, or painting are nonetheless morally corrupt to the core. The evil scientist is not just a creature inhabiting science fiction; some flesh and blood scientists leave much to be desired from a moral point of view. College and university faculty members are certainly among the most educated members of society. Yet some faculty are moral disasters, if not indeed moral monsters, in their treatment of other people, whether it be their students, their fellow faculty, those who hold subordinate positions, members of their own families, or indeed almost anyone they come across in the course of their daily lives. On the other hand, most of us have known simple uneducated people who know little or nothing of any of the arts and sciences who are kind, considerate, honest, and unfailingly fair and just in their dealings with other people. Reflection on our personal knowledge of the aesthetes, scientists, faculty, and simple uneducated people we have known and on our first-hand knowledge of how they treat other people ought by itself alone to convince us that an educated person is not necessarily a good person, that an uneducated person is not necessarily a bad person, and that uneducated people can be and sometimes are better persons than educated people. And while we are engaged in such reflections, let us reflect also on the question of how we ourselves regard and treat the educated and uneducated people we come across in the course of our daily lives. Do we value and respect as persons and treat as kindly and considerately the uneducated people we come across as we do those who are educated? An honest and accurate answer to this question will reveal at least something about our own attitudes toward the value of civilization and that of morality—toward the value of being educated and the value of being morally good.

2. Being Good and Having Goods

The preceding suggests that values are divisible into two broad classes—into moral values on the one hand and all other values on the other, which may accordingly be referred to as non-moral values. Included among the latter are certain of the objects of education in the sense of the term in which I have been using it. The objects in question are divisible into two broad categories—those of professional or vocational education on the one hand and those of liberal education on the other. I shall speak first about the former.

One of the purposes of higher education is to provide students the education necessary to enable them to pursue some vocation or profession such as business, engineering, nursing, teaching, law, or medicine. Most students attend colleges and universities to prepare themselves to pursue a vocation that will enable them to earn more money over the course of their lives than they would probably otherwise be able to do. There is nothing especially bad about this, given that we do need businessmen, engineers, nurses, teachers, lawyers, and physicians. Were it not for this economic interest of students and the fact that colleges and universities attempt to satisfy it, enrollments would be considerably smaller than in fact they are. The number of students who enroll in colleges and universities primarily to obtain a liberal education that will enable them to increase their understanding of various aspects of God, man, and the world and their relationship to one another is quite small in comparison to the number who enroll mainly for vocational purposes, and those who enroll primarily for the latter purposes frequently wonder why and complain that they are required to take a certain number of courses in the liberal arts and sciences. I take it that the main reason is that faculty place some value on their students increasing their understanding of various aspects of God, man, and/or the world.

Despite what is sometimes said by partisans of the liberal arts and sciences, it is possible for a person to be a good businessman, engineer, nurse, lawyer, or physician without having much knowledge of the various liberal arts and sciences beyond what is necessary to enable him to complete his course of vocational education. Engineers, for example, need to know some mathematics and physics, physicians some chemistry and biology, and students preparing themselves for careers as engineers or physicians usually see the point of requiring them to study such subjects. A person engaged, however, in vocations of the sorts indicated can be quite skilled in that vocation without having any knowledge of the liberal arts and sciences beyond what is necessary to achieve professional competence. And, if what was said above is true, he can also be a morally good person without having any knowledge at all of the various liberal arts and sciences beyond what he needs to be good at his vocation. On the other hand, as was also maintained above, a person can have wide knowledge of such arts and sciences yet be morally corrupt. It is one thing to be educated, whether liberally or vocationally, another to be morally good. The possession of such education is neither a necessary nor a sufficient condition of being morally good.

The preceding is connected with what was said above about the distinction between moral and non-moral values, which in turn is related to the distinction made earlier between having goods of various sorts and being morally good. One can have goods of various sorts without being morally good, and one can be morally good without having goods of various sorts. I earlier marked this distinction by referring simply to having goods and being good.[2] The goods a person can have can be categorized as falling into various broad categories such as health, wealth, power, education, knowledge, and facial and bodily beauty. A person can have goods of these sorts without being good, and one can be good without having various goods of these kinds. Similarly, a person can be good at his vocation without being a good person, and a person can be a good person without being good at whatever he does to earn a living. Of special importance for our purposes here is the distinction between being educated and being good. Being educated is itself a good one can have, but it is neither necessary nor sufficient for being good.

The complete good of a person consists in his having various goods and in his being good. It is better that a person both have various goods and also be good than that he have goods and not be good or be good and not have various goods. Part of what is meant by saying that the complete good of a person consists in his having goods and in being good is that neither of these constituents of the complete good is reducible to the other and that neither is merely a means to the acquisition of the other. Having goods of various kinds is by itself neither necessary nor sufficient for being good, and being good by itself is neither necessary nor sufficient for having goods of various types. Having goods has a value in itself independently of any contribution it might make to a person's being good, and being good is valuable in itself independently of any contribution it might make to one's having goods of various kinds. It is good, although good in a non-moral sense, to have goods regardless of whether having them contributes to one's being good; and it is also good, in a moral sense of "good," to be good regardless of whether being so contributes to one's having various goods. Any view of the complete good for man that does not include both these constituents is one-sided.

Few people today would regard a person's good as consisting simply in his being good, regardless of whether he also has goods of various types. There have, however, been philosophers who have come close to doing so, such as certain of the Cynics and Stoics of classical Greece and Rome. Surely, however, a morally good person who is healthy, well-off financially, educated, respected, and graced with facial and bodily beauty is better off than a good person who is sick, impoverished, uneducated, held in contempt, and ugly both in face and body. The Stoic view, if we may so term it, is hopelessly one-sided, even though from a moral point of view it is one-sided in the right direction. This view, however, is not likely to be adopted by many of us today, any more than it was embraced by many people during the centuries Stoicism flourished as a philosophical movement. Our tendency today, like that of most people at any time, is to be one-sided in the opposite direction. As was indicated earlier, this has also been the tendency of much recent moral philosophy. This is the tendency to regard having goods alone as being intrinsically good and to regard being good only as extrinsically good as a means to the acquisition of various goods one can also sometimes have without being good. Thus we frequently find recent moral philosophers endeavoring to convince us that we ought to be moral because it is rational so to be. The concept of rationality they operate with, however, is a narrow one-sided egoistic or self-interested concept. For them practical rationality consists in acting in those ways that are most likely to enable us to acquire whatever goods we might happen to want, or those goods we would want if we were fully informed or knowledgeable about the consequences of their acquisition. On this view being morally good and acting rightly in a moral sense have no intrinsic value at all but instead have value only as a means to the acquisition of various goods.[3]

Most of us doubtless would agree that usually we succeed more fully over the course of a lifetime in acquiring various goods by generally acting rightly in a moral sense than by not doing so. Only a simpleton, however, would believe that no situation can ever arise in which he can acquire certain goods he wants by acting wrongly rather than rightly. Most people are not such simpletons. This is shown by the fact that there are many people who not only know that they can acquire certain goods they want by lying or cheating or stealing but who also, knowing this, proceed to lie or cheat or steal and do so successfully. Morality therefore rests on a foundation that will not unfailingly support it if it has no intrinsic value in itself but instead has value only as a means to the acquisition of various goods we might happen to want. Sometimes acting rightly is useful as a means to the acquisition of such goods. Sometimes, however, rather than being a means to their acquisition it is instead an impediment and is known to be so. Were this not the case there would be less lying and cheating and stealing than in fact there is.

Although most people seem to place more value on having goods than on being good, this does not mean that they place no value at all on the latter. Certainly most people want others to act rightly, if for no other reason than that they believe that they themselves will benefit if others do so act. Frequently people act rightly because they believe that they will be detected and suffer in some way at the hands of others if they do not. And sometimes people want others to believe that they are morally good and endeavor to deceive others into believing that they are, again because they fear that they will suffer at the hands of others if others believe that they are not. In all these cases, however, morality is valued only as a means to some other end and not as an end in itself.

Most people, however, do place some intrinsic value, slight though it might be, on morality itself. This happens whenever a person engages in a process of rationalization and attempts to convince himself that some act he wants to perform is not in fact wrong or that some act he does not want to perform is not in fact obligatory. It happens also whenever a person suffers the painful pangs of a guilty conscience because he believes that he has acted wrongly or badly. A person cannot engage in such processes of rationalization or suffer from a guilty conscience unless he believes that acts of certain sorts are right and acts of certain other sorts wrong, regardless of whether he also believes that his omission of acts of the first type or his performance of acts of the second type might enable him to acquire certain goods he happens to want. That most people place some intrinsic value, however slight, on morality is also shown by the fact that few people like to think of themselves as or to admit to themselves that they are bad persons even though in fact they are. This leads them to endeavor to deceive themselves into believing that they are not bad. Such an aversion to thinking of oneself as bad or to admitting to oneself that one is bad and such attempts at self-deception would be impossible if one placed no intrinsic value at all upon being oneself a good person.[4]

If the preceding is correct, most people do not in fact value as an end only the having of various goods. At least to some extent, they also value as an end being good. This means that they believe, at least implicitly, that the complete good does in fact consist of the two constituents indicated above and that neither constituent is reducible to or eliminable in favor of the other. This is not to say that they hold such a belief explicitly or that they would express it in the language I have used were they to become aware of the fact that they hold it at least implicitly. To say, however, that most people place at least some intrinsic value on being good is not to say that they value it as much as they value having various of the goods they happen to want. The relative value we place on each of these two constituents of the complete good is at least one of the factors involved in determining how we act in situations in which we cannot both have certain goods we want and also act rightly. In such situations we must choose between (1) getting the goods in question at the cost of acting wrongly and (2) acting rightly at the cost of forgoing the goods in question. To the degree to which we are bad persons we tend to choose the first alternative; to the degree to which we are good we tend to choose the second. Few, if any, of us are completely good; and few, if any, of us are completely bad.

Some people have goods of certain sorts that others do not have and do not have goods of certain other sorts that others do have, and some people on the whole have a greater quantity of various goods than others have. Similarly, some people are morally better in certain respects than others are and morally worse in certain other respects than others are, and some people on the whole are morally better than others are. The class of those, however, who on the whole have a greater quantity of various goods than others have is by no means identical with the class of those who are morally better than others are. At least one, but only one, of the requirements of ideal justice is that as many members as possible of the first class also be members of the second, so that as few as possible of those who on the whole have a greater quantity of various goods than others have are also those who on the whole are morally worse than others are. This is an ideal that has never been realized perfectly in this world, and it is also doubtless an ideal that never will or even can be realized perfectly on earth. From this, however, it does not follow that we do not have at least a *prima facie* duty to try to approach it as closely as we can. If what was said above about the complete good is correct, we do have such a duty.

Although the faculty of colleges and universities, like others, have such a duty with respect to the wider community of which they are part, in their role as faculty they have it most immediately with respect to their students. They stand in a relationship to their students in which others do not, and because of this relationship they have a specific duty to their students that others do not have. Their duty is to educate their students, and in their role as faculty it is primarily through fulfilling this duty that they fulfill their duty to the wider community. It is also through fulfilling their duty to educate their students that they fulfill their duty to contribute to the realization of the complete good of the latter. In their role as faculty it is only through fulfilling this duty that they can contribute significantly to the realization of the complete good of the wider community and to a closer approach to a realization within the wider community of the ideal of justice mentioned above.

3. Moral and Non-Moral Education

Two opposing views, however, can be taken toward the education colleges and universities have a duty to offer their students. One of these views I shall call the non-moral or amoral view, the other the moral view. On the first view colleges and universities fulfill their duty to their students and to the wider community by offering their students what in effect is an essentially non-moral education. On the second view they can fulfill their duty only by offering their students a moral education. As the secularization of society and education has progressed in the past several decades, the first view has come to be more widely held, perhaps more widely held today than the second view, which in earlier generations and centuries was the majority view, with the result that colleges and universities increasingly are offering their students only a non-moral education. The difference between a moral and a non-moral education corresponds to the distinction between the complete good on the one hand and having goods on the other. What the proponents of the non-moral view of education in effect are proposing, although they doubtless do not realize it fully, is that colleges and universities offer their students a one-sided education designed only to enable them to acquire goods of various sorts. On this one-sided view of education, colleges and universities have no duty to provide their students an education designed to help them become good persons. The moral view, on the other hand, is not one-sided in what may be referred to as the Stoic direction, since it does not hold that the only duty of colleges and universities is to help their students become good persons. It holds instead that their duty is to offer their students an education that will help them realize their complete good by providing them an education that will not only help them acquire various goods but also become good persons.

There are two major ways in which an approach can be made to realizing the goal of the non-moral view of education. One is through providing students a vocational or professional education that will enable them to earn more money over the course of their lives than they otherwise would probably be able to do and thereby to acquire greater quantities of goods of various kinds than they otherwise could acquire. The second way is through providing a liberal education or through supplementing a vocational education with courses in the liberal arts and sciences. In this way students might acquire a greater understanding and appreciation of various of the liberal arts and sciences than they otherwise would have. The goal of the non-moral view of education is therefore realized to the degree to which students are enabled to acquire two goods of some importance—the wealth to acquire various of the kinds of goods money can buy and an increased knowledge and appreciation of various of the liberal arts and sciences. These are doubtless goods it is good to have. But, as was argued above, to be financially well off and educated is one thing, to be a good person another. On the non-moral view of education it is not part of the duty of colleges and universities to help its students become good persons. This is the duty of their parents and/or of their church, if they have a church, or perhaps of some other institution. But it is not the duty of colleges and universities.

This view of education is related to certain other views. One is the view that there is no such thing as moral knowledge. Since the duty of colleges and universities is only to do what they can to increase the knowledge of their students, and since there is no such thing as moral knowledge, it cannot be part of their duty to increase the moral knowledge of their students. Given the argument of the previous chapters, I hope it will not seem too dogmatic if here I say simply that the trouble with this view is that it is false. There are many moral truths that many of us know.

A second view, allied to the first, is that it is not part of the duty of colleges and universities to teach values. Those who hold this view usually do so for either or both of two reasons. The first is that values, whether they be moral or non-moral, are subjective, so that beliefs about non-moral values, like beliefs about moral values, are neither true nor false. This reason, however, is not sufficient to support the view in question, for essentially the same reason that the view that moral beliefs are neither true nor false is unacceptable. Those who argue against teaching any values at all, whether they be moral or non-moral, are also confronted with a serious self-defeating predicament that does not confront those who argue only against teaching moral values. The latter group can simply refrain from teaching any moral values at all. The other group, however, must make certain value judgments in deciding what to have their students read and study in the courses they teach. Professors of literature, for example, want their students to read good literature worth reading, not bad literature not worth reading. Even professors of mathematics and of various natural sciences want their students to learn good mathematics and science worth learning, not bad mathematics or science not worth learning. In deciding on what and what not to have our students study in the courses we teach we inescapably make value judgments.

A second reason sometimes given in support of the view that values ought not to be taught is suggested by the frequently posed question: Whose values? The supposition on which this question rests is that there is insufficient agreement about values to justify teaching certain values as opposed to others. This question is most frequently raised in response to the view that moral values ought to be taught. There is, of course, some disagreement among moral philosophers concerning specific moral issues and about what counts as good moral reasons and what does not. There is also, however, some disagreement among art, literary, and music critics concerning the value of particular pieces of art, literature, or music. There is also some disagreement in various of the sciences concerning the value of particular theories and approaches, such as the disagreement among psychologists concerning the value of behavioristic as opposed to Freudian approaches to their discipline. And just as there is considerable agreement among art, literary, and music critics concerning the value of certain pieces of art, literature, or music that are all but universally recognized by the experts to be good, and considerable agreement among scientists that certain theories within their disciplines have been abundantly confirmed or decisively refuted, so also there is considerable agreement on the part of moral philosophers and on the part of the ordinary man in the street that certain traits of character are virtues and others vices. Indeed, the entire educational enterprise and scholarly and scientific inquiry depend for their flourishing upon the widespread acceptance by scholars, scientists, teachers, and students of the value of being honest, impartial, and hardworking and on the widespread acquisition and practice by them of these virtues.

Another objection that might be made to the view that colleges and universities have a duty to help their students become good persons is that it is impossible for one person or group to make another morally good. This objection, however, rests on a misconception. I agree that no person or group can make another morally good. Neither can one person or group make another a good poet, painter, musician, philosopher, mathematician, or scientist. From this, however, it does not follow that one person or group cannot help another to become good in one or more of these ways. Nor does it follow that one person or group cannot help another to become a good person. Just as one person helps another to become a good poet, philosopher, or scientist by teaching the other as much as he can about the discipline in question, so also one person helps another become a good person by teaching him what he can about what is involved in being such a person. Such teaching is not by itself sufficient to make another a good poet or philosopher or scientist. Nor is it sufficient to make another a good person. It is also necessary that the pupil attend to what the teacher is teaching him and endeavor to learn and practice and also improve upon what he has been taught. Such teaching is nonetheless helpful and sometimes necessary if the pupil is to become a good poet or philosopher or person. What use the pupil makes of what he is taught after the teaching is done is up to him.

In recent years it has been various of the professional schools that have given the most attention to teaching at least professional ethics through requiring or recommending that their students take courses in business, engineering, legal, or medical ethics. Liberal arts colleges have not given the same attention to teaching their students ethics through requiring or recommending that they take a fundamental course in ethics designed, at least in part, simply to help them become good or better persons. Such courses, however, though helpful, are perhaps not as important as it is that faculty themselves be good persons in their dealings with their students outside as well as inside the classroom. Young people become good or bad persons more by following the examples set them by their parents and teachers than by attending to what they are formally taught. And if their teachers themselves do not practice what they teach, their pupils have a most remarkable ability to see quickly through the hypocrisy. This means that teachers can most effectively teach their students to become good persons by being such persons themselves. It is through having a faculty consisting of such persons that colleges and universities can most effectively fulfill their duty to promote the complete good of their students by helping them to become not only more civilized through becoming more knowledgeable about the various arts and sciences but also morally better. It is through their promoting the complete good of their students that they can most effectively fulfill their duty to contribute to the complete good of the wider community of which they are but a part by helping to make it not only more civilized but also morally better and more just and thus to approach more fully the attainment of its complete good. This, however, is not a task that can ever be accomplished once and for all but is rather a task that will continue to confront us for as long as the human race endures.

Notes

Chapter 1

1. Ross, *The Right and the Good*, 157–58.

2. For a good treatment of various species of pro- and con-attitudes, not much mentioned in the recent literature, see Nowell-Smith, *Ethics*.

3. Brentano, *The Origin of Our Knowledge of Right and Wrong*, 3–46, 137–60; *The Foundation and Construction of Ethics*, 130–37.

Chapter 2

1. Ross, *The Right and the Good*, 113.

2. For a treatment of this distinction and of the nature of universals and particulars and their relationships to one another, see my *Metaphysical Investigations*, chapters 8–10.

3. For a more complete treatment of the issues discussed in this section, see my "Propositions, States of Affairs, and Facts" and my *Metaphysical Investigations*, chapter 4.

4. For a defense of this claim, see my *Metaphysical Investigations*, chapter 4, sections 1–3.

5. Hall, *What Is Value?* 12–16.

6. Butchvarov, *Skepticism in Ethics*, 16. Although I disagree with Professor Butchvarov on this issue, there is much in his excellent book with which I agree.

7. Ibid., 14.

8. Moore, *Principia Ethica*, 28.

9. Ibid.

Chapter 3

1. Lewis, *An Analysis of Knowledge and Valuation*, 382–85.

2. Husserl, *Logical Investigations*, Investigation III, 2: 435–80; see also my *Metaphysical Investigations*, chapter 10, sections 1, 2.

3. To punish a person is to inflict suffering on him, or at least to endeavor to do so. Such suffering, taken in abstraction from its being deserved, is bad. If,

however, it is deserved it is good that it be inflicted, since it is good that a person receive what he deserves. This is not to deny that it is bad that more suffering be inflicted on a person than he deserves. Thus a state of affairs consisting of (1) a person's doing something that deserves punishment and (2) his suffering more punishment than he deserves, rather than being good, is instead bad. For a more extended treatment of retributive punishment, see my "A Defense of Retributivism" and my *Rights, Goods, and Democracy*, chapter 4.

4. For a treatment of the nature and ontological status of intentional objects, see my *Metaphysical Investigations*, chapters 5 and 6.

5. Some such wholes would be scattered objects. For a recent treatment of scattered objects, see Chisholm, *On Metaphysics*, chapter 9.

6. Lewis, *An Analysis of Knowledge and Valuation*, 385–96, 403–14, 432–34.

Chapter 4

1. Moore, *Principia Ethica*, 114.

2. See chapter 2, section 1 of this book.

3. Prichard, *Moral Obligation: Essays and Lectures*, 92–93; Ross, *The Right and the Good*, 105.

4. For a good discussion of Moore's treatment of self-evidence in *Principia Ethica*, see Noah Lemos, "Self-Evidence and *Principia Ethica*."

5. Cf. ibid., 460–61.

Chapter 5

1. Moore, *Principia Ethica*, 148. See also 25, 106, 147, 150, 169. Moore does not present such question-begging definitions of these terms in his later book, *Ethics*.

2. Ross, *The Right and the Good*, chapter 2.

3. "The Concept of Natural Right" and *Rights, Goods, and Democracy*, chapter 3.

4. This does not mean that a third party beneficiary, *c*, of *a*'s duty to act compatibly with *b*'s acquiring something to which *b* has a right therefore necessarily also has a right *a* has a duty to respect. Thus if I promise someone, Smith, to feed his dog while Smith is out of town, Smith has a right to my keeping my promise by feeding his dog, and I a duty to do so, but his dog does not therefore necessarily have a right to my keeping my promise to Smith or to being fed by me.

5. See my "Concept of Natural Light" and *Rights, Goods, and Democracy*, chapter 3.

6. Ross, *The Right and the Good*, 7.

7. This, however, does not mean that the motive moving a person to act is morally good only if the person believes that the act is right, morally bad only if he believes that the act is wrong. Instead, one person's compassion for another that moves him to act to relieve the suffering of the other would seem

to be morally good regardless of whether the agent regards the act he performs as being right or obligatory, and one person's envy of another that moves him to harm in some way the other would seem to be morally bad regardless of whether the agent regards the act he performs as being wrong.

8. For a more complete treatment of the distinction between objective and subjective duty and rightness, see my "Duty and Ignorance" and *Rights, Goods, and Democracy,* Appendix.

9. Chisholm, *Brentano and Intrinsic Value,* 102.

Chapter 6

1. For an account of the nature and ontological status of kinds, see my *Metaphysical Investigations,* chapter 6, section 1.

2. Moore, *Principia Ethica,* 43.

3. Kant, *Foundations of the Metaphysics of Morals,* 9.

Chapter 7

1. Findlay, *Values and Intentions,* 416.

2. Ross, *The Right and the Good,* 138–40.

3. Brentano, *The Foundation and Construction of Ethics,* 172–84.

4. For a good brief discussion of this issue see Nozick, *Anarchy, State, and Utopia,* 42–45.

5. Rachels, *The End of Life,* 46–47.

Chapter 8

1. *A Treatise of Human Nature,* book 2, part 3, section 3.

2. Moore, *Principia Ethica,* 99.

3. For a similar argument, see my *Rights, Goods, and Democracy,* chapter 2.

Chapter 9

1. It might be thought that although it is (1) appropriate to like something good and to dislike something bad and (2) inappropriate to like something bad and to dislike something good, it is (a) not necessarily good to like something good or to dislike something bad and (b) not necessarily bad to like something bad and to dislike something good. Such a view, however, would seem to neglect the fact that appropriate likings and dislikings are good and inappropriate ones bad and that it is good to like or dislike appropriately and bad to like or dislike inappropriately.

2. Sometimes an object is liked or disliked far more than it merits because it is believed to be far better or far worse than in fact it is. Such excessive likings and dislikings are proportioned, or at least might be, to the degree of goodness or badness the object is believed to have, and in that respect might be said to be appropriate or fitting relative to the beliefs in question. Given, however, that the latter are mistaken, such excessive likings and dislikings are intrinsically bad, since they are far out of proportion to the degree of goodness and badness the

214 Notes to Chapters 9–10

objects liked or disliked do in fact possess, and the beliefs in question are at least extrinsically bad as occasioning the intrinsically bad likings and disliking.

3. If, however, the argument of section 1 in chapter 4 is sound, this cannot be *all* that is meant by saying of something that it is intrinsically good or intrinsically bad.

Chapter 10

1. Chapter 6, section 6.
2. Ibid.
3. Chapter 8, section 2.
4. Chapter 7, sections 5 and 6.

Works Cited

Brentano, Franz. *The Foundation and Construction of Ethics.* English edition edited and translated by Elizabeth Hughes Schneewind. London: Routledge & Kegan Paul, 1973.

———. *The Origin of Our Knowledge of Right and Wrong.* Edited by Oskar Kraus. English edition edited by Roderick M. Chisholm, translated by Roderick M. Chisholm and Elizabeth H. Schneewind. London: Routledge & Kegan Paul, 1969.

Butchvarov, Panayot. *Skepticism in Ethics.* Bloomington and Indianapolis: Indiana University Press, 1989.

Chisholm, Roderick M. *Brentano and Intrinsic Value.* Cambridge: Cambridge University Press, 1986.

———. *On Metaphysics.* Minneapolis: University of Minnesota Press, 1989.

Findlay, J. N. *Values and Intentions.* London: George Allen & Unwin; New York: Macmillan, 1961.

Hall, Everett W. *What Is Value?* London: Routledge & Kegan Paul, 1952.

Hume, David. *A Treatise of Human Nature.* Edited by L. A. Selby-Bigge. Oxford: Clarendon Press, 1888.

Husserl, Edmund. *Logical Investigations.* 2 vols. Translated by J. N. Findlay. London: Routledge & Kegan Paul, 1970.

Kant, Immanuel. *Foundations of the Metaphysics of Morals.* Translated, with an introduction, by Lewis White Beck. Indianapolis: Library of Liberal Arts, 1959.

Lemos, Noah M. "Self-Evidence and *Principia Ethica.*" *The Southern Journal of Philosophy* 23 (1985): 451–64.

Lemos, Ramon M. "The Concept of Natural Right." *Midwest Studies in Philosophy* 7 (1982): 133–50.

———. "A Defense of Retributivism." *The Southern Journal of Philosophy* 15 (1977): 53–65.

———. "Duty and Ignorance." *The Southern Journal of Philosophy* 18 (1980): 301–12.

———. *Metaphysical Investigations*. Rutherford, Madison, Teaneck: Fairleigh Dickinson University Press; London and Toronto: Associated University Presses, 1988.

———. "Propositions, States of Affairs, and Facts." *The Southern Journal of Philosophy* 24 (1986): 517–30.

———. *Rights, Goods, and Democracy*. Newark: University of Delaware Press; London and Toronto: Associated University Presses, 1986.

Lewis, Clarence Irving. *An Analysis of Knowledge and Valuation*. La Salle, Ill.: Open Court, 1946.

Moore, G. E. *Ethics*. London: Oxford University Press, 1912.

———. *Principia Ethica*. Cambridge: Cambridge University Press, 1903.

Nowell-Smith, P. H. *Ethics*. London: Penguin Books, 1954.

Nozick, Robert. *Anarchy, State, and Utopia*. New York: Basic Books, 1974.

Prichard, H. A. *Moral Obligation: Essays and Lectures*. Oxford: Clarendon Press, 1949.

Rachels, James. *The End of Life*. Oxford: Oxford University Press, 1986.

Ross, W. D. *The Right and the Good*. Oxford: Clarendon Press, 1930.

Index

abnormality, 94–95
abstracta and concreta, 31
acts: and actions, 79–80; and intentions, 129–30; intrinsic goodness and badness of, 129–30; moral goodness and badness of, 79–80, 85; rightness and wrongness of, 79–80, 85
altruism, 169
Anselm, St., 51, 89
anthropocentrism, 190
Aristotle, 147, 170
ashamed, being, 7–12
assumptions, 70–71
attitudes, pro- and con-, 12
authenticity and inauthenticity, 107

belief, truth and falsity of, 15–16
better or worse: the concepts of, 174–76; intrinsically, 35–39
better than, the concept of, 65
blessedness, 170
Brentano, Franz, 13, 119, 121
Butchvarov, Panayot, 29, 211

Carritt, E.F., 132
Chisholm, Roderick M., 90, 212
civilization and morality, 196–200, 209–10

concepts: evaluative, 60–67; moral and value, 72; naturalistic, 60–63; non-evaluative, 60–63
conscience, guilty, 204
consequentialism, 84–85
contradictions, believing, 138–39, 145
Cynics, the, 202

deception, 104–8, 126–30, 134–43, 204; and silence, 126–30
definitions: circular, 67; evaluative, 60–67; naturalistic and non-evaluative, 60–63
deformity, 94–95
deontology, 85
diabolical, being, 112
duties, 130–34
duty: absolute, 73–74, 77; definition of, 72–74; objective and subjective, 85–86; prima facie, 73–74, 77–78; and rightness and wrongness, 73–78

education: liberal, 200, 206; moral and non-moral, 199–202, 206–10; professional or vocational, 200, 206
egocentrism, 190
egoism: deontological, 163; teleological, 163–68; unmitigated, 158–68

evaluating, 2–13, 62
evils, natural and moral, 87–90

facts, 15–19; goodness and badness of,
    21–29; value, 61
fact/value distinction, the, 61
fallacy, the non-evaluative, 64
Findlay, J. N., 121

God, 51–52, 89–90; attitudes toward the
    existence of, 117–22
good: as being beneficial, 166–67; being
    morally, 113–14, 170, 201–10; the
    complete human, 170, 202–10;
    regarding things as, 3, 6, 12–13, 62,
    166–67; as a transcendental concept,
    172
goodness and badness: and appropriate-
    ness and inappropriateness, 213; as
    emergent properties, 30–33;
    indefinability of intrinsic, 60–67;
    intrinsic, 164–68; and liking and dis-
    liking, 167– 68, 172–86, 189–95; of
    lives, 179–81; moral, 78–86; and
    moral concepts, 72, 78; of persons,
    179–81, 193; proof of intrinsic,
    67–71; supervenience of , 64
goods: having, 113–14, 170, 201–10;
    moral and non-moral, 200–210

Hall, Everett, 29
happiness, 170; goodness and badness
    of, 180–81; of lives and persons,
    179–81
hatred: and envy and dislike, 114
Hegel, G. W. F., 97 ,154
Holy Spirit, the, 118–20
Hume, David, 148–49
Husserl, Edmund, 41–42

indifferences, 176–86, 189–95
indifferent, the: extreme views of
    attitudes toward, 176–82; moderate
views of attitudes toward, 181–86,
    191–95
intolerance, 186
intuitionism, 132
is/ought distinction, the 61

James, William, 144
judgments, value, 61
justice, ideal, 205–6

Kant, Immanuel, 115, 170
Kierkegaard, Søren, 153
kinds: goodness of normal instances of,
    91–97; value of, 186–89; value of in-
    stances of, 186–89
knowledge: of intrinsic goodness and
    badness, 67–71; moral, 207; and
    proof, 67–71; and seeing, 70–71; value
    of, 117, 121–26, 143–47; without
    proof, 69–71

Leibniz, G. W., 51–52
Lemos, Noah, 212
Lewis, C. I., 39, 52–58
liking and disliking, 2–14, 52–58, 62;
    species of, 13
likings and dislikings: excessive, 175,
    213–14; goodness and badness of,
    172–86, 189–91
love, Christian, 115–16, 178
loving and hating, 13–14; and goodness
    and badness, 108–16; goodness and
    badness of, 109–16; and virtues and
    vices, 108–16

magnanimity, 68, 178, 184, 190–95
mean-spiritedness, 68, 193–95
Meinong, Alexius, 15
Moore, G. E., 31–33, 49, 60–61, 63,
    67–68, 72–73, 94, 163, 212
moralism: extreme, 153–54, 157–60,
    168; moderate, 154–60, 168
morality: and civilization, 196–200,

209–10; and education, 199–202, 206–10; egoistic view of, 150–68; non-egoistic systems of, 154–61; non-egoistic view of, 151–52, 168–71
motives, 79–80; morally good and bad, 212–13

non-egoism, unmitigated, 158–62, 168–71
normality, value of, 94–97
Nowell-Smith, P.H., 211
Nozick, Robert, 213

objectives, moral: and moral facts, 81–82; value of, 81–86
objects, intentional, 4–5, 9–12, 16, 18, 49–50
objects and objectives, 15
organic wholes, principle of, 31–33, 49
ought, the concept of, 65, 75–77

particulars, 15, 29–33, 91–94
Pascal, Blaise, 123
persons, good, 80–81, 170, 202, 205–10
philosophy, moral, and value theory, 72, 81
Plato, 170
pleasure and pain, goodness and badness of, 164–66
pragmatism, 144
preferability, 66, 76
Prichard, H. A., 65, 132
proof: and assumptions, 70–71; of intrinsic goodness and badness, 67–71; and knowledge, 67–71; and seeing, 70–71
properties: dispositional, 100–102; evaluative and non-evaluative, 61–63; excellent-making, 97–98; good-making and bad-making, 94–98; natural and non-natural, 61–63
propositions: goodness and badness of,

24–28; true, 18–19, 24–28; truth and falsity of, 16–19
psychological phenomena: intentionality of, 7–12; levels of, 4–12, 62; moral goodness and badness of, 78–79
punishment, 45–46, 211–12

Rachels, James, 144
rationalism and moralism, 149–62, 168
rationality: antecedent impartial concept of practical, 161–62, 169–71; axiological, 147; egoistic view of practical, 149–62, 168, 203; epistemic, 147; Humean view of practical, 148–49; non-egoistic view of practical, 151–52, 158–62, 168; practical and theoretical, 117, 122–26, 142–47
rationalization, 204
rightness and wrongness: definition of, 72–74; and duty, 73–77; objective and subjective, 85–86
rights, morals, 77–78
Ross, W. D., 11, 15, 65, 73, 79, 127, 132
Rousseau, Jean-Jacques, 197–98

Schopenhauer, Arthur, 52
self-deception, 134–42
self-respect, 105
states of affairs, 15–24; goodness and badness of, 19–24, 28–33, 54: obtaining and non-obtaining of, 19–24, 28–33, 54
Stoicism, 202–3, 206
supererogation, 74–77

terms, primitive, 67
tolerance, 184–86
true belief, value of, 121–26

understanding, value of, 121–26, 137, 143

unhappiness, goodness and badness of,
    180–81
universals, 15; exemplification of, 29–33,
    54, 91–94; goodness and badness of,
    29–33, 54, 91–94; non-evaluative, 63
utilitarianism, 84–85
utility, 39–41, 53, 56–58

value: calculus of, 38–39; contributory,
    33–34, 41–52; definability of the con-
    cept of, 60; definability of intrinsic
    59–67; economic or monetary, 38; ex-
    trinsic, 33–60; inherent, 52–58; instru-
    mental, 33–44, 48, 50–60; intrinsic,
    33–39, 59–67; negative, 2–5, 35–39,
    43, 45–52, 60; neutral, 2–5, 46, 60;
    objectivity and subjectivity of, 54–58;
    positive, 2–5, 35–39, 42–43, 45–52,
    60; sentimental, 187; total, 34–39;
    units of 37–39
values, 1–3: agreement and disagreement
    about, 208; competing, 132–34; moral
    and non-moral, 200–210; subjectivist
    views of, 207–8
valuing, 1–13, 62
virtues, the: contempt for, 106–7; good
    and bad use of, 114–16; honoring,
    104–7
virtues and vices: as dispositions,
    100–108; as good- and bad-making
    properties, 100; inward and outward
    manifestations of, 101–8
whole, the all-inclusive, 50–52, 82–83,
    120
wholes and parts, 31–33, 41–52
will, good and bad, 115
wisdom, practical and theoretical, 125,
    147
world, the created, 51–52, 82–83, 120
worlds, value of actual and possible,
    86–90
wrongs and wronging, 77–80